SO-BIB-508

WITHDRAWN
L. R. COLLEGE LIBRARY

This

Dynamics
of a City Church

What the soul is to the body Christians are to the world. The soul is distributed in every member of the body, and Christians are scattered in every city of the world. The soul dwells in the body, and yet it is not of the body. So, Christians live in the world, but they are not of the world.

LETTER TO DIOGNETUS

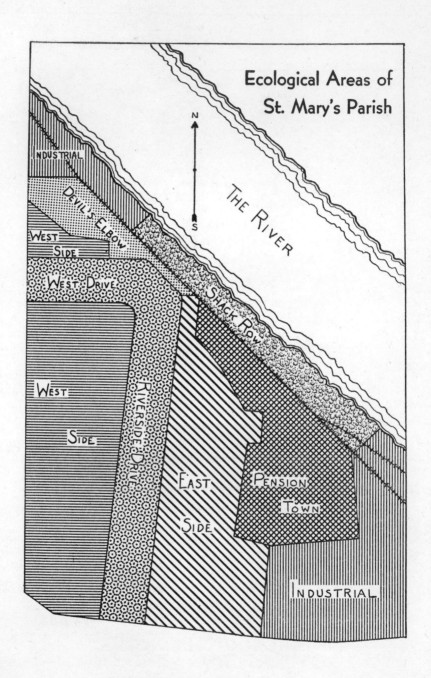

Ecological Areas of
St. Mary's Parish

THE RIVER

INDUSTRIAL

DEVIL'S ELBOW

WEST SIDE

WEST DRIVE

SHACK ROW

WEST SIDE

RIVERSIDE DRIVE

EAST SIDE

PENSION TOWN

INDUSTRIAL

Dynamics
of a City Church

By

JOSEPH H. FICHTER, S.J.

THE UNIVERSITY OF CHICAGO PRESS

CHICAGO · ILLINOIS

Carl A. Rudisill Library
LENOIR RHYNE COLLEGE

IMPRIMI POTEST: HARRY CRANE, S.J., *Praepositus Provinciae Neo Aurelianensis*

NIHIL OBSTAT: J. GERALD KEALY, D.D., *Censor Librorum*

IMPRIMATUR: ✠ SAMUEL CARDINAL STRITCH, *Archiepiscopus Chicagiensis*

Chicago, March 14, 1951

BX
1407
.S6
F5
1951
v 1

34577

January 1957

THE UNIVERSITY OF CHICAGO PRESS, CHICAGO 37
Cambridge University Press, London, N.W. 1, England
W. J. Gage & Co., Limited, Toronto 2B, Canada

Copyright 1951 by The University of Chicago. All rights reserved. Copyright 1951 under the International Copyright Union. Published 1951. Composed and printed by THE UNIVERSITY OF CHICAGO PRESS, *Chicago, Illinois, U.S.A.*

THIS VOLUME IS DEDICATED
TO
THE MOST REVEREND WILLIAM T. MULLOY, D.D.
Bishop of Covington, Kentucky

Foreword

FATHER SCHMIDT, who was born and reared in the parish and is now a high-placed cleric in the diocese, warned me at the beginning of this study: "The Pastor is going to dislike you because the facts will show that St. Mary's Parish is a hollow shell of Catholicism." It was a friendly warning, and at times during the course of our investigation I felt that it might have been wise to heed it. Social research of an empirical nature makes certain demands on the virtues of patience and forbearance which are outside the ambit of technical competence and analytical insight.

As far as I can judge, Father Urban did not come to dislike me, but he frequently exhibited an extreme distaste for the evidence we uncovered. He questioned our techniques, our methods, even our arithmetic, but in the end—like the truth-loving person he is—he accepted the facts. He still disagrees with some of our interpretations and conclusions. Neither he nor we have come to the conclusion that his parish is a "hollow shell of Catholicism." We still think that St. Mary's should be ranked high among the successfully operating parishes of the diocese.

Every attempt has been made to conceal the location of St. Mary's Parish and the identity of its priests and people. Minor descriptive changes have been introduced everywhere toward this end, but none of them has been sufficient to distort in any way the total picture of the parish. This anonymity, however, has its drawbacks. It makes it impossible for us to give due credit to the even-tempered co-operation of the Pastor, Father Urban, and his two assistants, Father Dominic and Father Paul. We cannot appreciate sufficiently the forbearance of the Sisters in the school, the officers and members of parochial organizations, the individuals and families of the parish. They were aware of our presence from the beginning but not at all certain of the purpose in our ubiquitous observation and our innumerable interviews.

The same need for anonymity does not apply in regard to my competent and faithful assistants during the twelve months' research.

Under assignment, the "raw data" of research were gathered during the week and presented for a thorough group discussion of several hours' duration every Saturday morning. The researchers and participants in these discussions were Eldon Bonnet, Rose Dalferes, Dorothy Dean, Mary Lee DiCarlo, John Elsner, Carmelo Graffagnini, Daniel Quinn, Ferdinand Schlumbrecht, Bettye Sykes, and Gerard Walsh. Through the kind co-operation of the Very Reverend Harry Crane, S.J., Superior of the Southern Province, we had the assistance of several young Jesuit Fathers for a period during the survey. Fathers John Capelle, Louis Hiegel, Fabian Johnston, C. Franklyn Lynette, Michel Majoli, and Julius May obtained valuable information in personal interviews with parishioners. The tedious work of typing, compiling data, drawing graphs, checking cross-references, and correcting proofs was efficiently performed by Joan Forshag.

My indebtedness to the great social scientists of our times is too large to recount here. The following men, through their personal encouragement, professional counsel, and many writings, have helped me to formulate the concepts and techniques upon which this research project is based: I express my deep gratitude to Gordon Allport, Joseph Fitzpatrick, Harlan Gilmore, Everett Hughes, Clyde Kluckhohn, Franz Mueller, Bernard Mulvaney, Talcott Parsons, Liston Pope, T. Lynn Smith, Pitirim Sorokin, Samuel Stouffer, Rupert Vance, Joachim Wach, W. Lloyd Warner, and Carle Zimmermann.

Finally, it is with a sense of appreciation and pleasure that I make the following acknowledgment. This research project, as reported in this and subsequent volumes, was made possible in part by a research committee at Loyola University, New Orleans, Louisiana, from funds made available jointly by the Carnegie Foundation and Loyola University. It must be understood, of course, that I, and not the University or the Foundation, am solely responsible for the statements made in these volumes.

J. H. F., S.J.

New Orleans, Louisiana
Holy Thursday, 1951

Table of Contents

Table of Contents

Chapter One

The Parish and the Good Society

THERE are two important concepts which have influenced both the origin and the growth of this study in parochial sociology. The first is a strong belief that the reintegration of modern Western society, particularly on the American scene, can take place only through the agency of Christianity in the form of the Roman Catholic Church. The second is an accepted supposition to the effect that the parochial system of the Church is the most likely sociological factor for strengthening the inner structure of the Church and for channeling the influence of Christianity to the larger community and nation.

CONVICTION

Every student of society knows the concept *anomie*, a sociological byword made famous by Émile Durkheim. One need not be an alarmist to recognize that this normlessness, in all its manifestations, is a characteristic of contemporary American life. The lack of stable standards of human thought and behavior is recognized even by those who enthusiastically proclaim this lack as a glorious expression of the free human spirit.

The most important aspect of *anomie* for the sociologist and social psychologist is that it is the state of mind of people who are wanting in social solidarity. In human society complete independence from one's fellow-men is an impossible ideal, if indeed it can be called an ideal. Human beings depend on one another, and human relations must reflect this mutual dependence if society is to function with any degree of stability. Now, if it is true that men behave toward one another on the basis of individually accepted norms, it seems a truism to conclude that commonly accepted and observed norms are imperative for the successful function of the larger society.

Elton Mayo has pointed out that norms of social behavior are main-

I

tained, or at best are only slowly changing, in an established society. The primary institutions which are preserved in that form of society make possible a high degree of social skill. On the other hand, the adaptive society, now common to urban America with its tremendous technological progress and secular rationale, is destructive of both the habits of social skill and the primary institutions in which they best flourished.

In so far as men like Mayo and his disciples are interested in social reform, they proceed on the assumption that the present technological structure is here to stay. They apparently despair of any progress in the primary institutions of family and kinship relations, rural, small business, and neighborhood relations. While approving the kind of scientific research done by Le Play among the European workers, they seem to accept the questionable theory of the "cultural lag." Human beings must adapt themselves to the demands of modern industrial institutions. It seems much more reasonable to suggest that institutions be eventually adapted to the needs of human beings.

There are other economic approaches to social reform, all of them much cruder and simpler than the above. The Marxist is generally convinced that the form of production is the basis of the whole social structure and that, if he can tinker sufficiently with that form, he can change society. Here again there would be a need to conform man to institution. The various other simple and sovereign economic remedies need not detain us here. Suffice it to say that the primacy of the economic (and therefore of the material and sensate) is not even questioned in large segments of our Western civilization today.

Another feature of our current culture that must be briefly mentioned is the political element. Perhaps the restlessness of man will be allayed, and stable norms of thought and behavior restored either in the security of the completely rationalized state or in the freedom of the unplanned democratic state. The enthusiasm with which people in the democratic countries seem to accept political parties and candidates is, matched only by the gullibility with which citizens of totalitarian nations seem to accept the promises of their dictators.

On the other hand, it cannot be said that the forms of economic and political institutions are irrelevant to the good society. Social reform is largely bound up with these elements as techniques, or means to the better life. But it must be said that the emphasis placed upon them has been a factor of social disintegration. They cannot serve as ends in themselves, for without the support of higher means and a more worthy end they are logically self-destructive.

My conviction is that *anomie* is primarily (though not solely) a moral problem that can best be understood through the approaches of ethics and religion. This does not mean that a host of subsidiary factors can safely be ignored. Modern society is too complex to allow a single supreme approach. People who place their whole faith in universal education frequently forget to ask on what values or norms that education should function. The same is true both of scientists who ignore the fact that science as such is sociologically sterile and of jurists who depend completely upon a legal order of evolving principles. Certainly, education, science, and law are important directive agencies in the social order; but, like economics and politics, they are logically fissiparous, unless they are subsidiary to a higher integrating principle.

I think that Clyde Kluckhohn had this same conviction in mind when he declared that "there appear to be only two social forces powerful enough to bring some semblance of order and stability to Western society: the one is the ideology of Communism, the other is that of Roman Catholicism." Those words have no meaning to the person who views communism merely as an economic or political system and Catholicism merely as a formal social structure. "Ideology" is the all-important concept. The difference between these two moral philosophies is much deeper than that existing between the capitalist and the Communist economics or between the totalitarian and the democratic states.

Pitirim Sorokin wisely insists that a culture cannot be understood without primary reference to its system of meanings and values. Regardless of what the values are, so long as they are internally consistent, a society in which they are widely held and commonly practiced will be an integrated and balanced structure. He sees the debacle of Western culture in the fact that absolute norms (even of a sensate kind) have been abandoned and that the values which still remain are logically inconsistent. This social chaos would largely disappear under the relatively uniform moral philosophy of either Marxism or Christianity.

The vacuum left in the social and cultural system by our contemporary moral relativity promises to be filled during the next half-century by one of these ideologies. If the decision is left to Christian people, there is really no choice. The Marxian morality is professedly a materialistic, this-worldly system of values which does not pretend to measure means against absolute norms or direct them to spiritual and supernatural objectives. Arnold Toynbee is in no dilemma about this fact. "I am not sanguine about man's ability to make a good moral decision if he aims only at a worldly goal. Love of mankind has been a force in history—but only when it was a by-product of an intense love of God. The great need of the modern world is a re-birth of supernatural belief. Without it, man—unregenerate man—is hardly to be trusted with the dangerous toys his laboratories have hatched."

Christopher Dawson is even more forthright and specific on the function of organized religion in the modern world. "Religion is the only power that can meet the forces of destruction on equal terms and save mankind from its spiritual enemies. . . . Wherever Christianity exists there survives a seed of unity, a principle of spiritual order, which cannot be destroyed by war or the conflict of economic interests or the failure of political organizations. . . . The one thing that it demands is faith, and lack of faith is the only thing that even defeats the divine purpose. Thus the hope of the world rests in the last resort on the existence of a spiritual nucleus of believers who are the bearers of the seed of unity."[1]

The sociology of religion, however, does not deal exclusively in supernatural beliefs or in value systems as such. In fact, it borrows a knowledge of these from priests and theologians. The sociologist is interested in these norms only in so far as they effect and affect patterns of behavior, institutional structures, social relations and functions. In essence, then, a systematic understanding of the role of Catholicism in modern society requires a study not only of its values and meanings but more especially of the "vehicles" employed to activate them and of the agents who believe in these values and employ these vehicles.

All that I have been saying up to now leads to this brief conclusion: I am convinced that Roman Catholicism is the institution with the best possible prospect of reintegrating Western culture. This is the broad underlying conviction which urged me to undertake a study in parochial sociology. I will not even bother to support this conviction or to argue about it in this book. I take it as an objective fact that must be proved elsewhere. Sociologists are free to consider it a mere postulate, an assumption which has its roots, if any, outside the field of scientific investigation. Even if Christianity actually fails in the foreseeable future to replace our materialistic ethics and to reconsolidate our society, I think that it has within itself the power to do so.

1. Christopher H. Dawson, *The Judgement of the Nations* (New York: Sheed & Ward, 1942), pp. 220–21.

HYPOTHESIS

The direct and essential objective of Catholicism is the eternal salvation of all human beings. Without this end, the Church is utterly without meaning. The Church may at times seem to intrude upon, and pursue, a great number of minor objectives of a social and temporal character, but these can be only secondary ends related in some way to the primary supernatural purpose.

The supernatural means employed by the Church are equally clear cut and simple, and much of the effort of professional ecclesiastics is spent in the preservation, protection, and clarification of these means. And this is readily understandable, for, like the purpose, the means are necessarily contained in the divine commission given to the Church by Christ. Certain truths must be believed by all members of the Church. These constitute the Christian creed. There are also certain patterns of conduct, called "the Christian code of behavior," outlined basically in the Ten Commandments, the counsels of Christ, and the precepts of the Church. Third, the Christian cult, or form of worship, comprises the sacramental, liturgical, and devotional system of the Church. Finally, the Christian communion of all members with one another idealizes the essential social nature of the Church.

It cannot be emphasized too strongly that this fourfold instrument of creed, code, cult, and communion must be accepted as existing data by the social scientist. It will not do to reject as mythical, or as an unwieldy transcendental, this whole structure of supernatural means-end relations. On the other hand, we need not become theologians or attempt to intermingle the sciences of theology and sociology. At this point a false dilemma may be constructed as an objection: If Catholicism is really a supernatural institution, it cannot be subjected to the research methodology of social science. If, on the other hand, it is simply another social institution, human and fallible, we can dispense with all these pretensions to divine factors and purposes.

Both of these contentions are erroneous because they ignore the traditional distinction between the "order of grace" and the "order of nature." There is no way of measuring the influence of divine grace conferred upon a Catholic through the sacrament of penance. There is no psychoanalytical method to discern where the inspiration of the Holy Spirit leaves off, and natural eloquence takes over, in the pulpit preacher. No one can determine scientifically how much of a foreign missioner's success is attributable to himself and how much to the prayers of a cloistered contemplative back home. All these questions are imponderables that belong in the supernatural order.

These imponderables make much more difficult the problems of evaluation and predictability which face the empirical social scientist. It is simple enough to measure the numbers and frequency and to weigh the statements made by those who participate in the functions of the parish. These are externals which can be compared with the high, ideal behavior proposed by the Church for its members. Only by inference from this evidence can we evaluate the internal adherence to the Church's ideals, the degree of sanctity of parishioners, etc. Operating ideals of a whole group may be discerned and discussed, but the supernatural state of any person's soul is open to the scrutiny of God alone. This handicap of evaluation is not simply a failure of the "tools of research." The most proficient psychoanalyst recognizes this stumbling block in the area of supernatural relations.

Another complex problem for the social scientist is that of predictability of human behavior. We cannot say in any absolute sense that the present patterns of religious behavior will be continued by St. Mary's parishioners in the future. Besides the many other dynamic factors which variously operate in any given social structure, there is the constant factor of self-directing personalities. A basic expectation of every institutionalized religion is that people are personally able to improve their religious values and behavior. For centuries the philosophers and theologians have wrestled with the problem of cooperation between free will and divine grace, on the one hand, and the prediction of human behavior, on the other. By constant research, analysis, and comparison, the social scientist can hope for at best a degree of probability in his projection of present religious behavior.

"Grace builds upon nature," says the theologian, and this latter foundation is susceptible to the detailed scrutiny of the social observer. It is in the "order of nature," that is, in the structures and processes of human relations, where the Church has at times been a quite expert psychologist, sociologist, and anthropologist, even long before the names of these social disciplines were known. In other words, quite distinct from its essential and constantly utilized supernatural means, the Church has employed every variety of legitimate, this-worldly, natural means.

Some of these instruments have been so successful in bringing the Church's influence to bear on modern society that they have been individually singled out as *the* most important factor. Here we get closer to the matter of the underlying hypothesis of the present study.

Which of these instruments is likely to be the most effective as an auxiliary to the indispensable supernatural means? In an absolute sense, no answer can satisfy the question; hence there must be a choice among hypothetical statements. For example: "Catholicism can restore social integration to the world today only if it makes full utilization of the radio (or the press, or the colleges)."

Now there can be no doubt that radio broadcasting is an important modern medium of religious propaganda, that thousands have heard the Mass and various devotions for the first time, and that millions have listened to snatches of Catholic doctrine and prayer from the lips of radio preachers. Although the Catholic press reaches a smaller audience who must make greater effort to learn the truth, it too has been a valuable channel for communicating Catholic influence to the world at large. The collegiate and university system of the Church, especially in the United States, has trained great numbers of men and women in the doctrines and practices of Catholicism. In fact, it may be said that all three—radio, press, and higher education—are simply variants of the one same function of the Church: the work of teaching religious truths. But all of them generally reach people (even in the colleges) who are hardly known to one another, come from different places, and have varying cultural backgrounds. The Christian system of values and meanings is conveyed to them, but not in the sociological setting where it can be transformed into Christian life and behavior.

Let us consider this same problem from a structural aspect. It is sometimes said that Catholicism will flourish in so far as the Pope is a learned, holy, and vigorous leader—or as long as the episcopal sees in a nation enjoy competent administrators—or to the extent that national organizations of lay people, like the Knights of Columbus, the Sodality of the Blessed Virgin, and similar guilds and associations, are active and numerically strong. Whether one speaks of an ecclesiastical office or its incumbent, of a lay association or its members, he can have no reason for belittling their importance and influence. All these elements, however, constitute at best a minute minority of the vast Catholic population. They are genuinely concerned with leadership functions, both lay and clerical, but they most frequently operate on a level quite removed from the sociological bases of Catholicism.

All the above discussion simply clears the way for the following hypothesis: In so far as the "order of nature" is employed, Catholicism will succeed or fail in the imperative job of reconstructing and reintegrating modern society mainly on the basis of the strength or weakness of its individual parishes. In other words, a vigorous parochial system not only bespeaks an internally strong Catholic social structure but also promises solidarity for the larger community and the nation in which it exists. It is therefore the accepted supposition of this book that the sociological roots of Catholicism are in the parish.[2]

In this connection, Cardinal Suhard emphasizes the same hypothesis: "We are drawn, inevitably, to the heart of the problem, which is the rechristianizing of the life of our people *at its source*. Even though Catholic Action is a privileged instrument of this task, we have to admit that only the parish, *the local and universal seat of the Redemption*, can become the adequate means."[3] The parish is where the people are. It is the place where the great majority of people, both Catholic and non-Catholic, have their only contact with the Church. It is the locus of life and work and play for pious Catholics and renegades, for prospective converts and hardened sinners. The beliefs, the behavior, and the worship of the Catholic faith are exhibited here in the parish, or they simply are not exhibited at all.

It is a curious fact that so-called "total" community studies in recent sociological research missed this point almost completely. To be sure, they give references to the various churches, or even a whole chapter to religion, but they do not contribute any serious analysis to the purposive inner functions of Catholicism, Protestantism, or Judaism on the basic level of the congregation itself. This cavalier treatment of an important social phenomenon by otherwise competent scientists means one of two things. Either the parochial unit has really ceased to wield dynamic influence in the culture of its own community or, as Dawson remarks, "the great fundamental realities— the truths on which everything depends and which are more real than the things we see and touch—are dismissed as words, mere pious formulas that have no relevance to modern life."[4] If the influence of the local community church is dead, the social researchers do well in ignoring it. If it is not dead, then the failure to focus it properly in "total" studies may be merely a reflection of the secular culture of our times.

2. This does not mean that the American city parish has actually succeeded in maintaining an integrated social group. A subsequent volume will analyze the specific problems of congregational solidarity.

3. Cf. his Preface to Abbé Michonneau's significant and penetrating book, *Revolution in a City Parish* (Oxford: Blackfriars, 1949).

4. *Op. cit.*, p. 133.

Chapter Two

What Is the Parish?

THE original intention of this study was to select a group of three or four parishes in order to allow experimental control and comparison among them. It was hoped that a number of parishes could be found to correlate closely in those structural and institutional patterns which are outside the (immediate) control and influence of the Church; that is, they would be as similar as possible in ethnic and racial composition, in occupation and income, in cultural and educational background, and in general residential characteristics. Furthermore, it was thought best that these parishes be located in a southern city which has been relatively long established and yet has not been changing so rapidly as the larger cities of the East, Midwest, and Far West.

When the general location of the research had been chosen and episcopal approval obtained, a preliminary study was made of all the parishes therein. This careful survey of existing parochial units showed that great diversities exist. Not even two were found sufficiently similar for detailed comparative purposes. All differ in some degree not only in their secular components but also frequently in their religious components (excluding, of course, the essential worship and sacramental functions of the Church). Hence, it must be emphasized here that St. Mary's Parish is not presented in this study as a model or generic type of southern urban parishes. It may be considered, at best, a point of departure for those who have a practical interest in the real, informal operation of the Catholic parochial unit.

The actual selection of this parish was made with certain positive criteria in view. There was no intention of seeking out a "broken-down" social unit according to the fashions of sociologists who study divorce rates, delinquency, slum areas, etc. These researches yield valuable knowledge of society, and these negative elements must be studied even when one is determined to observe a successfully functioning social unit. In a sense, the negative approach was a useful instrument for the selection of this parish, for it helped us to eliminate many parishes from further consideration.

Thus, these negative characteristics were employed as follows: Parishes in the hotel and business districts and those in slum areas were not considered susceptible of fruitful study because of the transitory and sometimes unstable character of their congregations. Negro and national "parishes," and those operated by religious orders or in conjunction with educational institutions, were regarded as exceptional units. Of the remaining parishes, some were excluded because they were only recently established; others because the pastor was either on the inactive list or had not been in office long enough. Three parishes emerged as potential material for the study, which were then measured against certain positive criteria for a successful parish.

These criteria were as follows: In general, we looked for a parish in which the majority of its members are overtly behaving as Christians according to their orthodox inner beliefs and values. A well-financed and up-to-date physical plant at the parochial center was not considered an essential mark of success, although it is a partial indication of the laity's virtue of generosity and the clergy's capacity for leadership. However, in so far as Catholic conduct can be measured in a scientific way, the following characteristics were used as positive norms: religious vocations coming from the parish, attendance at Mass, sacraments, and weekday devotions, type and activities of parochial organizations, a functioning parish school, number of converts, presence or lack of juvenile delinquents, proportions of mixed marriages (also divorces and separations), and size of families. Besides the observation of all these elements, we solicited the opinion widely of the diocesan priests to discover which of the three parishes they thought the "best" and what reasons they had for choosing it.

St. Mary's was finally chosen after all the aspects of the three parishes were weighed and correlated. Even before we started the study we were reasonably certain that its "reputation" as a Catholic parish was good among both the clergy and the laity of the diocese. Other churches in the city are more beautiful architecturally, and several are much larger with greater crowds in attendance. St. Mary's is not the most efficient in its material vehicles and buildings. Our choice was not greatly influenced by these outward manifestations of secular success.

The contemporary universal organization of the Roman Catholic

Church on the bases of dioceses and parishes is the result of a long evolution of social structure within the Church. In view of centuries the present territorial pattern is relatively new. As Christianity spread through Europe, the rural communities were arranged in fixed ecclesiastical districts, called *parochia,* each under the jurisdiction of a bishop. Gradually, during the centuries following the breakup of the Roman Empire, these "parishes" were subdivided and each section was placed under the direction of a priest. The word "diocese," which in Constantine's day referred to a province of the empire, was not definitely and widely used to designate an episcopal see until the twelfth century.

At about the same time the Church began to subdivide the jurisdiction of urban areas, but this did not become general practice until long after the Council of Trent (1545–63). Even though this Council prescribed as a universal law the division of all cities into parishes with pastors to manage them, there were still large Italian cities in the seventeenth century which did not obey the law.[1] The new code of canon law of 1918 has made it an absolute law that all dioceses must have both their rural and their urban territories organized on the parochial scheme.[2]

As far as can be determined historically, says Harbrecht, the present parochial system seems to be "the last stage in the evolution of the local organization of Catholicism, and it is likely that no new form will evolve out of the changed conditions of our modern times. For the Church seems convinced at present that fifteen centuries of experience have fully shown that the parish organization has successfully met every condition, crisis and problem when the processes, institutions, and relations held in custody by the Church Universal, have been applied to the individual unit."[3]

It is obvious, therefore, that the parish is a *human* institution in the sense that it is the result of the Church's administrative experience and genius. Since neither the parish nor the office of parish priest was known during the first three centuries of the Church's existence, it is

1. Rev. John J. Harbrecht, S.T.D., *The Lay Apostolate* (St. Louis: B. Herder Book Co., 1929), pp. 18–19.
2. Canon 261, 1.
3. *Op. cit.,* p. 20. This question seems to have been reopened by the missionary activities of some of the priests in urban European parishes. Abbé Depierre thinks that a new sort of structure may emerge in which the priest will "become the parish priest of a sort of personal parish made up of all those proletarians who want to be Christians, but not like those other Christians who in their eyes represent a class that has exploited and enslaved them" (cf. Masie Ward, *France Pagan* [New York: Sheed & Ward, 1949], p. 214).

clear that the parochial system cannot claim origin in Christ in the way that the papacy and the episcopacy can. The parish is a man-made institution, developed for practical purposes of administration and maintained as an operative area within the total social structure and hierarchy of the Church.

But the parish does not appear "spontaneously" when a sufficient number of Catholics settle in a given location, nor does it function independently at any time during its growth. The ecclesiastical defi-nition of the parish depends rather upon the arbitrary decision of the code of canon law: "The territory of every diocese is to be divided into distinct territorial units; and each unit is to have a special church with a designated people, and a special rector is to be given charge over it as its proper pastor for the necessary care of souls.... Such units are parishes."[4]

A declaration of the Sacred Consistorial Congregation gave more minute details in 1919 when it insisted that a canonical parish should have not only fixed boundaries and an officially appointed pastor but also a permanent residence for the priest and the assurance of suffi-cient income to support the parish.[5] Every newly established parish must now have a decree of erection by the bishop of the diocese in which it is contained. Hence the parish does not come into being by the will of the Catholic people. It exists, in the strict sense, not as the voluntary association of lay people but only by the formal decision of the local bishop.

It appears, then, that four elements are necessary to constitute a parish: (a) an appointed pastor, (b) a church or rectory, (c) certain territorial limits, and (d) a designated group of persons. Actual con-ditions, particularly among American urban populations, give rise to various complications. One of these is the ethnic diversity of the Catholic lay parishioners. For example, it is not uncommon that the members of three different Catholic congregations occupy the same section of the city. Although the Bishop has divided the city into de-fined parishes, there may be several Catholic churches for Negroes established in various parts of the city. The same may be true of parish churches frequented by nationality groups: French, Mexican, Italian, etc. Thus, while tentative boundaries are drawn for each of these racial and ethnic congregations, they necessarily overlap with one another and with the strictly defined territorial parish.

Looked at from the point of view of the pastor, this arrangement does not appear quite so complicated. The three church buildings and

4. Canon 215, 1–3.
5. *Acta Apost. Sed.*, XI, 346.

rectories may exist within two city blocks. Each will have territorial boundaries and a designated congregation, but both boundaries and people will differ for each parish. The pastor of St. Joseph's will have care of all Catholics except Negroes and Italians within a limited area. The pastor of St. Henry's will be in charge of all Catholic Negroes in a larger but clearly defined area. The pastor of St. Lucy's Church will care for all of Italian descent within the whole city.

The differences in ethnic and racial groups, recognized by the Church, constitute only one kind of difficulty in the formulation of a sociological definition of the parish. Canonically, the parish is defined as a distinct spatial unit with a church and rectory governed by an appointed pastor and attended by Catholics living within the area. In the popular mind, following this traditional legal concept, the parish is thought of primarily as a place. To the social scientist this notion of spatial dimensions is of much less importance. It is true that territorial limits help to provide a locus of his research, but the sociological problem of definition begins only after the area has been located.

Our tentative postulate at the beginning of this research was that the persons constituting the parochial unit were somehow "informed" by a distinctively Catholic ideology. In order to be sure that the parish can be termed a social unit,[6] this system of meanings and values had to serve a double function: (a) as a bond of solidarity which united this specific group of persons into a parochial congregation and (b) as a recognizable characteristic which distinguished this group from all other non-Catholic religious groups and from all secular social units.

A social unit, whether religious or secular, is composed of people; and in the canonical definition we are told that these are "designated people." Quite aside from the problem of racial or national "parishes," this term is generally understood to include all those Catholics who live within the limits arbitrarily set up by the bishop for this parish. But even this information is of little value, for it does not give us a definition of a Catholic. Is he anyone who has been baptized and has never publicly announced his withdrawal from the Catholic religion? Or shall we say that he is anyone who, when asked about his religion, will answer: "I am a Catholic." This was a serious problem for us, for we had to know who was to be excluded from the study as a person not fulfilling the definition and who was to be included.

6. The data reveal that this postulate is open to serious question in the urban parish. Except for the inner core of solidaristic people, the parishioners do not exhibit a strong and distinctively Catholic bond of unity.

We employed three different techniques in attempting to answer this question. (*a*) In a house-to-house canvass of the entire area covered by the parish we found a little less than eleven thousand white persons who listed themselves as adherents of the Catholic faith. (*b*) A detailed census schedule was then brought to all those households listed as white Catholic in the preliminary canvass. Many of these refused the schedule because they "no longer practiced the faith." From this survey it was discovered that 6,436 persons[7] could be considered members of the parish. (*c*) Meanwhile we were counting the attendance at Sunday Masses in the parish church. The highest count taken was that of Easter Sunday, when 4,468 attended Mass. If we add to this number the 1,155 white Catholic children below the age of seven, who are not obliged to attend Mass, over six hundred adults who admit they never go to Mass, as well as the adults who may have been ill or out of town on Easter Sunday, we reach approximately the same total as the census.

The whole white population of the parochial area may thus be divided into three categories: (*a*) non-Catholics, (*b*) dormant or former Catholics, and (*c*) actual parishioners. For practical sociological purposes only this last group can be considered for further study. Since marginal Catholics and non-Catholic spouses in mixed marriages are inextricably involved in the parochial life of their families, it seemed reasonable to include them in the parochial group. It may be said that all these 6,727 persons are sociologically identified as members of St. Mary's Parish.

Professor Donovan adds another sociologically relevant concept in his definition. "The Catholic parish must be conceived of as a real social group composed of the Catholic clergy, religious, and laity within certain territorial boundaries who share a unity founded on common religious beliefs and who participate in socioreligious relationships institutionally defined by the parent-organization of the Church."[8] Just as the parish gets its origin and continued existence from the mother-church, so also does it get its essential religious functions and institutions.

The primary function of the parish is always and everywhere the same as that of the Roman Catholic Church, the parent-organization. It is functionally the ecclesiastical microcosm, the "Church in miniature." In a true sense, also, the formal structure of the parish is every-

7. This figure excludes 291 non-Catholic spouses in mixed marriages.
8. John Donovan, "The Social Structure of the Catholic Parish," a paper read at the Tenth Annual Convention of the American Catholic Sociological Society, St. Louis, Missouri, January, 1948.

where the same, since it is imposed by the traditions and legislation of the universal Church. Canon law requires a regularly appointed pastor, whose duties and privileges are fixed on a relatively rigid basis and are both protected and enforced through episcopal supervision. In the same way the pattern of religious relationships of the laity, both to one another and to the parochial clergy, is fixed in a more or less formalized structure and embodied in traditional practices as well as in the precepts of the Church and the decrees of the diocese.

All the above represents at best an "ideal" structure of relations within a parish. It gives a formal definition of the parish as it ought to be rather than as it is. No adequate sociological understanding of a parochial system can be obtained until this formal and ideal definition is subjected to the test of real relations among Catholics on the level of actual living conditions. These introductory remarks cannot point out the divergences between the two orders of being, but they must insist that the structure and function of a Catholic parish are important only in real-life situations. One of the major objectives of this research was to discover the obstacles to the realization of the "ideal" parochial system. But it cannot remain merely negative in its approach. The knowledge of those elements and factors which tend to the successful operation of the parish are of the utmost importance.

The distinction between clergy and laity is emphasized by the various roles the priest plays and by the total status he enjoys and is even symbolized by the distinctive garb he wears. Yet the pastor is not the parish. Ideally, he may be expected to have the same paternal spiritual relationship with all his parishioners. Here arises a further difficulty, for all the laity are not the same. On the other hand, he cannot think of them merely as discrete individuals, aside from the various strata and groupings to which they belong.

Except in instances of purely religious public worship, it can be safely said that all the lay parishioners never act together as a group. Even conceptually, there are levels of action that must be observed: (a) the person-in-action in so far as his activity is consonant with his status; (b) the active relation of the person to other persons and to groups; and (c) the various subgroups, both formal and informal, in which people act. This complex of subordinate social structures exists within every parochial system, even one in which the pastor has banned all associations, societies, or organizations. The very nature of social relations, especially in contemporary urban communities, requires informal groupings, cliques, and associations based on kinship, sex, age, occupation, education, etc.

The sociological definition of the parish, therefore, highlights the human relations which exist therein between the clergy and the laity and among the persons and groups within the laity itself. Hence, the "appointed pastor" (and other priests) and the "designated people" mentioned in the canonical definition are the specific foci of our social research. The two other elements, "church building" and "geographic boundaries," are important only to the extent that their description and analysis contribute to a clarification of the central human relations.

It is obvious that St. Mary's fulfils the canonical definition of a Catholic parish in all details. We shall be able to analyze separately the "territorial parish" with regard to its total population, both Catholic and non-Catholic, and also its ecological description. Of more importance for our purpose, however, is the fact that this parish is well suited to investigation from the point of view of the sociological definition. Formal associations are active in varying degrees, and there was at least a reasonable certitude that we would be able to "get at" the informal structures.

The present book is a study of functions rather than of structures. The accumulated data of the whole research project have become so large that they could not be presented within the limits of a single volume. Specifically and primarily, the present book investigates the religious and supernatural activities of the parishioners of St. Mary's in so far as they could be externally observed and measured. The various parochial organizations, the family life and school, and the participation of parishioners in extra-religious and community activities are left for future consideration.

The conceptual scheme of procedure in this volume is simple. Each major religious function of the parish is measured against the "ideal" set forth in the teaching and legislation of the Catholic Church. For example, in the sacrament of matrimony the "ideal type" would be found in two devout and well-instructed Catholics, unhampered by impediments, married by an authorized priest at a nuptial Mass in their parish church. To what extent are there deviations from this criterion by invalid marriages, mixed marriages, and afternoon ceremonies? What is done by the Pastor and parishioners to approach more closely the full realization of this criterion? From these investigations emerges a concept of various circles, the inner core of which represents the most "Catholic" parishioners and the outer circles the "marginal" Catholics. When all the religious functions were combined, it was found that the same persons and families occupy roughly the same position in relation to one another in all of them.

Chapter Three

The People of St. Mary's

Sт. маry's сhurch is located in Riverside, a long-established neighborhood which is part of a large southern city. A random sample of opinion among a group of leaders in the city showed that Riverside ranked sixth among the city's nineteen "neighborhood" districts. It was considered a "pretty good place" in which to live, made up of people who are predominantly white Catholics of remote German ancestry. According to this general opinion, there are no really poor people and no crucial social or civic problems in the area. Actual evidence gathered during the study showed that these generalizations were not reliable. They had been formulated in the minds of white people who apparently based them only on a knowledge of the better residential areas, the progressive business district, and the various civic organizations of Riverside.

Generally throughout the diocese the reputation of St. Mary's Church matches that of the community of Riverside. It is considered a "good parish" to work in as a curate and is rated an excellent appointment for the priest awaiting promotion to a pastorate. Riverside Drive is considered an upper-class section of the city, and, since the church buildings are located there, the Drive lends an aura of social prestige to the parish. A few of the "old" families of considerable wealth live there, and this is also supposed to give "tone" to the position of pastor.

Father Urban, the present Pastor, has been in office since 1933. He is a short, stockily built man in his fifties who was born in Hungary and who came to the United States at the age of thirteen and still speaks with a slight foreign accent. Father Dominic, the first assistant, has been in the parish for eight years, ever since his ordination. He is of remote Irish ancestry and was born and reared in the city where St. Mary's is located. Father Paul, the second assistant, has been ordained only two years. He is of remote French parentage from a large rural family which has its residence about sixty miles from the city.

The priests are the only ones who live in the rectory, a two-story, brick building adjoining the church. A female white secretary is employed part-time to do the office work. Charlie, the Negro cook and porter, has a room next to the two-car garage; while Emmaline, the housemaid, comes in to work "by the day." The rectory staff includes Arnold, the sexton, and his wife, who take care of the church building, and three white women who are janitors in the school. The convent, which is around the corner from the rectory and behind the school, houses nineteen Sisters and a white lay woman who cooks for them.

This center of religious activity is surrounded by the community of Riverside, which contained 23,621 persons when we first began to study it. Of these, 18,094 were white (76.6 per cent) and 5,527 were Negroes (23.4 per cent). St. Mary's is a white Catholic parish. In the same year the large city of which Riverside is a neighborhood community was estimated to have a population which was approximately 32 per cent Negro. Hence, Riverside, from a numerical point of view, is supposed to have a smaller "Negro problem" than the rest of the city. Of course, the sociological definition of the Negro is used here and refers to anyone of some known Negro ancestry, even though a majority of the Negroes living in the community are more than half-Caucasian in ancestry. We estimate that in a northern city where their family backgrounds are unknown about 5 per cent could pass for Nordic whites and another 10 per cent for Latin-Americans.[1]

The religious composition of the whole population shows that the Catholics number 12,292 (52.03 per cent), the Protestants 10,006 (42.36 per cent), the Jews 506 (2.14 per cent), and that those who had no religion or whose religion is unknown total 817 (3.45 per cent). If one considers the whole biracial population from this aspect, the concept of a predominantly Catholic community must be altered considerably. When this religious composition is redivided according to race, it is seen that the great majority of Negroes (70.67 per cent) are Protestants (mainly Baptist and Methodist), while the majority of whites (60.49 per cent) are Catholics. Figure 1 shows the relative numbers in the Riverside population.

There are thirty churches within the territorial limits of St. Mary's

---

1. This estimate is made from several actual counts of passers-by on Main Street, based on a numerical and "complexion" scale, combined with the results of interviews among the Negroes of the community.

Parish (eight white and twenty-two Negro). Of the eight white churches, one is Catholic and seven are Protestant; there is no Jewish synagogue or temple. Only the two Catholic churches claim territorial boundaries, and those of St. Benedict's, the Negro Catholic parish, extend over an area almost five times as great as Riverside. The statistics for the number of worshipers in all these churches (except

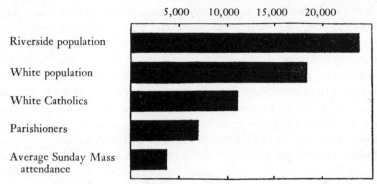

Fig. 1.—Relative numbers in the total population (23,621), whites (18,094), white baptized Catholics (10,946), St. Mary's parishioners (6,727), and average attendance at Sunday Masses (3,465).

St. Mary's) do not give a true account of the size of their congregations. Some of them are situated near the edges of the community and draw their members from surrounding areas, while others are

TABLE 1

	White	Negro		White	Negro
Baptist	0	15	Methodist	1	2
Catholic	1	1	Nazarene	1	0
Christian Scientist	1	0	Presbyterian	1	0
Evangelical Lutheran	1	1	Protestant Episcopal	1	0
Evangelical and Reform	1	0	Spiritualist	0	2
Holiness	0	1			

"class" churches to which people come from all over the city. The denominations of these churches according to race are shown in Table 1.

The churches of Riverside are scattered all over the area except on Shack Row along the river, where there is at the present time no church building. The five white churches with the largest congregations are situated on Riverside Drive. The twenty-two Negro churches, with the exception of St. Benedict's, are mainly small storefront establishments with part-time preachers, generally placed in or near Devil's Elbow and Pension Town. The Nazarene Church is on the outskirts of Devil's Elbow, the Evangelical Lutheran is on the West Side near the cemeteries, while the remaining white church, the Christian Scientist, has a beautiful structure on the main highway on the South Side.[2]

The parish of St. Mary's, as a sociological unit subject to analysis, does not include all the 10,946 white persons who said that "they were Catholics." On the other hand, since the parish must be considered a unit composed of Catholic families, we cannot completely exclude the 291 non-Catholic spouses in mixed marriages. Thus, St. Mary's Parish has 6,727 persons, but for practical administrative and religious purposes the priests of St. Mary's are directly charged with the care of 6,436 souls.[3] The remaining thousands are, at best, nominal or dormant Catholics who appear to be unwilling to practice their religion and are thus only an indirect responsibility of the priests.

What kind of people are these parishioners of St. Mary's? How do they compare with, and in what ways do they differ from, other recognizable social groups in Riverside? In many ways they are, of course, physically and socially integrated in the larger community and seem to be marked by all the common patterns of thought and conduct existing in Riverside. The *only* distinguishing characteristic in which we are interested is their Catholicism. Even in those areas of social activity by Catholics where we have difficulty in discerning it, this is the central feature of our study. Every other factor and element must in some way be related to this religious adherence.

Catholicism is not a uniform characteristic manifesting itself in the same way in every parishioner of St. Mary's. By the criterion of church attendance alone, there are "Easter Catholics" and "Sunday Catholics" and very devout Catholics. This means that there is a discernible religious composition of the persons within a single denomination and within a single congregation. For example, 4,468 persons

2. St. Mary's and St. Benedict's are the only churches of Riverside that are in any sense biracial. While there is no question of organizational participation by either Catholic group in the other's parish, there are almost always a few Negroes who attend Mass at St. Mary's and a few whites who attend St. Benedict's.

3. This includes 86 children below the age of fourteen whose parents have not yet brought them for baptism. The 291 non-Catholic husbands and wives are to some degree integrated into all the sociological patterns of the parish, with the exception of the purely sacred functions of the Catholic religion. Furthermore, all figures exclude the Sisters who teach in the parochial school and the priests who administer the parish.

attended Mass on Easter Sunday, an average of 3,465 attend on all Sundays of the year, while about 2,807 attend on holy days of obligation. The same differentials may be observed in the frequency of confession and Holy Communion.

Parishioners vary widely, too, on the materialistic criterion of their contributions to the support of the parish. Generally speaking, the devoutly observant Catholic is also a steady contributor in proportion to his income. St. Mary's uses the "envelope system" wherein each employed parishioner is supposed to receive a packet of envelopes, one for each Sunday and feast day in the year. There are in the parish 2,481 employed persons, but only 1,123 individuals had received packets of envelopes for the year in which the count was taken. Actually, however, only 886 were regularly putting the envelopes in the collection basket. But even this number is not representative of either families or employed people. The envelopes are distributed in January to anyone who asks for them. Some families have three or four; other families have none; some retired persons and children receive them, while many workers do not.

The internal diversities of the parish constitute one of the key concepts of this book. In each aspect of religious behavior which we studied, the Catholic Church presents a recognizable ideal. The complete acceptance and practice of all these ideals is sanctity. Variations from the ideal may be roughly categorized and placed on a scale so that a general view of the parish's success or failure in its primary religious functions may be obtained.

The criteria mentioned above—Mass attendance and financial contribution—are merely two examples of the kind of complex activities which must be studied in order to distinguish Catholics from non-Catholics and parishioners among themselves. A further difficulty must be taken into consideration right from the start—the fact that some parishioners tend to fulfil their religious duties in other parish churches. From the census we learned that in 21.8 per cent of the parish households one or more persons attended Sunday Mass regularly at some other parish church. This means that at least 374 persons escape most of the criteria which we employed. Most of these live on the periphery of St. Mary's Parish and adjacent to three neighboring white parishes.[4]

The comparison between St. Mary's parishioners and the other

4. Since St. Mary's Church is situated on a transportation line, it is convenient for persons coming from other parishes for services. Numerically, these "outsiders" probably equal the parishioners attending other Catholic churches.

residents of Riverside may be carried further at this point. By noting three factors—crowding of household, homeownership and telephone subscription, and occupational status—we may gain a general idea of

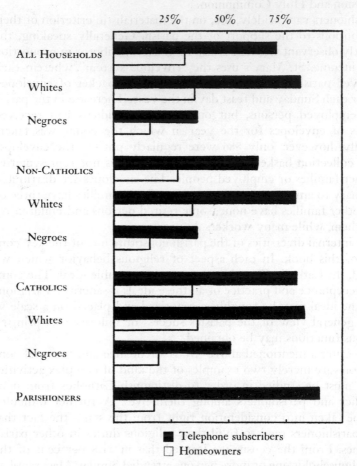

Fig. 2.—Percentage comparisons of the various householders in the Riverside community having telephones and owning homes.

the socioeconomic differences existing in the community (Fig. 2).

The socioeconomic difference between Negro and white households is immediately apparent in all except the matter of housing. Although the average per dwelling unit is only 3.26 as compared to 3.31 for whites, this is explained by the smallness of the Negro residences, the great majority of which contain only two rooms in which it would be a physical impossibility to accommodate larger numbers. The parishioners of St. Mary's have a larger number per unit than any other group (3.92). Actually, there are ninety-one identifiable family units doubling up with relatives. The average for dwelling units and family units cannot be used as an indication of the birth rate or of the number of children. In many instances there are relatives (a widowed mother or father, cousins and boarders) present to increase the number.

Taken separately, neither crowding, homeownership, nor telephone subscription can be employed as a clear criterion of socioeconomic status in the community. The statistics show that the parishioners of St. Mary's have a larger percentage of telephones than any other group but that their homeownership is down almost as low as the percentage for Negroes in general. A large number of parishioners live on the East Side, where two-family and four-family houses are the rule. Hence their tenancy rate is high.

In a modern urban American community the most reliable index to both social and economic status appears to be the occupation of the head of the household. As might be expected, occupational status in Riverside is weighted heavily in favor of the white people, who hold the greatest number of well-paying positions, while the great majority of Negroes are in the semiskilled and unskilled categories. From the religious point of view, however, there is a reversal within each race. The white non-Catholics are in better positions than the white Catholics, while the Negro Catholics have the advantage over Negro non-Catholics.

The comparisons in Figure 3 indicate that St. Mary's parishioners swell out the ranks of the lower middle class. The large percentage of heads of household engaged in clerical and sales operations and also those in the skilled and semiskilled categories substantially exceed the averages for the white population of Riverside. The percentage of professional people (lawyers, teachers, doctors, etc.) is appreciably lower than that for the whole white community. The highest and the lowest occupational categories are underrepresented by St. Mary's parishioners.

All the information in Figures 2 and 3 must be combined in order to form an estimate of the social stratification of both the Riverside community and the Catholic parish. It must be remembered, however, that "society" in the sense of a class structure wherein people have varying degrees of social access to one another cannot be judged in

Riverside except on a biracial basis. In this regard the two races must be analyzed separately. No Negro family in the area ranks with the very top group in the city's Negro class structure, but several Catholic

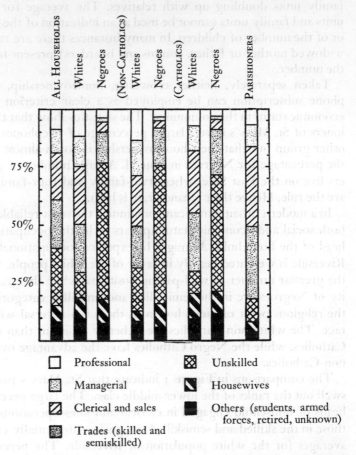

FIG. 3.—Percentage comparisons of the occupations of heads of households by race and religion.

Negro families, because of their educational and professional status, rank high among the Negroes of Riverside.

With the exception of the very top rank, the class structure of the whites is similar to that of the whole city. Two white Catholic families may be termed part of the "highest society" of the city, while several other families rank quite high. Within the Riverside community the West Side contains the greatest proportion of persons who are socially mobile and verging on the upper class. Except for the families living on or near Riverside Drive, the greater proportion of persons in the East Side (where many of the parishioners live) are of the lower middle class with no serious social aspirations.

The comparative statistics for the age composition of the various groups show that the parishioners of St. Mary's are a substantially

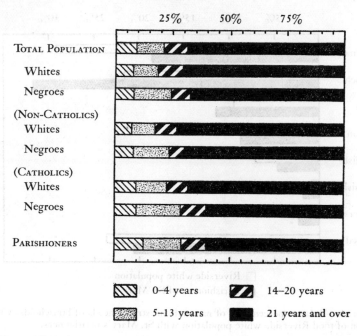

Fig. 4.—Relative percentages of age groupings by race and religion in the Riverside community.

younger population. The age grades are given in Figure 4. This figure shows that the Negro population is younger than the white. This may be accounted for partially by the recent influx of rural Negroes with their relatively large families and also by the fact that Negroes in their twenties and thirties have been migrating from the South. The religious proportion among Negroes is the same as that of whites. The Catholic Negroes have a larger proportion of children in the preschool and grammar-school ages than the non-Catholic Negroes. The parishioners of St. Mary's have a larger percentage of preschool children than either the nominal Catholics or the total white population.

The sex composition of the population of Riverside is typical of urban centers of the South. The widest distribution is among the Negroes and the narrowest among the parishioners of St. Mary's. The sex ratio for the whole population is 90.39, for whites alone 90.8, for Negroes alone 89.08, and for St. Mary's parishioners, 98.96.

In the preponderance of females in all groups Riverside is similar to

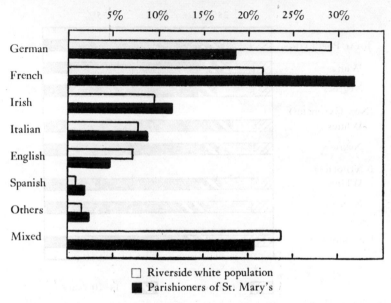

Fig. 5.—Relative percentages of national ancestry of heads of households. Comparison of total Riverside white population with St. Mary's parishioners.

other long-established communities in the South. The disproportion in the sexes among Negroes is a common phenomenon, since Negro men have been migrating in greater numbers than women to the industrial centers both within the South and in the North. The opportunities for domestic service generally have helped to keep the Negro women more or less stable in the southern cities.

The ethnic diversity of the Riverside population is of considerable background interest. The predominant nationality groups are German, French, Irish, and Italian. By asking the nationality of heads of households, we were able to make a comparison between the community at large and the parisioners of St. Mary's (Fig. 5).

The statistics in Figure 5 do not include the nationality background of the spouses of heads of households. The fact that only 1,270 out of

5,464 heads of white households in Riverside, and only 353 out of the 1,715 heads of parishioners' households, were of mixed national ancestry seems remarkable. But more than half of the spouses of "pure" national background are now married to persons of different national origin, so that in the next generation the proportion of "pure" heads of households will be very much smaller.

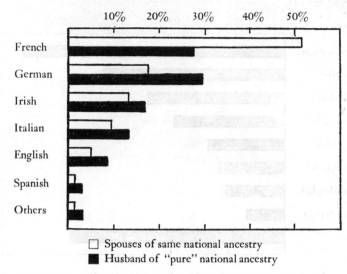

FIG. 6.—Ethnic composition of St. Mary's parishioners. Percentage comparisons of households in which both spouses are of same nationality and households where husband is of "pure" nationality.

The immigration of Germans into Riverside was heavy right from the beginning of the community's history, more than one hundred years ago. They continued to come in large numbers even when the migration of French had practically ceased. The Irish came mainly in the second half of the last century, and at the present time there are practically no foreign-born Irish in the community. The Italians constitute the largest group of foreign-born, the majority of them having migrated to Riverside since the beginning of this century. Those of English descent are mainly Americans from other parts of the country, most of them from the rural areas of the South (Fig. 6).

A further analysis of the ethnic composition of St. Mary's Parish shows the kind of "mixture" that has taken place. There were 718 households (41.86 per cent) in which both spouses were of the same nationality; 644 (37.55 per cent) in which the husband was of pure national origin; and 353 (or 20.58 per cent) in which the husband was of mixed nationality. These three categories, when analyzed further, show that French persons tend to marry each other more than twice as often as Germans and almost four times as often as Irish. Germans and French married each other more frequently than others, while French-Irish and German-Irish marriages were next in order of frequency (Fig. 7).

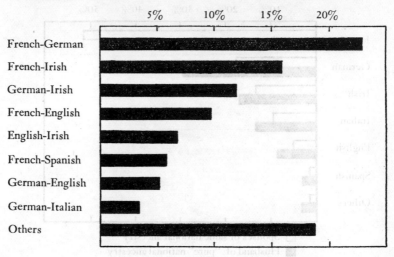

Fig. 7.—Ethnic composition of St. Mary's parishioners. Percentage comparisons of husbands of mixed national ancestry.

Scattered throughout the parish there are representatives of many other ethnic strains. Among the "Others" who are of pure nationality there are Scotch, Rumanian, Cuban, Danish, Slav, and Swiss. Among the "Others" of mixed nationality there is a great variety of combinations, some of them showing as many as four different ethnic backgrounds.

It is obvious, of course, that the children of these marriages are contributing to the amalgamation of the various groups. The children of 997 households are now of mixed ancestry. In another generation this process will have moved forward quite rapidly, and thereafter it will be practically useless to attempt an unraveling of nationality backgrounds. Germans seem to have become more thoroughly assimilated than the French. This may be attributable to a noticeable migration from rural southern areas where small French communities have been relatively isolated. Some of these moved in when they were already married, while single persons seem to have preferred spouses of their own national extraction. The impact of ethnic custom is losing its force, however, in the rapidly changing culture of this urban parish. We shall discuss in another place what still remains of probable ethnic influence on religious observance.

The political composition of the people of Riverside is approximately what one would expect in a southern urban community, and

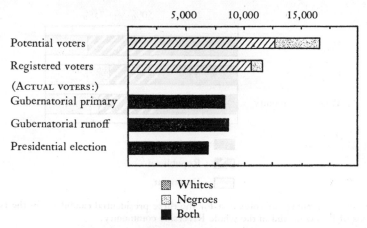

FIG. 8.—Numbers of potential and registered voters in Riverside by race. Total numbers of actual voters in three elections.

that of St. Mary's parishioners does not differ significantly from the rest of the community. The extent of participation in political affairs is a criterion of civic-mindedness, while the way in which the parishioners voted and the candidates they supported are an even more important index of their social attitudes and values. For the most part, the people are nominally Democrats, having their own intergroup divisions on the state and local levels. The Republicans come to life politically once every four years at the presidential election.

Both the gubernatorial and the presidential elections were held while the study was in progress. Figure 8 shows the extent of participation. Approximately 50 per cent of the potential voters elected the governor and about two-fifths voted for President.

There is a noticeable stratification in the political structure which appears to be sociologically as well as territorially significant. Riverside Drive is the official dividing line between the two city political wards which comprise the community. Considering this rough division, the ward leaders remark that the whole West Side is politically unpredictable and that the hardest work has to be done there to get out the votes. The East Side is usually well under the control of the city machine, with deviations appearing only when there is a shift in the power centers of the machine.

There is a three-way split among the Democrats on the municipal level, and this split extends into Riverside. In point of numbers and influence generally, the city machine is the best-knit and most strong-

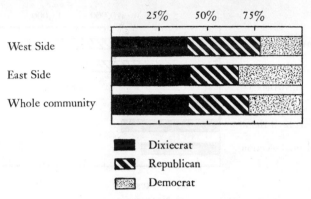

FIG. 9.—Percentage of votes cast for the three presidential candidates in the two sections of Riverside and in the whole Riverside community.

ly organized in the community. Typical, year-round politicians are active in this group, and they usually deliver the vote in the East Side. The reformers, now in power, are also a municipal group gradually building a professional organization in opposition to the city machine. Its most active members are generally of the better-educated upper class, who think of themselves as the "natural" leaders of the community. For the most part, their influence is strongest on the West Side, where residential and economic conditions are somewhat higher. Finally, the state faction has also had a foothold in Riverside during the last decade. It is supported by the lowest-income groups and contends with the city machine for control of the East Side.

The political and social mentality of the Riverside population was brought into sharp focus by the presidential election of 1948. Of the fifteen precincts in both wards, ten went for Thurmond, four for Dewey, and only one for Truman. In a comparison of the East and West Sides, the actual percentage of voters for each candidate is probably a better gauge than the location of the precincts (Fig. 9).

The anti-Truman sentiment was strong in the West Side, where the voters seemed to hesitate between Thurmond and Dewey. In the senatorial race six of the nine precincts on this side of the community went Republican. On the East Side there seemed little desire to break the southern tradition by voting Republican, and the real choice was between Thurmond and Truman. The only precinct, however, which gave Truman a plurality was the Fifth on the East Side, comprising some of the worst residential area (i.e., part of Pension Town) in the community.

There is no direct method of discovering accurately the political sentiments and affiliations of the members of St. Mary's Church. However, the areas of concentrated Catholic households may be matched with the vote returns in the various precincts. The East Side, in which the influence of the city machine is most strongly felt and where the Republicans have the least success, is also the most Catholic area. The mayor of the city lives on Riverside Drive, and some of his reformers are among the upper-class Catholics in the better residential sections. The previous mayor, a Catholic of Italian extraction and a close friend of Father Urban, was the power behind the city machine, but his votes were most often obtained among the Catholics in the poorer sections.

There are Catholic precinct leaders and ward leaders in all political parties, even in the Republican group which is revivified every four years. A list of the Catholic precinct leaders for each party shows that their economic and educational background is of more significance than their adherence to the Catholic religion. In other words, there seems to be no "Catholic vote" as such or a distinctive "Catholic political philosophy" in operation among the parishioners. In the three Democratic parties on the local level, the reformers' party generally drew its workers from the upper-class Catholics, the city machine from a combination of middle- and lower-class Catholics, and the state faction from the support of the lowest-income groups.

The national presidential election demonstrated a peculiar split in the civic mentality of Catholics. The so-called "intellectuals" and business groups in the parish rejected Truman completely and were placed in the dilemma of choosing between Dewey and Thurmond. As far as could be ascertained by casual questioning among the parishioners, the professional and business people tended toward Dewey. The Pastor told many of his friends that he would vote Republican, and he probably influenced them. Very few seemed to have any ethical qualms over the racist aspect of the Dixiecrat program.

The comparative picture of the parishioners of St. Mary's may be summarized as follows: While Riverside is predominantly white and more than half of the people are Catholics, the parishioners constitute a little more than a third of the white community. Their family and household units are larger than those of either Negroes or of the whole white group. Their homeownership is below the average, and their telephone subscription is above the average for the whites; but they are above the average in both when compared to the Negroes. They have a smaller percentage in the professional and managerial occupations than the whole white group but more than the Negroes. They have a higher percentage in the clerical and trades categories than either the other whites or the Negroes.

St. Mary's parishioners are a younger population than the other groups, having a significantly larger percentage in the age class 0–13 years. Their sex distribution is closer to a balance than that of both other groups. In their ethnic background the people of St. Mary's have a slightly smaller percentage of mixed nationality. They have a smaller percentage of persons of German extraction than the community as a whole but a larger percentage of French, Irish, and Italians. In their social and political attitudes they tend toward the traditional and conservative ideas prevalent in Riverside.

Chapter Four

Recruitment to the Parish

The Catholic life of an individual begins at the moment of his baptism. It is at this time that he becomes a friend and child of God, a participant in the supernatural order of which the Catholic Church is the earthly custodian, a member of the Mystical Body of Christ, and a parishioner. Unlike the various religious sects which count their membership only from the reception of confirmation, or by the signing of a letter of application, or by some form of public "witness of faith," the Catholic Church insists upon the sacrament of baptism as the essential beginning of parish membership.

As we have already seen, the baptized Catholic is supposed to be an integral member of the parish wherein he resides. From a sociological point of view, however, it is fruitless to include in the parish unit of St. Mary's those thousands of baptized Catholics who do not observe the rules of membership in the Church. These people constitute the problem of "leakage" from the Church. Baptism leaves an indelible mark on the soul, and no one can cease to be baptized no matter how he conducts himself or how greatly he regrets that he was baptized. Only in a wide sense, however, can such persons be termed Catholics or parishioners.

Since the Church, by the intention of Christ, is all-embracing in its membership, the ideal condition for any parish would be the recruitment and maintenance in membership of all human beings (23,621) living within its territorial boundaries. The presence of non-Catholics and of dormant Catholics in the geographical parish of St. Mary's indicates the extent to which it falls short of this ideal. While the parish has shown a steady numerical increase over the century of its existence, its proportional increase is probably not so great as that of the total population of Riverside.

Two important questions must be asked at this point: How does

33

the parish of St. Mary's gain in membership? How and why does it lose members? There are three ways by which the parish grows: (a) by migration of Catholics from other parishes, (b) by infant baptisms, and (c) by adult conversions. There are also three ways by which the parish loses membership: (a) by migration to other parishes, (b) by deaths,[1] and (c) by individual defections, or failure to observe the essential conditions of adherence.

Since the conditions and factors of spatial mobility are not directly the result of the parish priest's work, we need not discuss them here.[2] Proximity to the church and school is in some instances the reason why a family selects a certain location for its residence. By and large, however, there is nothing which the priests of St. Mary's have done in order to influence the migration of Catholics into the parish. There has been no large-scale residential construction within the parish borders in which they have participated in any way.

Infant baptism, the second way of gaining members to the parish, is of extreme importance because through it the largest number of souls come into the parish. Catholic parents usually bring their children to the parish church within a month of their birth, and for this reason the birth rate of St. Mary's parishioners takes on great significance. The Catholic parish grows much more by births than it does by either migration or conversion. The moral implications of birth prevention and the relatively higher fertility of Catholics will be treated in another part of this study.[3]

Of much greater importance than the physical is the spiritual birth of children into the parish by way of the sacrament of baptism. The official records of the parish show that 276 infants were baptized at St. Mary's during the year of the study. Taking the total population of the parish as 6,727, we find that this is an infant rate of 40.93 per thousand, an obviously absurd figure as compared to the actual birth rate of 24.08. If, however, we use as a base figure the whole white Catholic population of Riverside, which includes many dormant Catholics, we reach an infant rate of 25.21 per thousand.

This discrepancy led us to the following conclusion. While the birth rate and the infant baptism rate may not necessarily coincide in

---

1. See below, chap. 11.
2. Urban mobility and its relation to religious observance are treated in a subsequent volume. Cf. Joseph H. Fichter, S.J., "Urban Mobility and Religious Observance," *American Catholic Sociological Review*, XI, No. 3 (October, 1950), 130–39.
3. Cf. Joseph H. Fichter, S.J., "Catholics in the United States: How Many Are We?" *America*, LXXXII (February 4, 1950), 523.

any given parish because of family mobility or of failure to have the child baptized or because former parishioners may bring children back to St. Mary's for baptism, these two rates ought to be fairly the same. In other words, the number of children born in twelve months to the Catholics of St. Mary's Parish ought to be roughly equal to the number of infants baptized in St. Mary's Church. In the census of parishioners there were 162 infants; in the baptismal records there were 276 infants, a little more than the number of infants (255) reported in the census of all white Catholics of Riverside. The conclusion must be that dormant Catholics still follow the custom of having their children baptized even though they maintain no other connection with the parish.

It may be said, therefore, that in the administration of the sacrament of baptism the priests of St. Mary's serve not only their parishioners but also the nominal Catholics of Riverside. This "extension" of the pastoral activity must be kept in mind in the following description and analysis.

The traditional liturgical preparation for the birth of a child to Catholic parents is no longer observed in St. Mary's Parish. The Catholic ritual provides a special blessing for pregnant women, but as far as can be ascertained no prospective mother during the last ten years has availed herself of this blessing, nor has there been any effort on the part of the parish priests to inform lay persons of this ceremony. The same may be said of the old ceremony of the "churching" of women, a special ritual for women who have given birth to children. These are pious practices which have fallen almost entirely out of usage in this urban community.

The sacrament of baptism, however, is still considered of great importance even among so-called "dormant" Catholics. This sacrament is administered every Sunday afternoon in the baptistry of St. Mary's Church by the assistant pastors. On special occasions and for special reasons the Pastor himself or some visiting priest may administer baptism. During the year of the study, Father Urban performed 18 infant baptisms, Father Dominic 109, Father Paul 122, and visiting priests 27.[4]

The baptistry is a small alcove, about eight by ten feet in size, at the right of the entrance of the church. On Sunday afternoon at two

4. This is a total of 276 baptisms compiled from the parish records at the end of the year. This differs from the total of 255 infants in the families of both dormant and parochial Catholics, as learned from the census made in the beginning of the study.

o'clock the infants are brought to the church by their godparents, usually attended in each case by three or four relatives and friends. At times as many as eleven children are presented for baptism, and the group crowded in the back of the church may number seventy-five persons. The ministering priest writes on separate sheets of paper the name of each child, its birth date, and the names of parents and godparents. He does this slowly in order to give all infants time to arrive at the church.

The "assembly line" technique is then employed. The godparents, with the godmother holding the child, are asked to line up along the wall at the back of the church. The priest asks all to answer the questions simultaneously. He says the prayers in the plural for all the infants at once and performs the necessary individual actions by stopping along the line at each child. He then asks that the infants be brought one at a time into the baptistry, where the actual pouring of water occurs. As they go out, the godfather hands the priest a sealed envelope containing the stipend,[5] usually one or two dollars.

The whole ceremony, even when conducted in this mass fashion, is over before three o'clock. The priests are informal in their manner and are undisturbed by the wailing of infants. Most of the children remain quiet, but every Sunday there are one or two crying babies, whose godmothers appear flustered and embarrassed. The priest smiles and assures them that these cries "are praise for God in His house." He puts all the people at their ease and finishes with the remark, "Well, here's another good Christian," or "See that he is brought up a good Catholic."

There appears to be a growing conflict and confusion between the sacred and the social aspects of baptism. This is indicated in some instances by a lack of knowledge concerning the function of godparents. According to Catholic tradition and practice, the godparent enters a special spiritual relationship with the infant, whereby he assumes responsibility for his religious training in the event that the parents are unable or unwilling to perform this duty. Many parents seem to be losing sight of this function, and they tend to select as godparents friends or acquaintances to whom they wish to do honor. A frequent choice is a business associate who may be expected to take a special future interest in the prospects of the infant. Most often, however, the godparents are selected from the immediate family of the husband or wife. When a non-Catholic appears as godparent, the

---

5. The stipend is a voluntary, but expected, donation accepted by the priest as a personal gift. It is in no sense a fee, or charge, for the baptismal service.

priest must explain that the relationship and its obligations are impossible for him.[6]

The practice of "christening parties" seems to be on the ascendancy in St. Mary's Parish. The parents invite a number of guests to their home, or perhaps to a restaurant, for a Sunday-afternoon cocktail party to celebrate the baptism of their child. Occasionally the priest is invited to these parties, but the invitation is rarely accepted. As far as could be learned through interviews, approximately 40 per cent of the baptisms are followed by social events of this kind.

The social importance attached to the ceremony may be one of the reasons why many Catholics who do not practice their religion insist

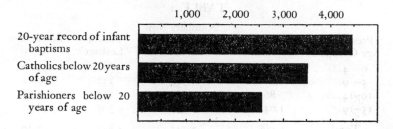

Fig. 10.—Comparison of number of infants baptized during twenty years at St. Mary's Church with the number of acknowledged Catholics and of actual parishioners below the age of twenty years.

on Catholic baptism for their children. Apparently they do not fully comprehend the sacramental significance of the ceremony. The community in which they live does not particularly disapprove their own lack of religious observance, but it looks askance at people who do not have their children baptized. This practice is still well imbedded in the family mores. A clue to the persistence of this pattern of behavior is found in the number of godparents who address the priest as "Sir" instead of "Father." Their general ignorance of the Church customs and the purpose of baptism indicates a proportion of ill-instructed and nonpracticing Catholics.

The statistics for baptisms lend a strong support to this observation. The parish register shows that during the course of twenty years prior to the study there were 4,426 infant baptisms performed at St. Mary's Church. On the other hand, the parish census made in the year of the study gave a total of 2,545 persons below the age of twenty. The census of Riverside showed that there were 3,540 per-

6. On several occasions during the year people asked whether they could have non-Catholics as "sponsors" at baptism.

sons of this age living in families that listed themselves as Catholics (Fig. 10).

Here we are confronted with a very serious problem: What has happened to the 4,426 children who were baptized at St. Mary's during the last twenty years? The normal mortality for a population group, 0–20 years of age, is 6 per cent. Thus 265 of these baptized children may be said to have died. There remain, then, 4,161. Of this number, 3,540 are listed as Catholics, even though about one thousand of them neither are themselves active Catholics nor belong to active Catholic families. Of this number, there still remain 621 persons below the age of twenty who are unaccounted for. Have they, with their

TABLE 2

Present Age Group	Infants Baptized	Numbers Now Reported in Census	Loss or "Leakage"	Percentage Loss
0– 4	1,443	812	631	43.70
5– 9	1,077	745	332	30.82
10–14	865	452	413	47.74
15–19	1,041	536	505	48.51
Total	4,426	2,545	1,881	42.49

families, completely lost the Catholic faith so that they are no longer identifiable as even dormant Catholics? Or have they, as the Pastor suggests, "moved out of Riverside"?

This last explanation is hardly plausible. Both the community of Riverside and the parish of St. Mary's have grown considerably in the course of twenty years. Our statistics on mobility show that the parish itself has increased by about five hundred families in the ten years prior to the study.[7] We can hardly assume that large numbers of families with children moved out of the parish while still greater numbers of families without children replaced them.

The explanation seems to lie in the facts mentioned above, namely, that these children are lost to the Church immediately after baptism. They are submitted for baptism in infancy by parents who feel that "it is the thing to do," but who either have no intention of rearing them as Catholics or want to allow them to "choose for themselves when they get older."

This picture of the loss of children to the parish is seen most clearly when the figures from the baptismal records are placed side by side with those of the parish census (Table 2). Assuming that each age

7. Cf. Fichter, "Urban Mobility and Religious Observance," *op. cit.*, pp. 130–39.

group was baptized in the year of infancy which corresponds to its present age, we find that there are great discrepancies between the two figures.

If we consider infant baptism as the beginning of membership in the *parish* of St. Mary's, we see that over a period of twenty years there is a 42.49 per cent loss of parishioners. If we subtract from this the approximate mortality loss of 6 per cent for the age group 0–20, we still note a membership loss of 36.49 per cent. Actually, these children are from the families of dormant Catholics who cannot in any realistic sense be termed parishioners. Hence the children "enter the Church" by baptism but never really "enter the parish" as such. It is no mere accident that this percentage of youthful "leakage" from the Church closely coincides with the percentage of self-styled Catholics in Riverside who are dormant or lapsed. Our statistics show that 4,219 or 38.49 per cent of all white Catholics in Riverside are nonparishioners.

The conclusion that we must draw concerning leakage from the parish during the early years of life is corroborated by the study we have made of school children. The parish census shows 1,034 children in the age group 5–13 years. The corresponding number of infant baptisms for this age group was 1,774. Making allowances for mortalities, we find that approximately seven hundred elementary-school children who ought to be members of the parish have "disappeared" from it since baptism. This is close to the number of children (755) who actually attended St. Mary's Parochial School during the year of this survey. The capacity of the school would have to be more than doubled to take care of all children baptized in St. Mary's Church. Large numbers of children have simply "dropped out" of the Catholic parish before they reach school age.

Finally, what steps are taken in an action program by the parish priest to save these infants to the Catholic Church? At St. Mary's Church no record is made of the parents' address, nor are any questions usually asked concerning their practice of the Catholic faith. When other sacraments are administered, for example, Holy Communion, confirmation, and matrimony, careful investigation is made and instruction is given. The results are usually gratifying, or at least the priest feels that he has done all in his power to advance the spiritual life of the recipient of the sacrament. It has been suggested in some parishes that at infant baptism a questionnaire be filled out concerning the parents and that a follow-up be made in an attempt to recall the dormant Catholics among them to the practice of the Faith. This may provide at least a partial solution of one of the most vexing problems of the urban Church.

Besides migration and infant baptisms there is a third way by which new members may be added to the Catholic parish. This is the conversion of non-Catholic adults to the Catholic faith. We are speaking here only of this type of conversion, because there is no record kept of the spiritual conversion, or return to the Church, of dormant Catholics. As was noted above, a large harvest for this latter kind of conversion work lies within the shadow of St. Mary's Church.

There are at the present time 136 adult converts to Catholicism in St. Mary's Parish; 84 are women and 52 are men. Without other studies on which to base a comparison, there is no way of telling whether this proportion is high or low. We were interested in discovering how and why non-Catholics enter the Church, and we found that marriage, or prospective marriage, to a Catholic was the most important factor. In only six marriages were both husband and wife converts. Of the 136 converts, only 34 were baptized while still single and with apparently no thought of matrimony in mind. Forty-nine became Catholics at the time of their marriage, while 53 entered the Church after they had married Catholics.

Thus, it would seem that the attitude of Catholics and the constant teaching of the Church concerning mixed marriages had the most important influence in bringing 102 (or 75 per cent) of these converts to the Church. The remaining 25 per cent became converts mainly after a period of association with lay Catholics or after attending a Catholic school. Some had become interested through reading Catholic pamphlets and books, but only three declared that they had been influenced by the direct proselytizing efforts of priests.

All the above information came from the census-taking and informal questioning of the parishioners. When we turn to the parish records, we find that over a period of twenty years there were 175 adult baptisms, of which 77 were males and 98 were females. This is an average of 8.75 persons each year. When compared to the number of infant baptisms, the yearly increment to the parish through adult conversions is exceedingly small. When compared to the 7,048 white citizens of Riverside who are non-Catholics and the 4,219 who are dormant Catholics, the number seems almost infinitesmal.

There is no organized effort in the parish for the specific purpose of bringing converts to the Catholic Church. The diocese operates an information bureau in the downtown area of the large city, and several of the other city churches conduct weekly inquiry classes for non-Catholics. As far as could be observed, the priests of St. Mary's have no specific plan for attracting non-Catholics to the Church. In advertising the two-week mission conducted during Lent, they asked the parishioners to bring their non-Catholic friends to the sermons, but there is no way of knowing the extent to which this invitation was accepted.

When a person presents himself for instructions, or is brought to the rectory by a future husband or wife, the priests are very gracious. Father Urban, of course, has the greatest amount of experience in the instruction of converts and conducts the individual lessons in the Faith with care and patience. Usually the person under instruction is given a catechism of the kind used in Catholic high schools and a few pamphlets in Apologetics. The length of time and the number of lessons depend upon the state of knowledge of the future convert. Some Protestants have a fairly complete knowledge of the teachings of their own Church, while others know hardly more than the fact of God's existence.

The length of time spent in preparation for adult baptism may vary from two to eight months. No matter how well prepared he may be, a non-Catholic is hardly ever accepted for baptism at St. Mary's Parish with less than two months' instructions. Coming to the rectory on two or three nights a week, he listens and discusses the main truths of the Catholic faith. The outline of the catechism is generally followed by the priest-instructor, who will give explanations and examples wherever they are required. The priest judges not only the state of knowledge of the future convert but also his spirit of faith and his general prospect of future fidelity to the Church.

As Father Dominic says, "It's better to give them thorough instructions now before they enter the Church. They may never have a chance like this again." All three of the priests try to make their instruction periods do double duty whenever a non-Catholic is under instruction for baptism before marriage. They believe that the "review" of religious truths can help also the engaged Catholic, and, unless one of the parties objects to the arrangement, they ask that both be present.

The actual ceremony by which an adult formally becomes a member of the Catholic Church and of the parish is more complicated than that of infant baptism. Most adults have held some sort of religious faith and many have been baptized in Protestant religions before deciding to become Catholics. Therefore, three formal steps are required of them: (1) abjuration of previous heresy, (2) baptism, and (3) confession.

Adults are not accepted as Catholics into St. Mary's Parish at the usual Sunday-afternoon period reserved for infant baptism. At any other time convenient to the priest and the convert they and two witnesses meet in the church itself. The priest wears cassock, surplice, and stole, lights the candles, and seats himself usually inside the Communion rail. The convert kneels, places his hands on the altar missal, and reads a renunciation of all heretical doctrines and an acceptance of all Catholic doctrines.

The two sacraments of baptism and penance are then administered conditionally. If the convert had been validly baptized in his previous religion, he now needs the sacrament of penance to remove all the sins committed since baptism. If his previous baptism was invalid, his present baptism is sufficient to remove not only original sin but all the personal sins committed during his whole life. The Church provides for either contingency and safeguards both the recipient and the sacraments.

After the formal abjuration of error and the profession of faith, the group goes from the sanctuary to the baptistry. There, unlike the infant who needs someone to respond for him, the convert gives all the answers and makes all the necessary prayers and statements. Otherwise the baptism ceremony proceeds much like that of a child. After this is completed, the priest and new convert go to the confessional, where the penitent makes a "general" confession, that is, an acknowledgment of all the sins of his whole life. He is usually well prepared for this by the priest during his course of instructions and is free to choose as confessor some priest other than his instructor. Such choice is readily available in an urban parish like St. Mary's, where there are three priests, but most converts prefer to confess to the priest from whom they learned the truths of Catholicism.

Adult converts are not required to undergo another series of instructions in preparation for their first reception of the Eucharist. They usually receive Communion with the other communicants at the next Mass they attend. Neither do they usually take special instructions before receiving the sacrament of confirmation, but, since this latter sacrament is administered only by the Bishop at a designated time, the adults receive it publicly at the same ceremony with the children.

After this discusison of infant baptisms and adult conversions, it may be remarked that the degree of net growth of St. Mary's parish cannot be judged unless consideration is made also of those persons who leave the parish by migration, death, or defection. In other words, net gain cannot be measured unless the annual losses are subtracted from the annual gains in membership. This problem has been touched upon above in the consideration of losses after infant baptisms and will be treated at greater length in another place.

Chapter Five

The Confessional

As a supernatural ideal for the everyday life of its adherents, the Church proposes that Catholics should strive always to be in the state of grace and of friendship with Almighty God. This means that Catholics are urged not only to live a virtuous life but also to receive frequently the sacrament of penance for the removal of whatever sins they have committed. Although the ideal of complete sinlessness among members of the Church on earth is unattainable, the priests of the Church constantly urge Catholics toward the ideal.

The sacrament of penance not only removes sin; it also strengthens the penitent in the supernatural life. It re-establishes sanctifying grace in the soul of the person who has committed mortal sin and gives special supernatural assistance for the avoidance of sin. Thus, the confessional is a pivotal experience for good Catholics. The person who goes to confession frequently is almost always the Catholic who best exemplifies the personal and social behavior demanded by Christianity. There are exceptions, of course, but these are due mainly to ignorance or to a misunderstanding of the actual application of the Church's moral teaching in contemporary society.

The normal procedure for the removal of sins is the use of the confessional. There the penitent kneels to tell his sins to the priest, receives the sacrament which absolves him, and expresses his own contrition and purpose of amendment. For the faithful Catholic the weekly reception of the sacrament becomes almost a matter of routine. For the marginal Catholic, who makes only his annual Easter duties, it becomes an ordeal to be postponed to the end of the paschal time. For the dormant Catholic it is a fearful and unknown experience.

Even the least-informed parishioner of St. Mary's knows that by Church precept he must confess his sins once a year. He may think that he is excommunicated unless he fulfils this duty and undoubtedly

44

realizes that he is on the verge of leaving the Faith. Good faithful Catholics are distressed when a member of the family fails to make his paschal confession, and they pray for his "return to the sacraments." There were 1,117 persons in the parish who are known to have missed their Easter duties during the year of the survey. In almost every instance this serious sin of omission is known only to the parish priests and to the immediate family. Some of these persons are involved in invalid marriages and cannot receive absolution until they cease to live in sin. Others have been "away for years," while still others have been "drifting away" gradually.

By the time the Catholic child is in the second grade of school he is presumed to have reached the age of reason and is therefore capable of sin. His obligation to confess his sins starts at that time. In the regular catechism classes the Sisters of the parochial school undertake to teach the children how to go to confession. This is usually done during the year preceding the child's first reception of Holy Communion. Catholic children attending the public schools receive the same instruction in the release-time program of the Confraternity of Christian Doctrine. Adult converts learn the procedure from a priest during their course of individual instructions.

In almost all instances the child's first experience in the confessional comes the day before he receives his first Holy Communion. At St. Mary's this occurs on the eve of St. Joseph's feast day, March 19. The children make a spiritual retreat for two days. Our observer noted: "Sister brought the girls to the church and began the catechism on confession. She explained just what had to be done and gave a review of sins the child might have to confess. She then had the children stand up and sing a hymn. Sister followed this with a story about Martha and Mary getting their home ready for Jesus; getting the place all clean just as they were going to do when they go to confession. They don't want to have cobwebs in their souls when Jesus comes."

On the morning when confessions were heard, "some of the little girls were afraid, while others kept telling them there is nothing to be afraid about. One girl said, 'What do they do to you in there?' I tried to reassure those who were frightened and worried by telling them the same things Sister told them yesterday: that the priest was simply taking God's place, and they were telling God what they had done wrong; that the priest would help them if they didn't know what to do; that he couldn't remember what he was told because he had so many people going to confession, and besides he couldn't see who it was making the confession.

"The boys had been much less frightened than the girls. They had seemed eager to get their turn in line and were more sure of themselves. Most of the boys had gone to the Communion rail to say their penance, and some of them stayed up there talking to each other. Many of the girls came out of the confessional with a happy smile on their faces and were then very quiet and angelic. They all returned to the back pews to say their penance.

"Sister Mary Anne complained several times during the day about how hard the public-school children were to handle, and particularly the boys. She said you could pick them right out of the crowd. When they went to confession, she sent them to Father Dominic, who had taught them in the release-time catechism classes. Later she told me that Father Urban did not think they were well enough prepared or knew what to do, but Father Dominic had taught them and could get along with them."

In approximately one-fifth of the sermons preached in St. Mary's there was some mention made of the confessional. The priests of the parish urged the people to receive this sacrament frequently, particularly during Lent and in the few weeks preceding Trinity Sunday. On April 4, Whitsunday, the Pastor said: "This is the day on which Our Lord gave to His disciples the power to forgive sins in confession. Today you should all be joining together in thanksgiving to God for the sacrament of penance. Look at the years of consolation we Catholics have had from the power of penance. We are privileged beyond all words. Think of the Protestants: How do they get along when they are in sin? They don't: They close their eyes to the words of Christ. They do not realize that telling your sins directly to God is not sufficient. They and we must do what Christ told us to do. If you refuse to go to confession, it's because you're too proud or because you don't want to give up your sins. The sacrament of penance is a sign of God's mercy on us, and it shows that He is an all-kind Father."

The two missions preached by the Lazarist Fathers during March were concentrated on the theme of bringing back sinners to God and of strengthening others in the friendship of God. The sacrament of penance was emphasized as the divinely established means for accomplishing this purpose. "Anyone with mortal sin on his soul," said the missioner to the men, "should not leave this church with it tonight. Pray to St. Peter, the keeper of the keys, to help you make a good confession, and tell God that you are truly sorry for having offended

Him. There will be no chance to go to confession after death. Come back to God before it is too late."

In the women's mission the priest talked about the qualities needed for a good confession. He tried to inspire them with faith in God's mercy. "The important thing to think about is the future, not the past. Do not worry yourself sick about what you have done in the past. Trust in God and plan for the avoidance of all sins in the future."

Since the actual process of going to confession may also be termed a form of social interaction, we observed and described the persons-in-action during the regular confession periods over a period of four months. The "typical" penitent takes about fifteen minutes from the time he enters the church until he leaves it. The first five minutes are used in the prayers and examination of conscience in the pews near the confessional. He then looks for the confessional with the shortest line and stands there for a few minutes waiting his turn to go to confession. After telling his sins and receiving absolution, he returns to his seat to say his penance and may add a few prayers.

This typical confession is not representative of all the great variety of personalities who enter the church to go to confession. Some individuals kneel in the pew for a half-hour before going to confession; others go immediately to the confessional line upon entering the church. High-school girls usually come in pairs and trios and sometimes talk and giggle the whole time they are in the church before and after their confession. About 15 per cent of the penitents kneel at the altar rail or before one of the statues while saying their penance. Some older people who wish to confess in French always go to Father Paul's confessional, while others prefer Father Dominic, who is "quicker."

Most of the time, especially on Saturday afternoon, there is no great delay for those waiting to go to confession. But on those occasions when large numbers wish to confess the priests can hear an average of forty-five confessions an hour. Father Dominic hears more than this number; Father Paul, fewer. In the monthly confessions for the parochial school children each priest may hear as many as sixty confessions per hour, with the Pastor lending occasional assistance.

There are four confessionals in St. Mary's Church, and they are located at the four corners of the church. The Pastor's confessional is in the front at the Gospel side of the church, and, with the exception of Sunday mornings and the vigils of important feasts, it is not used. At the rear of the church on the same side is an "extra" confessional, which is used by visiting priests assisting at Christmas and Easter time. The regular confessionals are on the Epistle side of the church, Father Dominic's, the first assistant, at the front, and Father Paul's at the back.

These two priests hear most of the confessions of the parishioners of St. Mary's, and they are noticeably different in their habits. The younger priest, Father Paul, comes to his confessional at four o'clock and stays there until six; he returns promptly after dinner and remains until there are no more penitents. Even though he is slower, he hears more confessions on any given Saturday and has more people who confess regularly to him. His penitents say that he is serious, patient, understanding, and given to pious counseling. His youth attracts younger people to his confessional, and his seriousness (as well as his ability to speak French) attracts the older parishioners.

Father Dominic's popularity as a confessor is greatest among penitents who are in a hurry. On Saturdays he frequently arrives late— and leaves early. He seems to hear confessions "in spurts," finishing with those who are in the line and then going to the church steps for a smoke and a chat with the people who enter or leave the church. Parishioners remark approvingly of his friendliness on these occasions. On hot summer afternoons he will treat a couple of the school-boys to "snowballs" and eat with them on the steps of the church. The men of the parish think he is a "card," and they tend to go to his confessional. They say he "doesn't take all day to give absolution."

The Pastor is for the most part free of the "drudgery" of the regular Saturday confession periods, but he "helps out" once in a while. The younger parishioners, and particularly the school children, say that he is severe to his penitents. Others report that they like a priest to "bawl them out" for their sins and that Father Urban is not "always making excuses for sinners."

The two Lazarist missioners and the visiting priests who sometimes assist in hearing confessions had the dubious advantage of "not knowing" their penitents. Some parishioners announce that they prefer to go to confession to "strange" priests who come to the parish. Actually, they have no way of knowing the reputation of the priest as a confessor, whether he is severe or lenient, abrupt or patient. Generally speaking, these parishioners are not the weekly or monthly penitents, and they seek out other churches and other priests for their infrequent confessions.

In a discussion about confessions several ladies of the parish thought that priests in other parishes are "more broad-minded; you can talk things over with them and reach some satisfactory agreement." Some of the men said they prefer to go to the priests at a certain downtown church, because "they are very understanding and up to the minute on everything." One lady ended the conversation with the remark that she was "looking for a priest who understands no English or is hard of hearing."

Since the sacrament of penance is so important in the life of practicing Catholics, it may serve as a rough index of the spirituality of St. Mary's parishioners.[1] If they go to confession frequently, they are likely to be good Catholics. Several cautions, however, must be kept in mind before applying our statistics for this criterion of Catholicism. The first is that a small number of fervent parishioners have regular confessors and spiritual advisers in other parishes of the city. Second, a relatively large number of those parishioners who are employed in downtown offices receive the sacrament at a downtown church where confessions are heard all day long every day. Third, there may be as many as two hundred confessions heard by the parish priests at odd times during the year and on sick calls. They are not recorded here. Finally, since the confessional is open to any Catholic who desires to use it, the figures will include numerous confessions of persons from other parishes.

Hence, for an accurate estimate of the confessional customs of St. Mary's Parish, the figures given here must be revised upward. If judged, however, from the point of view of the parish priest, the figures give a fairly accurate record of their service to the people in this regard. With these conditions kept in mind, we may analyze the year's record of confessions in the parish.

First Fridays.—The habit of monthly confession is instilled in the parishioners at an early age when they are urged to receive Holy Communion in honor of the Sacred Heart of Christ on the First Friday of every month. On the preceding day the school schedule is so arranged that one class at a time is released to go over to the church for confession. Of course, the assumption is that practically all receive the sacrament. Thus, while the children are not "forced" to go to confession, they are given the opportunity to develop a monthly habit of doing so.

Besides the children's confessions on Thursdays before the First Friday, there are also regular confession periods for adults in the late

1. The problem of inducing the 4,219 dormant Catholics to return to the Church through the sacrament of penance is not considered here. They do not "even attend Mass on Sundays."

afternoon and evening. Table 3 and Figure 11 give the record of the year for both children and adults.

There are two important observations to be made concerning these figures. The first is that the "habit" of going to confession on the Thursday before First Fridays does not carry over into the summer-time, and, second, it does not seem to carry over into adult life. The average monthly Thursday confessions of school children during the vacation is only 119 as compared to the monthly average for the school year (446.5). There can be no doubt that the convenience of

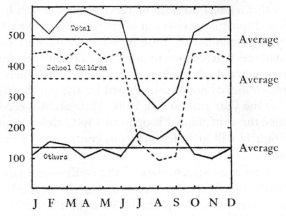

Fig. 11.—Monthly variations in the numbers of confessions before First Fridays for school children, nonschool persons, and total.

TABLE 3

Month	School Children	Others	Total
January	446	116	562
February	452	159	511
March	435	145	580
April	480	102	582
May	428	131	559
June	449	105	554
July	147	187	334
August	98	163	261
September	112	202	314
October	445	116	516
November	452	100	552
December	432	128	560
Total	4,376	1,554	5,930
Monthly average	364.6	129.5	494.1

going to confession in a group and within the school day accounts largely for the high average during the school year. On the other hand, the children have not become accustomed to the late-afternoon and evening periods for confession. Furthermore, there is a general lull in all parochial spiritual activities during the summer months which can be partially accounted for by the fact that about half of the Catholic families leave town for a week or two of vacation.

This latter fact does not seem to apply to adult confessions before First Fridays. July and September show the two highest numbers of confessions for them. The contrast between children and adults is, however, remarkable. When these older people were children in the parochial school, they, too, followed the custom of monthly confession before First Fridays. Their failure to continue this habit becomes even more noticeable when we compare the populations from which these two groups come. There are 647 children of grammar-school age (above the age of seven) in the parish. The monthly average of Thursday confession for them is 364.6. This means that 56.19 per cent of these children go to confession for the First Friday. On the other hand, there are 4,781 persons above grammar-school age. Their monthly average is 129.5, representing only 32.50 per cent of the total.[2]

Saturday confessions.—The traditional time for hearing confessions in the parish is on Saturday afternoon and evening. There were fifty-two Saturdays during the year of the survey, but two of these are omitted because they were Christmas and the Feast of the Circumcision, when no confessions were heard. Table 4 and Figure 12 give the monthly total of Saturday confessions and also the average, since the number of Saturdays varies with the months.

The two months which stand out with the most Saturday confessions are March and May. The last Saturday in March was the day before Easter, when 539 confessions were heard, the largest number on any Saturday of the year. There were two reasons why the month of May shows unusually large numbers of confessions: Mother's Day, when many parishioners receive Holy Communion in honor of the Mother of Christ and their own mothers; and Trinity Sunday, the fourth Sunday in May and the last opportunity to receive paschal Communion. There seems to be no suitable explanation why February shows the lowest weekly average. It also happens to be the

2. This percentage would be increased if we could include the high-school and college students who go to confession at their institutions and the other persons who go at the downtown churches.

month with the smallest total sum of confessions. Three of the Saturdays of this month were during Lent, a time when some greater spiritual effort would be expected from Catholics.

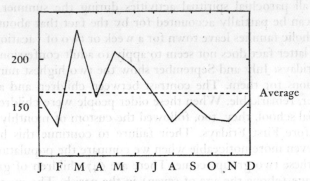

FIG. 12.—Average number of Saturday confessions heard at St. Mary's for each month and for the year.

TABLE 4

Month	Saturday Confessions	Average per Saturday
January	648	162
February	516	129
March	921	230
April	645	161
May	1,036	207
June	668	142
July	825	165
August	539	135
September	614	153
October	699	140
November	544	136
December	468	156
Total	8,123	164

Feast days.—Besides the confessions for First Fridays and for Sundays, a third category may be made of those in preparation for feast days. There are six days of "obligation" in the United States when Catholics are bound to attend Mass. In preparation for these days the priests at St. Mary's hear confessions on the previous afternoon and evening. An announcement to this effect is always made from the pulpit on the preceding Sunday. Figure 13 includes the confessions before Holy Thursday, even though the latter is not a feast day of obligation.[3]

It is to be expected that confessions for Holy Thursday (224) and Christmas (542) would be numerous. Many people seem to choose one of these feast days on which to receive their annual or semi-annual Communion. The liturgical significance of the other feast days seems to have dwindled in the modern urban parish where no special preparations are made for them. In other words, the habit of Saturday confessions is so strong in regular penitents that they tend to make their confession on that day even in a week which contains a holy day of obligation. Weekly penitents who go to confession on the eve of a feast day usually do not go again on Saturday, and vice versa.[4]

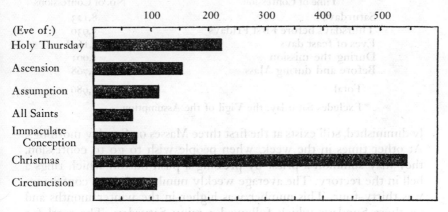

Fig. 13.—Numbers of confessions heard at St. Mary's in preparation for the holy days of obligation and for Holy Thursday.

The mission.—A fourth category of confessions is that of the mission which was conducted at St. Mary's Church during the second and third weeks of March. The missioners were visiting priests of the Lazarist Order who stressed the importance of frequent confession. Parishioners occasionally wish the opportunity to confess their sins to strange priests, and the Pastor urged them to take advantage of this opportunity. As a result, the missioners heard all the confessions of

3. Ordinarily, it would also include confessions before the Feast of the Sacred Heart, celebrated on the Friday of the week following the Feast of Corpus Christi. In the year of the study the Feast of the Sacred Heart coincided with the First Friday of June, and the number of confessions is already included there.

4. The Vigil of the Assumption was a Saturday. This figure (112) has already been enumerated among the Saturday confessions.

school children on the third day of the children's mission. This was a total of 385. During the week of the women's mission they heard 379 confessions, and in the men's mission 237. Thus, in the course of two weeks the sizable number of 1,001 confessions were heard by these visiting priests alone.

Before and during Mass.—At the beginning of the century when St. Mary's Parish included an area far beyond its present limits, it was often impossible for parishioners to come to town on Saturdays for confession. To serve these people, the priests heard confessions on Sunday mornings before and during Mass. This custom, while great-

TABLE 5

Time of Confession	No. of Confessions
Saturdays	8,123
Thursdays before First Fridays	5,930
Eves of feast days	1,164*
During the mission	1,001
Before and during Mass	1,768
Total	17,986

* Excludes Saturday, the Vigil of the Assumption.

ly diminished, still exists at the first three Masses on Sunday mornings. At other times in the week, when people wish to go to confession, they may summon a priest by pressing a push button which rings a bell in the rectory. The average weekly number of these confessions was thirty-four. This number was higher in the winter months and on those Sundays which followed a rainy Saturday. The total for the year was 1,768.

Table 5 is a summary of all the confessions heard at St. Mary's Church during the year of the survey. These statistics give us an opportunity to estimate the spiritual habits of the parishioners in the penitential aspects of their sacramental life. Remembering the caution that many of the parishioners may receive the sacrament of penance at downtown and other churches, we may note that there are 5,281 persons in the parish who are subject to attend to this duty.[5] If we divide this number into the sum of the confessions heard at St. Mary's, we find that there is an average of 3.4 confessions per person per year (once every 105 days; or once every fifteen weeks; or once in about three and a half months).

The frequency of confession pertains not only to the average

5. From the total parochial population of 6,727; this excludes 1,155 children below the age of seven and 291 non-Catholic partners in mixed marriages.

attendance of the whole parish but also to smaller segments of the population. There are four general classifications of parochial penitents. (*a*) The *weekly* penitents are the smallest group, comprising persons who are known as the most fervent Catholics. Generally speaking, they may be called the most faithful adherents to all parochial ideals and activities. (*b*) The *monthly* penitents are much more numerous and include in large part the children in the parochial school and the active membership of the parish societies which receive Holy Communion in a body once a month. (*c*) Those who went to confession *semiannually* comprise about one-third of all the parish-

TABLE 6

Classification of Penitents	No. of Persons	Per Cent	No. of Confessions	Per Cent
Weekly	131	2.48	6,812	37.87
Monthly	492	9.32	5,904	32.83
Semiannually	1,729	32.74	3,458	19.23
Annually	1,812	34.31	1,812	10.07
Never	1,117	21.15	0	0.00
Total	5,281	100.00	17,986	100.00

ioners seven years of age and older. They seem to have the habit of receiving this sacrament only at Christmas and during the Easter time. (*d*) Finally, the *annual* penitents fulfil their obligation by going to confession between the beginning of Lent and the end of the paschal time.

Table 6 is an estimate of the various classifications of parishioners measured according to the frequency of their reception of the sacrament of penance. The figures for the weekly and monthly confessants are based on the actual count of confessions made during the year. The figure for those who did not go to confession at all is taken from the census of the parish. The statistics for the annual and semiannual confessions are simply a distribution of the remaining numbers of confessions as obtained by count and of penitents as taken from the census. Of course, there may be some parishioners who go to confession three or four times a year, but their numbers are probably small enough to be statistically insignificant.

The assumption is usually made by priests that most Catholics (excepting daily communicants) make their confession previous to each Communion they receive. Using the estimates in Table 6, if we combine the number of persons who went to confession weekly with the number who went monthly, we find 623 persons who confessed one or more times a month. On the other hand, 2,362 parishioners, in answering the questions on the census schedule, claimed that they receive Holy Communion one or more times a month. This means that approximately seventeen hundred persons are not included in the estimated number of penitents who confess at St. Mary's each month. They fall into one of the three following explanations: (*a*) some of them go to confession at other churches; (*b*) some receive Communion more frequently than they go to confession (contrary to the assumption of the priests); and (*c*) some probably exaggerated when they answered the census schedule.

These estimates of different groupings give us a more or less dependable view of the supernatural stratification of the parish. This view is limited, of course, by the fact that we use only one criterion—the frequency of confession—to judge the position of persons. It gives us at least an indication of the proportion of parishioners who are trying hardest to achieve the supernatural ideal of sinlessness and friendship with God through the confessional. This statement claims too much only if it is interpreted absolutely and rigidly and without the limiting qualifications already mentioned.

It is conceivable that persons in the second or third category lead a most virtuous life between confessions. But, in spite of expectations, the general proposition seems valid: the more a Catholic uses the means instituted by Christ for removing and avoiding sins, the more likely is he to be a faithful, religious person. This statement may be safely made also about the persons who receive Holy Communion daily or weekly.

It may be said that the parish is adequately served in the matter of the sacrament of penance. The parishioners are aware that even in cases of emergency there is always a priest available for confession. Almost eighteen thousand confessions were heard in this one year, a fact which indicates not only that the sacramental facilities of the parish are properly offered by the priests but also that the parishioners of St. Mary's make proper use of them.

Chapter Six

Communion with God

THE reception of the sacrament of the Eucharist is the most intimate relationship a Catholic can have with God. Receiving the Body and Blood, humanity and divinity of Christ, under the appearance of a wafer constitutes a spiritual and physical union of the highest supernatural order. To many converts this experience is the ultimate test of faith in the Catholic religion. To practicing Catholics it is the sustenance of their faith and the greatest support for their moral behavior.

Sanctity may be defined as union with God. Since the purpose of the Church's existence on earth is the sanctification of human beings, it is quite obvious that Holy Communion is its central medium to that end. The Catholic who receives Communion intelligently, devoutly, and frequently is certain to be a person who approaches the ideal of behavior which the Church proposes. The highest spiritual status in the social structure of the Church is occupied by this saintly person. This is true even though the individual's position may not be recognized as such either in the external formal hierarchy of the Church or in the social stratification of parish and community.

When one has committed serious sin, the preliminary to Communion is confession. That is why the preacher's urging to "go to the sacraments" means to "go to confession and Communion." Frequent communicants are also frequent confessants, because they realize that both sacraments bring special graces to the soul. But confession is necessary before the reception of the Eucharist only when a person has committed a mortal sin. In practice, however, a realization of the supreme value of the Eucharist influences devout Catholics to approach the altar with a virtuous state of soul, previously cleansed by sacramental absolution.[1]

1. In St. Mary's Parish there was one confession for every three and one-third Communions (see the remarks in chap. 5, pp. 55-56).

We may assume therefore that interest in, devotion to, and frequency of Holy Communion in St. Mary's Parish constitute a valuable index to the Catholicism of the parishioners. In other words, it is one of the criteria by which we may judge the successful functioning of the parochial structure. It is only a partial standard, however, since it is also extremely important to ask whether the actual behavior of parishioners reflects the high spirituality that frequent Communion connotes. Of course, the ideal, apparently unattainable, would be the widespread devotion to the Eucharist accompanied by the expression of complete sanctity in human relations.

The young Catholic child is introduced to these ideals from the beginning of his parochial school education and usually receives his first Holy Communion in the second grade. St. Mary's Parish follows a local custom of long standing, making a distinction between "Little" Communion and "Big" Communion. The latter refers to a ceremony of great solemnity, when the child receives Communion on the day of his confirmation at about the age of eleven. The following account refers only to the "Little," or First, Communion, received at the age of seven or eight years.

The parochial school children make a spiritual retreat of two days before their First Communion, which the public-school children must also attend. The previous pastor had followed the traditional pattern whereby the first group received the Sacrament on the Feast of St. Joseph, March 19, while the public-school children received for the first time on the day before Trinity Sunday. The present Pastor, however, changed this custom. The Confraternity of Christian Doctrine, in the release-time program, prepared the public-school children during the year. The children are then permitted to come to the Catholic school for the retreat, and both groups receive Communion together on the Feast of St. Joseph.

On the Friday before the retreat started, the Principal called children to her office in groups of twelve or fifteen to test them on their knowledge of the catechism. As our observer noted: "She told them why you could not see Jesus in Holy Communion. She explained it this way: Jesus is really present in the Host. He has arms and legs and is just like a little baby. Jesus knew that people wouldn't want to receive a real live baby, so He put Himself under the appearance of bread. She asked them if they wouldn't be afraid to receive a real live little baby. Jesus knew all this and did the best thing by putting Himself under the appearance of food."

On Wednesday morning the children came to the seven forty-five

Mass to begin their retreat. The combined Communion class from both public and parochial schools was 73 boys and 71 girls, but some of the public-school children were almost always late for the exercises. All had been warned that they must keep silence for two whole days, a warning which was relatively well obeyed by the children from the parochial school but hardly at all by those from the public school.

A great deal of time was spent in lining up the boys and girls separately according to size, the smallest in the front and the largest toward the back. Three times each day they practiced, boys and girls separately, the whole routine of marching into the church, genuflecting, finding their assigned places in the pews, approaching the altar rail, and finally marching out of the church. The transformation from a children's rabble on Wednesday morning to the relative orderliness of the ceremony on Friday morning required the combined efforts of Father Dominic, the school Principal, and two teaching nuns. The patience and effectiveness of these four persons were demonstrated constantly during an experience which would be an ordeal to most adults.

While the boys were practicing in the church, the girls were shepherded into schoolrooms for a review of the catechism, for pious stories, and particularly for preparation for their first confession. Over in the church the boys were shown the correct way to come in and genuflect, how to leave the pews, and how to line up along the Communion rail and genuflect together. After rehearsing the whole procedure several times, the boys went to the school and girls to the church. The girls were less distracted and noisy than the boys. They seemed to try harder and learned more quickly.

In the afternoon both groups went to the church for prayers and catechism lesson conducted by Father Dominic. The boys again were restless and troublesome. Father said to them, "Don't you know you're supposed to shut up on retreat? Now keep quiet and listen to me." Soon he decided they had better practice some more, and after singing the hymn "O Lord, I Am Not Worthy," they did so. This time both boys and girls practiced exactly as they were to do it on Friday morning. They were told to keep their hands folded when they genuflect and not to make the sign of the cross while doing so. Father reminded them that they were genuflecting to God. Several of the bigger boys seemed to be deliberately confusing the instructions, and the Principal threatened to use a paddle on them. To add to the confusion, various children were asking to be excused all the while the group was in church.

Finally, the Principal gave them advice about the actual reception of Communion. She warned them not to touch the Host, or chew or bite It, but to swallow as soon as possible. She had them repeat the prayer, the act of love, several times, and advised them to say it while receiving Communion. At the end of the afternoon, as the children marched out of the church toward the school, they saw six youngsters from the kindergarten standing in a row. One of the Sisters had posed them there with finger on lips as a sign that the retreatants should keep silence. This had the opposite of the intended effect, because the others mimicked the younger ones and laughed and made remarks about them.

On the morning of the second day, Thursday, the children attended Mass, went to the school for instructions by the Sisters, and then returned to the church at nine-thirty for a talk by the Pastor. He spoke to them mainly about confession. Fathers Paul and Dominic then came in to hear the confessions of the boys, while the girls went to the school auditorium. About an hour later the two groups of children changed places, the boys going out the front door and the girls coming in the side door of the church.

Over in the school auditorium the children listened to recordings which told the story of the child Jesus' life on earth. These kept their interest, especially when the Sister asked them afterward what the record had said. At lunchtime the three Sisters in charge had to take turns in getting their own lunch and had some of the eighth-grade girls assist in keeping order in their absence. In the afternoon the procedure was a duplication of the previous day's activity. Some of the mothers of children came and sat at the back of the church during the last practice. Their children were much better behaved after having made their first confession.

The First Communion Mass was at seven o'clock on the Feast of St. Joseph. The little girls wore wreaths on their heads, but only about half of them wore white dresses. A little more than half of the boys had white suits. This is "Little" Communion, and it did not require the uniformity of dress demanded by "Big" Communion. The children lined up in the school auditorium. Having learned by previous experience, the Sisters posted eighth-grade girls at the drinking fountains so that none of the youngsters would break the fast. In spite of this, one older boy wearing a tweed suit was not recognized as a first communicant by the watchers, and he took a drink of water. The

Principal saw him as he left the fountain and asked him to get his mother, who was informed that her son could not make his First Communion that day. The mother became quite angry. She sought out Father Dominic and demanded that he be allowed to go to Communion with the others. "After all, he wasn't thinking of what he was doing, and he only took a *little* water."

The Pastor celebrated the Mass. At the time for the Gospel, he ascended the pulpit and spoke first to the children. "You have prepared a long time for this First Communion. You are taking Jesus Christ into your souls and hearts. Now remember that your souls are clean and nice. Keep them that way by being good children. Jesus is coming to you from out of heaven, and you must come to Him. You must say your prayers and be good children. You must go to Mass on Sundays and not eat meat on Friday. If you are good boys and girls, you will be good Christians when you grow up; and, when you die, you will be happy with Him in heaven.

"Children, whatever you ask God today He will give you. He will hear your prayers sooner than He hears the prayers of grownups. Ask Jesus to bless your parents, your family, the Sisters, and the priests. Ask Him to bless your school, your city, and your country. And, children, ask Jesus to keep this country from another war. He can do it; so ask Him. Also ask Him for the special intention of Father Urban."

The Pastor continued by telling them to keep away from the occasions of sin and never to commit a mortal sin. After dwelling on this theme for a while, he turned to the adults and said: "Parents, here are your treasures. Keep them pure; train them to be good Catholics. You and they will both be rewarded in heaven." After more words of counsel to the parents he closed with a blessing for both children and parents.

After the sermon several children showed signs of nervousness. One little girl started to cry. As the Sister led her to the side door, her mother met her and comforted her. As she returned, another girl slumped in the pew and was carried out by the Sister. She revived very quickly in the open air. Finally, the boys began to receive Communion as a Sister stayed at each end of the railing to usher. One of the smallest boys refused to swallow the Host. The Principal saw him sticking his tongue out with the Host still on it, and she held her hand over his mouth. This apparently frightened the boy, so Father Dominic took him outside for a drink of water.

Father Dominic and the Sisters in charge agreed that the whole preparation of children for First Communion is an exhausting experience. The great reverence which they have for the Blessed Sacrament made them constantly alert to any possible, unintentional desecration on the part of the children. After the children have received Communion a few times, this tension relaxes. One incident, however, indicated the alertness needed by the priests in this regard. One Sunday morning several months after the First Communion, the Pastor was distributing the Host at the altar rail when he noticed that the child to whom he was about to give Communion had traces of egg on his chin. He asked the child, "Did you have breakfast this morning?" When the child nodded affirmatively, Father Urban, still holding the ciborium, said loudly to the whole congregation: "Please teach your children that they mustn't break their fast before coming to Communion!"

It is no longer required that the record of the names of first communicants be kept in the parishes of the diocese. We were able, however, to obtain the definite and accurate numbers, as well as the sex and age, of all children who made their First Communion during the last twenty years. There were 1,505 boys and 1,457 girls. This disparity is explained by the fact that more girls than boys attend private Catholic academies in the city and make their First Communion there. The average number of first communicants per year over this twenty-year period was 148.6. The highest number (234) was in 1929, and the lowest number (96) was in 1945. In this latter year the Bishop sent instructions to all pastors to increase the amount of catechism teaching and to be more strict in the examination of candidates for First Communion.

To what extent are the parishioners of St. Mary's failing to fulfil the obligation of receiving their First Holy Communion? There are sixty-three persons aged seven years and over in the parish who have not yet received Communion. Twenty-nine of these are seven years old and for the most part had been advised to wait until they were better prepared. This means that less than 1 per cent of the actual parishioners have failed in this regard.

We make a much more negative discovery if we compare the age cohort of 917 infants who were baptized in the five-year period 1937–41 with the 615 children who received their First Communion in the years 1944–48. This is a loss of 302 children (or 32.93 per cent) to the parish between baptism and First Communion. If we look at the same age group, 7–11 years, as counted from the census schedules, we find that there are only 588 children, another loss of 27 children in the few years after the reception of Holy Communion.[2]

All the above figures represent the First Communion classes of children. Adult converts to the Catholic faith in the parish are given individual instructions and seldom come to the rectory in a group, nor do they receive their First Communion together. Of course, all the practicing which children do is unnecessary for adults. The priest-instructor must use his own judgment concerning the amount of teaching needed in each case, and this depends largely upon the convert's previous state of knowledge. Thus, the First Communion of an adult may occur at almost any period in the year, but it usually coincides with one of the principal feasts of the Church. The work of conversion is a highly personal relation between the priest and the convert, and it is difficult to estimate from the opinions of converts which of the priests is most adept at this function.[3]

The records of the year's survey may be analyzed as to the reception of Holy Communion by looking at the different classes of days on which Communion is received. Sundays, First Fridays, and holy days of obligation show the largest numbers of Communions, since they are the days on which the largest numbers attend Mass. The three daily Masses in the parish church have a much smaller attendance, but we shall also consider the reception of Communion at these.

It will be seen from Table 7 and Figure 14 that the two highest months for the Sunday reception of Holy Communion are March and May. The mission for both men and women occurred in March, and the increase in Communions was especially noticeable at the closing of the women's mission, when 909 went to the altar rail. Easter Sunday, March 28, had the record number of 1,415, the largest for any day of the year. The month of May also had two important days. The first was Mother's Day, when 785 persons received Communion, and the other was Trinity Sunday (616), the last day on which the Easter duty could be fulfilled.

The months with the lowest record of Sunday Communions were during the vacation period in the summer when many families spend the week end out of town. It must be noted that January and February show low Sunday averages of 426 and 428, respectively. This is the "social season" in Riverside, a period when the largest balls, dances, and parties are held. At least among the adults, the late Saturday-

2. See chap. 4, pp. 37–39, for other information about this youthful leakage from the parish.
3. See chap. 4, pp. 40–42, for a discussion of adult conversions.

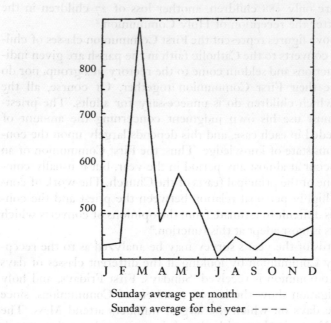

Sunday average per month ———
Sunday average for the year – – – –

Fig. 14.—The average Sunday reception of Holy Communion for each month and for the year at St. Mary's Church.

TABLE 7

Month	No. of Sundays	Sunday Communions per Month	Average per Sunday	Average per Sunday Mass
January	5	2,132	426.4	71.1
February	5	2,140	428.0	71.3
March	4	3,533	883.3	147.2
April	4	1,918	479.5	79.9
May	5	2,903	580.6	96.7
June	4	2,036	509.0	84.8
July	4	1,651	412.8	68.8
August	5	2,229	445.8	74.3
September	4	1,691	422.8	70.5
October	5	2,227	455.4	75.9
November	4	1,782	445.5	74.3
December	4	1,880	470.0	78.3
Total	53	26,122	492.9	82.1

night parties show their effect in lowering the average number of Sunday Communions.

The First Fridays of each month are dedicated to the devotion to the Sacred Heart of Jesus, and it has long been a custom of Catholics to receive Communion on these days for nine consecutive months. Those who follow the custom of monthly Communion frequently receive on the first Friday of the month and then again two days later on Sunday, without going to confession again. This, added to the

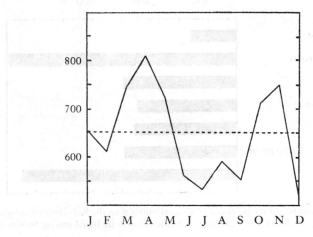

J F M A M J J A S O N D

Fig. 15.—Number of recipients of Holy Communion on the First Friday of each month and the average for all First Fridays of the year.

fact that the first Sunday of the month is "Communion Sunday" for some parish organizations, tends to increase the Communions in the beginning of the month.

Figure 15 shows how the number of Communions fluctuates throughout the year. Again, the summer months have a low record for the obvious reasons already mentioned. The First Friday of December had the lowest number of all (510), a fact explained by the inclement weather of that day.

The highest count of the year was that for April 2, when 812 persons received Communion. Probably two factors help to account for this relatively large number. The children who received their First Communion during the previous month were urged to start "making the First Fridays" at their earliest opportunity. Second, the spiritual effects of resolutions made at the Easter time on the previous week end may have carried over. Some persons may have decided to go to the sacraments more frequently and began to carry out their decision on the Friday after Easter.

Holy days of obligation form the third classification into which we may place the number of communicants. Since Holy Thursday is traditionally the Feast of the Last Supper, we have included it among the feast days, even though it is not a feast day of obligation. There were more Communions (989) on that day than on Christmas (948) (see Fig. 16).

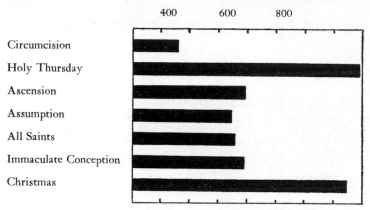

FIG. 16.—Number of recipients of Holy Communion on the holy days of obligation and on Holy Thursday. (The Feast of the Assumption is included among Sundays.)

It is to be noted that, according to the practice of St. Mary's parishioners, the three days in the year when the Sacrament is most received are Easter (1,415), Holy Thursdays (989), and Christmas (948). The only other day in the year which saw more than nine hundred approach the altar was the second Sunday in March, the closing of the women's mission. The Feast of Our Lady's Assumption happened to coincide with a Sunday during the survey, but there were many Sundays in the year when more Communions were received. It is true, however, that the Assumption had the highest number for the month of August (537), and it may be said that the coincidence of the feast day increased the normal amount of Communions for Sundays in August.

Finally, we must consider also the weekday Communions. Some parishioners still think that a daily communicant among lay people is an almost extraordinary character. It is true that the daily reception of the Sacrament has increased greatly in recent decades, but it is still a relatively limited practice. Besides the Sisters of the parochial school, who receive Communion every day, the average number of Communions distributed daily at St. Mary's Church is about fifty. But the number of parishioners who are weekday communicants throughout the year is less than thirty. Table 8 and Figure 17 give a monthly summary of Communions on weekdays, excluding First Fridays and feast days.

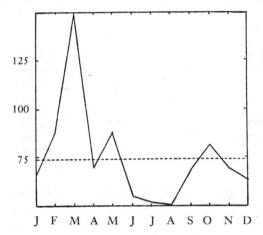

Fig. 17.—The average daily reception of Holy Communion (excluding Sundays, First Fridays, and holy days of obligation) for each month and for the year.

TABLE 8

Month	No. of Weekdays	No. of Communions	Average per Day	Average per Mass
January	23	1,520	66.08	22.02
February	23	2,001	87.00	29.00
March	21	3,089	147.09	49.03
April	29	2,009	69.27	23.09
May	23	2,005	87.15	29.05
June	23	1,290	55.65	18.55
July	29	1,525	52.95	17.65
August	23	1,122	49.65	16.55
September	23	1,560	67.80	22.60
October	29	2,377	81.96	27.32
November	22	1,522	69.18	23.06
December	26	1,688	64.92	21.64
Total	294	21,698	73.83	24.61

The large number of weekday Communions during March is accounted for by two occurrences. During the two-week mission, particularly that of the women, lay persons went to Mass and Communion almost every day. The other is the First Communion class on March 19, when many of the other children, as well as adults, received Communion. The Pastor uses this occasion to persuade parents to receive Communion with their children, and he maintains that this annual appeal brings back to the sacraments persons who have not received for years.

TABLE 9

Frequency of Communion	No. of Persons	Per Cent	No. of Communions	Per Cent
Daily	73	1.38	21,462	36.06
Weekly	492	9.32	25,584	42.97
Monthly	646	12.24	7,752	13.03
Semiannually	1,773	33.57	3,546	5.96
Annually	1,180	22.34	1,180	1.98
Never	1,117	21.15	0	0.00
Total	5,281	100.00	59,524	100.00

The small averages during the summer months simply follow the usual parochial pattern in the sacramental life. However, the relatively low averages for December may be somewhat surprising. Perhaps the colder weather discourages people from attending the early-morning Masses. The general preoccupation with "social life" during December and January may also be a partial factor in these low averages. Contrary to expectations, February shows a relatively higher average, possibly due to the influence of Lent. April, again, is a low month, probably a letdown after the spiritual efforts of Lent, while May, the month of Our Lady, shows a sizable increase.

Table 9 is an estimate composed from the statistics already assembled and indicates the classification of the parishioners according to the reception of Holy Communion. The totals for the daily, weekly, and monthly communicants are simply the averages of each group as shown above. The number who did not make their Easter duties (1,117) is taken from the census schedules.

The table is merely a rough estimate which attempts to relate all persons of seven years of age and older (except non-Catholic spouses in mixed marriages) with the total number of Communions distributed during the year. In actual practice the spiritual habits of the parishioners cannot be placed in such neat classifications. In answering the census schedules, 2,362 persons claimed that they received Holy Communion at least once a month. If the average numbers of weekly and monthly communicants are combined, they total a little more than half of that amount. We must conclude that many of the persons who made this claim to frequent Communion either received the Sacrament in other parish churches or exaggerated their spiritual practices when they answered the census.

Chapter Seven

Public Honor to the Eucharist

W<small>HILE</small> the reception of Holy Communion is the most important and most fruitful demonstration of the parishioners' love of Christ, there are other parochial functions which also exhibit this devotion. During the course of the year St. Mary's Parish conducts several kinds of religious functions which are specifically directed to the honor and praise of Christ in the Blessed Sacrament. They will be considered here in the five following categories: (*a*) Benediction of the Blessed Sacrament, (*b*) the Sunday Holy Hour, (*c*) devotion to the Sacred Heart, (*d*) the feasts of Holy Thursday and Corpus Christi, and (*e*) the Forty Hours' Devotion.

In one sense, these activities are a peculiarly apt criterion for measuring the extent to which the complete Catholic ideology is accepted by the parishioners. None of them is of obligation, as are the Sunday Mass and the annual Easter duties. In other words, the parishioners who attend these services are going beyond the absolute requirements of practicing Catholics. They do not commit sin if they refuse to attend. The fact of their attendance may be a partial index of their willingness to approach the Catholic religious ideal.

a) In the frequency of its repetition, Benediction of the Most Blessed Sacrament is second only to the Sacrifice of the Mass. Practically every public devotion occurring in the parish church during the year is concluded with Benediction, which is in itself a short ceremony requiring less than fifteen minutes. Mass with the Blessed Sacrament exposed on the altar takes place on only two occasions in the year—at the High Mass on the Sunday within the octave of Corpus Christi and during the Forty Hours' Devotion. These are also the only times when there is Benediction after the Mass, with the exception of Sacred Heart devotions every weekday morning in June and on First Fridays.

b) The weekly Holy Hour is conducted alternately by Fathers Dominic and Paul on Sunday evenings at five o'clock. The whole religious function usually lasts about three-quarters of an hour. The priest comes from the sacristy carrying the monstrance and preceded by two altar boys. After exposing the Blessed Sacrament for adoration, he goes to the pulpit and leads the congregation in all the prayers and hymns contained in the Holy Hour booklet. The members of the congregation have this twenty-two-page pamphlet, and they kneel for the prayers and stand for the hymns. Besides the seven hymns, all in honor of Christ, except one which honors the Holy Spirit, there are prayers to Christ in the Blessed Sacrament, a spiritual Communion, the Litany of the Sacred Heart, consecration of families to the Sacred Heart, prayer to Christ the King, a prayer for vocations, and a prayer for the souls in purgatory. The "Tantum Ergo" is then sung, the blessing given, the divine praises recited, and a final hymn which closes the service.

The practice of the Holy Hour had been an innovation of the present Pastor. Twenty-five years ago, when he had been assistant pastor, the parish conducted Vespers on Sunday afternoons, followed by catechism lessons for the children and Benediction. When he returned as Pastor, the Vespers had been omitted, but there was still an hour's catechism lesson beginning at three o'clock and followed by Benediction.

"Very few people came, not even most of the children. The people complained about giving up their Sunday afternoons. You know, it's the only time the family can go out together in the car. So I stressed the catechism in the school hours and figured I could get the public-school children after school. I changed the time to five o'clock, so the people could come from their picnics and stop in the church for devotions before going home to supper. I made it a holy hour and got those nice booklets we are using. I used to preach a short sermon, and it took me a couple of years to go through the sacraments and the other teachings of the Church."

The Pastor remarked that, if the sermon were still delivered, the Holy Hour would take a full hour instead of forty-five minutes. "There used to be good crowds. But, when I got sick, the doctors told me I'd have to cut down on my work; and then my assistants didn't keep up the sermons. Now the attendance has fallen way off; and I don't know what to do. They should have this devotion, but the people just don't come to it."

In an effort to bolster the attendance at the Holy Hour on Sunday afternoons, the Pastor and the Principal of the school decided to assign a school class for each Sunday. It was left to the individual teacher to decide how she would persuade the children in her charge to come to the services. There was to be no coercion or negative sanctions, although some small prizes could be given for attendance. Thus the children from the fourth to the eighth grades rotated. Since each grade is divided into two classes, the arrangement meant that each class would have its turn every tenth Sunday. Usually about half the class appeared at the church, with the younger classes showing a better attendance record than the older, and about twice as many girls as boys.

During the year of the survey there was an observer present at every Holy Hour. The average attendance was about the same as that at the six o'clock Mass on weekdays, which means that there were usually about seventy-five people there, including some of the nuns. Table 10 and Figure 18 show the average weekly attendance for each month of the year.

During March there was only one Holy Hour. Of the four Sundays in the month, two fell within the period of the missions and the other was Easter Sunday, when the service was canceled. The month of May had the highest absolute number and also the highest Sunday average attendance of the whole year. The second Sunday, May 9, was Mother's Day, but only forty-five lay persons (nineteen of them grade-school children) and fourteen nuns were in attendance. On the fourth Sunday of May the traditional crowning of Our Lady's statue took place at four o'clock in the afternoon. The beautiful procession of the Children of Mary and the Sodality was watched by an almost capacity congregation. When this ceremony was over, most of the adults left the church before the Holy Hour started. But many of the children remained for the service, so that the total attendance was 235 persons. On the last Sunday of May the Corpus Christi procession accounted for an attendance of almost two hundred at the Holy Hour.

One other Sunday, the first in October, is excluded from the above tabulation. It merits separate emphasis because the Holy Hour was on that day a city-wide affair, sponsored by the Bishop, and held at the municipal sports stadium. The Bishop had asked that a special demonstration of devotion to Christ in the Eucharist be made on that Sunday and that all the churches of the city prepare for it with a triduum of Holy Hours on Thursday, Friday, and Saturday nights.

At St. Mary's Parish the priests had made the usual announcements on the preceding Sunday, urging the parishioners to attend in large numbers. On Thursday night the service started at seven-thirty and was attended by 222 persons. It was conducted exactly as on Sundays. On the following night the congregation was augmented by those who usually come to the Novena services. After exposing the Blessed

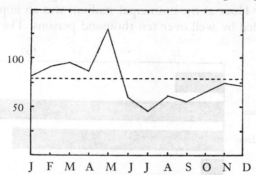

FIG. 18.—Average Sunday attendance at the Holy Hour service for each month and for the year.

TABLE 10

Month	No. of Holy Hours	Attendance	Average per Sunday
January	5	408	81.6
February	5	457	91.4
March	1	93	93.0
April	4	346	86.5
May	5	654	130.8
June	4	236	59.0
July	4	184	46.0
August	5	306	61.2
September	4	230	56.0
October	4	259	64.8
November	4	294	73.5
December	4	285	71.3
Total	49	3,752	76.6

Sacrament, Father Paul omitted most of the prayers and hymns of the Holy Hour booklet but recited the Rosary and the Litany of the Blessed Virgin. Benediction was then given, and the priest retired to the sacristy to remove the cope. Before he could return to the altar for the Novena services, all except a dozen of the 294 persons had left the church. The sexton was turning out lights and closing windows, and the organist, who felt ill that night, was leaving the choir loft. The Novena service was omitted. On the third night of the triduum the Holy Hour was again curtailed to about twenty minutes because of confessions. This latter fact accounted for almost three hundred persons being present for the service. Confessions started at seven o'clock and were continued by Father Paul while Father Dominic conducted the Holy Hour (see Table 11 and Fig. 19).

The Holy Hour at the municipal stadium was an impressive ceremony attended by well over ten thousand persons. The Sisters were

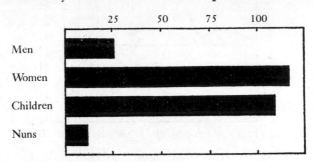

Fig. 19.—Comparison of average attendance of men, women, children, and nuns at the four Holy Hour services in the first week of October.

TABLE 11

Category	Thursday	Friday	Saturday	Sunday	Total	Average
Men	5	32	35	29	101	25
Women	70	118	122	154	464	116
Children	136	129	124	47	436	109
Nuns	11	15	17	5	48	12
Total	222	294	298	235	1,049	262

segregated, as were the Negroes, in the stands which form an approximate horseshoe around the field. The bands from the various Catholic high schools and grammar schools marched in, and the people rose to respect the American flag as each band passed (except when the bands from the Negro schools passed). The white Holy Name men of the city parishes occupied chairs on the field, as did the clergy in cassock and surplice, and the Boy Scouts in uniform.

The program did not follow the regular Holy Hour service. The Rosary was recited and a sermon delivered against communism. After some short delay, one of the priests, preceded by four altar boys with lighted candles and bells, brought the Blessed Sacrament onto the field and to the improvised altar. A procession started from the altar and made the circuit of the cinder track. All the persons on the field composed this procession, marching two by two. The Bishop carried the heavy monstrance under a canopy, flanked by uniformed Knights of Columbus and Catholic Foresters and preceded by the monsignors and other members of the clergy.[1] Meanwhile the people in the stands had lighted their candles. They sang hymns and genuflected when the Blessed Sacrament passed before them. When the Bishop had circled the field, he returned to the altar and finished with the usual Benediction. The whole congregation sang the hymn "Holy God, We Praise Thy Name" at the conclusion of the program.

The participation of St. Mary's parishioners in this public devotion to the Holy Eucharist does not seem impressive when we consider it only from the point of view of numbers. Four busses carried most of them from the parish church to the stadium, and the rest went in private cars. These 235 persons are indeed a small percentage of the Catholic members of the parish, but the small number of 29 men was a fairly good representation of the active Holy Name members of the parish. In comparison to other parishes of the city, St. Mary's had a better-than-average proportion of its people at the ceremony.

c) The devotion to the Sacred Heart of Jesus is intimately bound up with the Holy Hour, especially in the type of prayers and hymns that are used. There are, however, separate devotions every First Friday after the last Mass and also every day during June, which is the month of the Sacred Heart. The service on these occasions is always the same, consisting of the exposition of the Blessed Sacrament, the Litany of the Sacred Heart, and Benediction. The congregation at the last Mass on weekdays almost always stays for these devotions, hence the attendance is the same as that given for the seven forty-five Mass on First Fridays and all weekdays in June.

In the liturgical calendar the Feast of the Most Sacred Heart occurs on the Friday of the week following the Feast of Corpus Christi. During the year of the survey this feast coincided with the First Friday of June and the graduation Mass of the parochial school children. Because of this combination of circumstances, the church was unusually crowded at the seven o'clock Mass for the graduates. The Pastor gave a fifteen-minute sermon to the graduates in which he asked them to develop their appreciation of the Sacred Heart. "So, pray for devotion to the Sacred Heart to find peace and consolation and help for your whole life. The promise of the Sacred Heart to St. Margaret Mary is that God will never abandon those who have devotion to His Sacred Heart."

1. The Knights of St. Peter Claver, a Catholic order for Negro laymen similar to the Knights of Columbus, were not present in this procession.

d) Holy Thursday and the Feast of Corpus Christi are designed by the Catholic Church for promotion of interest in and love of Christ in the Eucharist. The latter feast is always celebrated on the Thursday following Trinity Sunday. In his sermon on that Sunday the Pastor told the congregation that the need to receive Holy Communion did not cease for people who received the paschal Communion. "You should please God by going to Communion frequently; so come on Thursday, the Feast of Corpus Christi. We shall have the procession and celebration next Sunday afternoon, but come anyway on Thursday and receive Communion."

Except among the school children who had been urged and instructed by the teaching Sisters, there was no increase in the number of communicants on the actual feast day. At five o'clock, the time for the Holy Hour service on Sunday, May 30, there were 198 persons in St. Mary's Church to do honor to the Body of Christ. The regular Holy Hour service was conducted until the time for Benediction. While the last prayers were being recited, the Sisters prepared the children for the procession.

This procession was led by a tall altar boy carrying a crucifix, flanked by two candle-bearing boys. Six small altar boys in white cassocks and capes followed the cross. The forty-two girls dressed in white and wearing white veils walked slowly with folded hands. These were followed by a double line of thirty girls from the first grade carrying small baskets of flower petals, which they cast on the floor as they sidled along. Over this carpet of flowers there walked twelve of the smallest girls from the kindergarten, about five years old, dressed in long white-satin gowns. Attached to their shoulders were small gold-trimmed satin wings.[2]

These little "angels" were followed by six altar boys carrying elaborate hurricane candles, reserved only for the most important liturgical occasions. The Pastor carried the Blessed Sacrament in the monstrance. He was accompanied by the deacon and subdeacon and preceded by two thurifers, who alternated in walking backward and swinging the censor toward the monstrance.

The people in the congregation watched the little girls for the most part until the priest came by with the Blessed Sacrament, when they bowed devoutly and seemed to pray earnestly. As soon as the priest

---

2. Before the procession, the mothers of these little girls hovered over them in the school building. They "made them up" as though for a stage show. Over the protests of the nuns, all of the flower girls and "angels" wore lipstick and rouge.

passed, they looked toward the other aisle where the children were slowly walking. The route of the procession was down the main aisle to the back of the church, then up the aisle on the Gospel side, across the front of the church, down the side aisle, circling the church. As the children came up the main aisle toward the altar, they went into their assigned pews, with the exception of the flower girls, who lined up along the pews until the priest brought the monstrance back to the main altar. The ceremony ended with Benediction.

The Feast of Holy Thursday, traditional reminder of the Lord's Last Supper, is completely dedicated to Christ in the Blessed Sacrament. Although it is not a holy day of obligation, there are more people in church and more communicants than on any day of the year except Easter. Only one Mass is celebrated on this occasion, a Solemn High Mass at seven o'clock in the morning. The doors of the church were opened at five-thirty, and when the "Angelus" rang at six o'clock more than four hundred were present to recite the prayer. Most of them received Communion when the two priests came out a few minutes later.

There was a lull when the priests had finished distributing Communion, hundreds of people leaving the church and others entering. At six-thirty, Father Dominic, accompanied by two altar boys with bell and lighted candles, took the ciborium over to the rectory to give Communion to the Pastor, who was then ill. Shortly afterward, Father Paul came out to distribute Communion to 174 persons who had to leave for work before Mass started.

Father Dominic celebrated this Mass, assisted by Father Paul and a visiting priest, as deacon and subdeacon. These two priests received Communion and then helped to distribute Communion to the altar-servers and congregation. At the end of the Mass a procession formed similar to that of the Feast of Corpus Christi. It proceeded down the main aisle, around the church to the Repository, which had been set up in place of St. Joseph's altar at the epistle side of the church. The Blessed Sacrament was then placed in this Repository, a beautifully decorated altar ablaze with candles and banked by bouquets of white flowers. The girls in the procession added their flowers to those already surrounding the altar.

From the time the Mass ended (at about eight-thirty) there was a constant vigil and public adoration of the Blessed Sacrament until the services on Good Friday morning. Holy Thursday is undoubtedly the greatest collective tribute by parishioners to the Holy Eucharist. Our observers were present all through the day and night, noting the formal, organized way in which this public adoration was conducted. Altar boys had been assigned for half-hour periods throughout the day until the sermon at night. From eight-thirty in the morning, these shifts of two boys changed each half-hour, the boys wearing cassock and surplice and kneeling in the first pew before the Repository.

The school children had been organized so that each class could come in for a half-hour of adoration accompanied by their nun teacher. The procedure for each group was the same; they recited the Rosary, led by one of the older boys, then they prayed the Litany of the Sacred Heart and sang the hymn "Sweet Sacrament." They meditated silently until their time was up and another group of pupils came in to replace them. All during the day older people came and went. Most of them stayed to pray between twenty and thirty minutes, a few remained less than five minutes, and others stayed as long as two hours. Most of them used rosaries and prayer-books, but many simply sat or knelt and stared at the altar of reposition. At almost all times during the day there were one or two persons making the Stations of the Cross.

At any time during the day there were more than a hundred persons in the church, including lunch period and the evening dinner hour. In the late afternoon and early evening before services the congregation was smallest. From early Thursday morning until Friday-morning services more than forty-five hundred persons were counted entering the church. Many of these were undoubtedly repeating their visits, coming for Mass in the morning, a period of adoration in the daytime, and returning for the sermon at night. The preponderance was composed of women and children, especially during the business hours of the day.

The night service started at seven-thirty with the singing of the hymn "O Lord, I Am Not Worthy" and the recitation of the Litany of the Sacred Heart, led by Father Paul. The choir sang "Come, Holy Ghost" while Father Dominic knelt in preparation for the sermon. There were 633 people present to hear him preach the year's most important sermon on the Blessed Sacrament. "Tonight we celebrate the anniversary of the Lord's last supper on earth. It was then that Christ instituted the sacrament of the Holy Eucharist to continue His work of salvation and love on earth. . . . Tonight we have a vivid reminder of this glory of Christ in the Repository. . . . But we, living in this nonchalant age, have taken this great supernatural gift for granted."

Father Dominic pointed out the need we all have for the "Food of

Angels"—the need to sustain, increase, and intensify the life of the soul. He expanded on the Church's doctrine of the real (not symbolic) presence of Christ in the Eucharist and explained that our very life and salvation depended on this sacrament. This sermon lasted for twenty minutes and was followed by the regular prayers and hymns from the Holy Hour booklet. At the conclusion of the service over two hundred persons remained to pray and adore. Most of these departed within a half-hour, but more than seventy others came in before nine o'clock.

TABLE 12

Hour	Men	Women	Children	Total
9:00 P.M.	58	55	10	123
10:00 P.M.	45	15	2	62
11:00 P.M.	39	8	1	48
12:00 M.	34	0	0	34
1:00 A.M.	27	0	0	27
2:00 A.M.	22	0	0	22
3:00 A.M.	31	0	0	31
4:00 A.M.	30	0	0	30
5:00 A.M.	53	0	0	53
Total	339	78	13	430

From this time on the men of the parish were present in greater numbers than women. This nocturnal adoration by the men is an annual function of the Holy Name Society.[3] More than three hundred men spent at least an hour each in church during the night. Symbolically they were visiting Christ in the prison of the tabernacle to commemorate the night on which Christ was imprisoned by the Sanhedrin before His death on the First Good Friday. Devoting a whole hour of one's time to prayer and meditation, especially after midnight, must be accepted as a reliable criterion of signal devotion to the Holy Eucharist. Table 12 indicates the extent of this devotion among the men of the parish.

These figures represent those who spent at least one hour in the church. In the period from nine until midnight there were frequent arrivals and departures of persons who made visits to the Blessed Sacrament of less than an hour's duration. Most of these persons joined in the praying of the Rosary or of the Litany of the Holy Name of Jesus, the Litany of the Sacred Heart of Jesus, or the Consecration to the Sacred Heart. Some of the men stayed two or three

3. The various activities of the Holy Name Society will be discussed in a subsequent volume.

hours and several remained in the church all night. Thus the figures given above repeat persons, and the absolute number of adorers is 324 men.

The doors of the church were opened about a quarter of six on Good Friday morning, and people began to arrive for the services in honor of Christ's death. We shall discuss this devotion in another place.

e) The Forty Hours' Devotion is conducted in every parish of the diocese once a year. The Bishop assigns the days for each parish so that there is a quasi-perpetual public adoration of the Blessed Sacrament going on at all times somewhere in the diocese. Father Urban made a special request of the Bishop this year so that he could have this three-day celebration in his parish immediately preceding the centennial celebration. The Bishop graciously acceded, and the dates were set for Wednesday, Thursday, and Friday, September 15–17.

Essentially there are three parts to this devotion: the Solemn High Mass each morning, adoration of the Blessed Sacrament all day, and the sermon and Benediction at night. This triduum had been well advertised in the announcements from the pulpit at all the Masses of the preceding Sunday. The priests had explained that public honor of this kind to the Divine Savior was a reparation for the serious sins being committed in the world. The parishioners should take this opportunity "to do honor to Christ in the Blessed Sacrament, to thank Him for all the graces given to the St. Mary's Parish for one hundred years, and to make up for the sins of the world."

The Solemn High Mass was celebrated each morning at six o'clock by the Pastor, with Fathers Dominic and Paul assisting as deacon and subdeacon. The school children's choir, directed by two of the nuns, sang the regular Mass at this time and then sang hymns during the next two Masses. After the first Mass the Pastor exposed the Blessed Sacrament above the tabernacle on the high altar. A large bouquet of white gladioli was placed before the tabernacle. Consequently, the seven and seven-thirty o'clock Masses were celebrated by Fathers Dominic and Paul at the Blessed Virgin's altar. Table 13 shows the attendance at Mass and the reception of Holy Communion during these three days.

Except for the children in the choir, the first two Masses were attended exclusively by adults. While the numbers seem small in comparison to the total adult population of the parish, they are higher than the usual attendance at daily Masses. The numbers for the seven forty-five Mass are high because they comprised for the most part school children who attended the Mass by grades in the regular formation and under the supervision of the Sisters as at the nine o'clock Mass on Sundays.

The adoration of the Blessed Sacrament during the day was very similar to that already described for Holy Thursday, except that the number who visited the church was much smaller. From a quarter to seven, when the first Mass ended, until seven-thirty in the evening, when the service started, there were always two altar boys present in the sanctuary. They changed shifts every half-hour, so that all except the smallest altar-servers had an opportunity to spend this time before the Blessed Sacrament. The children of the parochial school

TABLE 13

Mass	Total Attendance	Average	No. of Communions	Average
Six o'clock	244	81	118	39
Seven o'clock	168	56	94	31
Seven forty-five o'clock	977	326	99	33

also came to the church for assigned half-hour periods and prayed in unison as they had done on Holy Thursday. All during the day there were lay people in the church, the smallest number being sixteen in the early afternoon, and the largest number (over a hundred) in the hour before the evening service started.

On each night of the Forty Hours' Devotion a sermon was delivered by Father James, the pastor of one of the large city churches. His general theme was the divinity of Christ in the Eucharist. On Wednesday night he spoke of the crucifixion, saying that most people look at Christ either as the good thief did, recognizing and accepting Him, or as the bad thief did, scorning and rejecting Him. It is the same today—some recognize Christ's real presence in the Sacrament, others deny it. On Thursday night he spoke on the frequent reception of Communion, showing all the benefits that would accrue from this practice, using statistics to prove that Americans pamper their bodies at the cost of their souls. On Friday night Father James took for his topic the prayer of the blind man, "Lord, that I may see." He said that the people who saw Christ walk by needed the eyes of faith just as "we will need them when the Blessed Sacrament is carried in procession tonight."

The evening service started at seven-thirty with the recitation of the Rosary by Father Dominic on the first and third nights and by

Father Paul on the second night. After the third decade of the Rosary the people stood while the choir sang "Sweet Sacrament," and at the end of the Rosary the hymn "Come, Holy Ghost" was sung. Father James's sermon then lasted a little over a half-hour. After the sermon he led the congregation in prayers taken from the special Forty Hours' Devotion booklet which most of the people had. While these prayers were being said, the altar boys prepared the altar for Benediction, which was celebrated on the successive nights by Father Paul, Father Dominic, and the Pastor.

The attendance grew progressively better. On Wednesday night there were 268 (of whom 146 were children); on Thursday night, 375 (including 133 children); on the final night, 530 (of whom 121 were children). The school children gathered in the yard before the services, formed ranks according to grades, and walked into church behind the Children of Mary and the Sodalists. The Children of Mary numbered thirty-two on the first night, thirty on the second night, and fifty-one on the third. They wore white dresses and white berets. The Sodalists, who were mostly of high-school age, wore blue veils and dresses of various colors. On the successive nights they numbered eight, four, and seven.

The closing night of the triduum of devotions witnessed an elaborate procession similar to those already described elsewhere. It started in the sanctuary, led by an altar boy carrying the crucifix, flanked by two candle-bearing smaller servers. Then the Children of Mary and the Sodalists were followed by ten altar boys in red cassocks and eight altar boys in black cassocks. Thirty small flower girls, dropping petals on the floor as they walked along, preceded twelve small "angels" from the kindergarten. Father James walked before two thurifers, who took turns incensing the Blessed Sacrament. Father Urban carried the monstrance under an umbrella-like canopy held by a tall altar-server. At his side were the deacon and subdeacon, Fathers Dominic and Paul.

As usual the behavior of the congregation varied greatly. The parents of the little boys and girls in the procession stood on tiptoe to watch their children go by. They whispered to one another, smiling and nodding approval. Most of the adults made only halfhearted attempts to sing the familiar hymns which were played during the procession. It is remarkable, however, that as soon as the Pastor, bearing the Blessed Sacrament, came abreast of the pews in which they stood, the people genuflected slowly and reverently bowed their heads. The watcher from the choir loft saw this action almost as a wave rippling

down the church, each pewful of people genuflecting and rising slowly as the Pastor at the end of the procession went by.

When the procession had again reached the sanctuary, Benediction
of the Blessed Sacrament took place in the customary manner. The
people waited until the final hymn was sung and the priests had returned to the sacristy. About half of them were able to crowd out of
the front door before the children could make an orderly exit led by
two Sisters. Out on the sidewalk, parents and children found each
other and started for home, while the sexton closed up the church.

Thus ended the Forty Hours' Devotion, which really covered a
period of about forty-two hours. In other words, the exposition of
the Blessed Sacrament took place in the parish from a little before
seven in the morning until almost nine at night—approximately fourteen hours each day.

Finally, in summarizing the attendance at those parochial functions
which give public honor to Christ in the Eucharist, we may find a
yardstick to measure the variations in this devotion. There are 5,281
persons of seven years of age and older in the parish. An average of
55.6 received Communion daily in June, the month of the Sacred
Heart. An average of 76.5 attended the Sunday afternoon Holy Hour.
At the Corpus Christi celebration on the last Sunday afternoon in
May, 198 were present. An average of 262 attended the evening
services of the Holy Hour triduum in October. An average of 391
came to the evening services of the Forty Hours' Devotion in September, while 463 came to the daily Mass in the same period. The First
Fridays of the month had an average of 646 persons who received
Holy Communion. The public adoration of Christ in the Eucharist
on Holy Thursday brought approximately forty-five hundred persons to the church, although this figure includes numerous "dupli-
cations" of people who came two or three times. There were 324 men
present for the nocturnal adoration between Holy Thursday and
Good Friday.

A rough pattern emerges from these statistics. Single devotions, like
Holy Thursday adoration, and short-term devotions, like tridua, seem
to attract larger numbers than daily devotions, like the Sunday-afternoon Holy Hour. Besides the personal psychological reaction of
parishioners, the explanation of this may lie in the fact that more publicity and more elaborate preparations are given by the priests to the
occasional and special ceremonies. The concentrated effort that was
made to bring 324 men to the nocturnal adoration seems to be a
proof of this.

Except where the statistics include children, the general pattern seems to be that the attendance is larger in proportion to the lateness in the day. The Corpus Christi procession on a Sunday afternoon attracted only about 40 per cent of the numbers who came for a similar procession on the last night of the Forty Hours' triduum. The statistics for First Friday Communions seem to belie both of these patterns, but it must be remembered (*a*) that the average of 646 includes large numbers of school children and (*b*) that tradition and propaganda have for many years helped to promote the practice of First Friday Communions.

Chapter Eight

The Sacrament of Strength

Confirmation is the sacrament by which Catholics are supernaturally fortified in their beliefs and are given special divine graces to resist temptations against the holy faith. According to normal procedure and custom in St. Mary's Parish, this is the fourth sacrament which children receive. Their baptism takes place in infancy; the sacraments of penance and the Eucharist are first received when they are seven or eight years old, and they are customarily confirmed at about the age of eleven or twelve.

St. Mary's has followed a peculiar local custom in this regard for many decades. Among the parishioners the confirmation celebration is popularly known as Solemn Communion, or "Big" Communion. This custom was initiated more than a half-century ago in order to increase the amount of catechism the child learned and to stress the importance of the sacrament of confirmation. Formerly, many parents thought that their children had obtained sufficient instruction in the Catholic religion when they had received First Communion. They would withdraw their children from the parochial school and also fail to encourage them to attend Sunday school for catechism lessons.

To offset this trend, the priests began to postpone the "solemnization" of the Communion ceremony until the time for confirmation. The children were not dressed up and feted for their First Communion as they are in other parts of the country. The "official" First Communion photo is not made at that time, for which the child is posed in his white suit and holding a prayer-book, rosary, and candle. Children are thus kept in the parochial school for a longer time, and the public-school children come to the catechism classes for several more years of religious instruction.[1]

1. Formerly, the child could be accepted as a candidate for confirmation at the age of eleven. But in 1946 the Bishop ordered that only children who had reached at least the sixth grade could be confirmed. This accounts for the smaller-than-average number in the confirmation class of 1947.

The preparation for the reception of confirmation consists of nothing more than a thorough instruction in the truths of the Catholic Church. Parochial school children obtain this in their regular catechism classes; the public-school children get it in the release-time program conducted by the Confraternity of Christian Doctrine; and adult converts and those who have been delayed for some reason or other receive this instruction in personal interviews with the parish priest.

There is, however, a more proximate preparation for the school children which is both profane and sacred. All the external pomp surrounding the ceremony of "Big" Communion must be planned in advance. On Thursday, March 11, more than five weeks before the date set by the Bishop for the confirmation, the Pastor arranged for a meeting with the mothers of the children to be confirmed. The purpose was to place orders for the boys' suits and shoes and the girls' dresses, veils, and shoes. On the afternoon of the meeting the Pastor and our observer stood at the doorway of the school waiting for the parents' arrival.

"He said that this was 'the worst day of the year'—trying to get the mothers and children to reach a decision about apparel for Solemn Communion. He wanted them all dressed alike so that there would be no hurt feelings because one child has a very expensive dress or suit and the child next in line is practically in rags. He added that he would pay for the clothes of the children whose family cannot afford them."[2]

The Pastor had arranged with a downtown store to send two representatives with samples: a woman with two different girls' outfits and a man with two sets of samples for boys. He pointed out that he preferred to deal with local Riverside merchants but that last year the local store could not finish the work in time for the ceremony. The Pastor explained this to the assembled mothers and children in the presence of the Cohen Clothing Company's representatives and also told them why the children should all be dressed alike. "This is my church, and I have something to say about what goes on in it."

The mothers present looked at the dresses, and most of them agreed on the more expensive one, but there was much complaining about the price. "I could make three for the price they ask for this one." Another said, "I have material at home; I could make a dress like that."

2. Actually, the St. Anne Society paid for the outfits of three boys and two girls this year. This charitable work was done with the utmost privacy so that none of the other children or parents knew about it.

A third remarked, "I like the style all right, but I don't like the price." They looked at the suits for the boys and made similar remarks, although here again they showed a preference for the more expensive one.

At this point the Pastor was called from the auditorium by an urgent phone message from the mayor. "This was the signal for all the girls to run to me and their mothers. They didn't like the dresses and wanted our honest opinion about them. They said they were too big to be wearing such babyish things. (Some are tall, or fat, or said they were 'too old' for such dresses.) They told us that Mrs. Kaufmann, the sixth-grade teacher, doesn't like the dresses either. Some of the girls pouted when their mothers told them that they had to do what Father Urban said. The girls agreed among themselves that all they really liked about this 'stuff' was the veil."

When the Pastor returned, the auditorium was a babble of confusion, and he had a difficult time trying to restore order and get a hearing from these seventy-five or eighty women. He gave up this attempt and told the women separately to take their children to the Principal's office to be measured for the clothing. He also announced that any of the ladies who wanted to make the dresses themselves were invited to go down to the store to copy the pattern. "But, since none of you are shoemakers, we'll have to buy the shoes—white ones for the girls, and brown and white shoes for the boys."

During the ensuing weeks the catechism classes for these children were intensified in their studies. In both the release-time classes and the regular parochial school classes the children were warned to "get ready for the test." This was really a threefold examination. The various teaching Sisters were enrolled as examiners, and they had to give an individual oral examination of the main catechism questions to each child assigned them. The second test occurred during the pre-confirmation retreat when the Pastor asked questions of the whole group and picked children at random to answer them. Finally, on the night of the confirmation ceremony, the Bishop himself asked a series of questions of the whole group in the church.

The confirmation class, after a few had been eliminated because of ignorance of the catechism, numbered seventy-one girls and forty-nine boys when the retreat started on Friday, April 16. After morning Mass, which the whole school attended for the intention of the Bishop, the class went to the auditorium for the preliminary arrangements. Boys and girls were lined up separately according to their height, the smaller ones in the front and the taller to the back. Father

Dominic called the roll and then collected three dollars from each child to cover the confirmation expenses. Some of the children had forgotten to get the money from their parents; others had already given it to the Principal. While this was going on, the children were supposed to keep silence and study their catechism books. Some of them whispered among themselves, and others were engrossed in the new issue of the Catholic comic book, *Treasure Chest*.

The children returned to the church at nine-fifteen and said the Rosary while waiting for Father Dominic, who is frequently late for his appointments. When he arrived, the class went through the routine practice. Most of these children were in the sixth grade and did not require the repeated practice of marching into and out of the church, but they did have to practice three actions: the renewal of baptismal vows, going to Communion, and the actual confirmation ceremony.

After a fifteen-minute recess at ten-thirty the children returned to the church for a spiritual talk by Father Dominic. His words were simple and direct, and the children listened attentively. Father told them that they should make two resolutions and then ask God to give them the strength through the sacrament of confirmation to keep those resolutions. The first was: "I will work my whole life to get to heaven." The second resolution they must finish for themselves and according to their own conscience. "I am going to fight every day against the sin of. . . ." The priest continued: "This is a very important choice you have to make. Spend the day thinking about the sin that is keeping you from getting closer to God and might someday send you to hell. It may be a mortal sin, or it may be a venial sin that will lead to mortal sins."

Father then suggested some of the sins they might think about. "Some of you might be lazy about getting to Mass on Sundays, or you're always coming late for Mass. Maybe you are tempted to tell lies; and that can get you in trouble with God. If you're curious about things that don't concern you—especially in the Sixth and Ninth Commandments—you better look out for that, and make your resolution on it." This little sermon to the children had been well planned by Father Dominic, and the two points—the general resolution and the particular resolution—seemed to be understood and remembered by the children.

Back in the auditorium after this talk, recordings of Christ's life were played for the whole class. Groups were taken out at intervals to get their lunch under the supervision of a Sister. The constant coming and going, and the fact that the children had already heard these records, caused them to be somewhat restless and talkative. At this point our observer notes a conversation with one of the older Sisters:

"During the lunch period Sister Miriam came to talk with me. She said it wouldn't take much to win these children over to communism, if the Communists promised them lots of sweets and movies and comics and fun. She is glad she's near the end of her time because it will be a terrible experience to be living some years hence. She feels that the training, or lack of training, the children have received from their parents has a lot to do with the way they act today. Retreats today are different from the ones she knew years ago. All the children do now is to 'stuff themselves with candy and junk.' Father gave them an inspiring talk this morning, but it just went in one ear and out the other.

"Mrs. Kaufmann and Sister Berthold joined us. One of the boys who was misbehaving has an Italian name. Sister Miriam called him a bad, dumb boy who came from a family of ignorant Italians. Mrs. Kaufmann remarked that bad children are those who are morally bad and that all the pupils in her class are good. Sister Berthold said that poor Sister Miriam wanted the children to be more perfect than they could be. (Sister Berthold is herself from an Italian family, but she was sympathetic with the older Sister and not at all resentful at her remarks.)"

In the afternoon at one-thirty, Father Dominic had the children come to the church and told them he was going to give them their catechism "just the way the Bishop will on Monday night." This was a performance which interested the class very much. Whenever he asked a question in the exact words of the book, the whole class recited the answer in unison. When he asked questions in his own words, there was momentary silence, then a hand would go up here and there. There was some confusion about the difference between a mortal and a venial sin, and the children began to ask questions and give examples. One of the little girls wanted to know whether the priest remembers and tells the sins he hears in confession. In almost every instance when someone gave the wrong answer, Father Dominic was able to get other children to answer the questions correctly.

Finally, before dismissal Father Dominic told them all to keep silence even at home and to talk to their parents only if it was absolutely necessary. "Remember, now, no movies, parties, no Scout meetings; no talking between now and Monday morning." The boys were dismissed first. Sister Berthold kept the girls in the church for a brief talk, telling them that they would be received into the Children of Mary Sodality on Tuesday morning, the day after confirmation. She said she was disappointed in the way they behaved this first day of the retreat and asked them to do better on Saturday and Sunday. "You must learn to set a good example for the boys and men because, if you are not good, they won't be good either."

On Saturday, the second day of the retreat, the children were present for seven forty-five Mass and remained on the church property until three o'clock in the afternoon. Since there were three weddings in the church that morning, they had to do all their practicing in the school auditorium. Otherwise the whole day was almost an exact repetition of the previous day.

On the third day of the retreat the order changed completely. The confirmation class sat as a group in a separate section of the church at the nine o'clock Mass. The sermons at all the Masses that day centered around the sacrament of confirmation and the gifts of the Holy Ghost. The Pastor remarked that "the great sacrament of strength will be administered by the Bishop tomorrow night. The Holy Spirit will come down upon all those who will receive the sacrament. All Catholics should develop a devotion to the Holy Ghost. . . . He will inspire and strengthen us in our faith and service of God."

After their Mass, the children went to the school auditorium for a short catechism instruction by Sister Berthold and the Principal, Sister Mary Anne. They were then sent home with instructions to return promptly at two-thirty with their sponsors, so that the whole ceremony could be practiced to perfection. The afternoon practice took more than an hour and was observed by more than a hundred adults, parents, relatives, and friends of the children. The Pastor himself gave a catechism instruction and supervised the practice.

He discovered one twelve-year-old boy who had just applied that day for confirmation and had never been to catechism classes or to the retreat. After practice he took this boy over to his office and found that he had not even received his First Communion, was attending the public school, and was the son of a non-Catholic father. The Pastor told him that he could not receive Communion or be confirmed until he learned his catechism. When the boy burst out in tears, the priest softened immediately and said he would see what could be done. But he apparently did not trust himself to make the decision, so he called in Father Dominic to "see whether this boy knows enough catechism to make his First Communion and be confirmed." As was to be expected, Father Dominic was forced to reject the boy as a candidate for the sacraments.

On Monday morning at six forty-five, the children formed a line in the school auditorium. They walked to the church, preceded by four little girls from the first grade, dressed as "angels." As they came into the church, the organ played in full peal, all lights in the church were on, and candles blazed on the altar. The boys came first in their new light-tan suits and two-toned shoes. The girls followed in their white dresses and veils. There were forty-nine boys and seventy-one girls in the class.

The Pastor celebrated the Solemn High Mass, with the two assistant priests acting as deacon and subdeacon. At the Gospel time the celebrant spoke very briefly about the joy that should be in the children's hearts and in the souls of their parents. While they had all received their First Communion several years ago, they must cherish the memory of this public display of their affection for Christ. He congratulated the parents and asked that they co-operate with the priests and sisters in keeping their children close to God.

The reception of Holy Communion was a unique ceremony which is not duplicated at any other time in the parish. The children went up into the sanctuary, led by two little "angels," and ascended the altar steps where they knelt to receive Communion. They were then led back to their pews, while two more "angels" brought up the next row. All was done in a very orderly fashion as previously rehearsed, the boys going up first, and the girls afterward. During this whole procedure the children's choir sang the hymn "O Lord, I Am Not Worthy." After the Mass, the children lined up in the main aisle, genuflected in unison, and marched out to their waiting mothers and fathers.

Traditionally, this Solemn Communion Day is a day of festivity in the parish. The children go to a photographer's studio or have their picture taken at home. After a Communion breakfast with their family, they remain "dressed up" for the entire day. They go about visiting their different relatives and receiving gifts from them. As a result of this activity all day long, they sometimes return to the church for confirmation at night in a sad state of disarray. The Sisters had ordered them to come back promptly at seven o'clock in the evening. All the girls were fresh and clean, but four of the boys had to be washed and cleaned up before the confirmation ceremony began.

The Pastor was anxious to make the public ceremony as impressive as possible by having a number of priests and monsignors present in the procession and in the sanctuary. In order to get the clergy to the ceremony, he invited them to a dinner in the rectory at five-thirty. He arranged with a caterer to prepare and serve the meal, which was done in the finest taste. There were nine guests besides the Pastor and his two regular assistants, but three priests had to leave before the procession started.

The congregation began to arrive before seven o'clock and went into all the pews off the center aisle except the front pews reserved for the children and guarded by four ushers. The altar was massed with red flowers, the traditional color symbolizing the Holy Spirit. A large crowd stood outside the church watching the procession headed by Father Dominic in surplice and biretta. The boys followed him into the church, genuflected together, and entered the pews. Then four nuns came in, leading the girls, who genuflected in like manner. A tall altar boy carrying the crucifix was flanked by two smaller boys carrying lighted candles. Then followed twenty-six altar-servers ranged for size, the smaller ones wearing red cassocks, while the taller ones had black cassocks. Father Paul with two more altar boys led twenty-two ushers, who formed an honor guard through which passed four monsignors, the Pastor, four visiting priests, and the Bishop. When the latter had passed, the ushers returned to the back of the church.

The Bishop immediately started a short, twelve-minute sermon in which he briefly explained and praised the sacramental system of the Catholic Church. Baptism makes one a child of God; penance removes the obstacles to God; Communion unites one to God; and confirmation makes him a temple of God, the Holy Ghost. Then he asked the children to answer the catechism questions loudly and distinctly. For about thirty-five minutes he questioned them mainly about the sacraments and for the most part received answers from the whole group. Several questions were quite difficult and were answered by individual children when the group failed to respond. "How many times can you receive matrimony?" was greeted by dead silence. Then several hands went up, and one boy said: "You can marry, and, if that person dies, you can marry again, and keep on marrying as long as one dies." Another question, "Why did God not change the appearance as well as the substance of the Eucharist?" was left unanswered until a little girl said, "So that we can receive Communion like food." After the last question the Bishop told the children that he was sure that their Pastor, priests, teachers, and parents were proud of them. He then asked that they make the following promises to God: to say their prayers every day; to never miss Mass on Sundays and holy days of obligation; to persevere in a life of grace by going to confession and Communion once a month; and to be loyal to the Church and their parish until death.

While the Bishop took his place at the episcopal throne, the Pastor was seated on a chair on the platform of the altar. The children advanced from the pews three at a time. Each held a lighted candle in his left hand and kept his right hand over his heart until reaching the altar steps. The three then knelt together before the Pastor and placed their right hands on the Bible. In unison they repeated after him their baptismal vows, arose, genuflected, and made way for the next trio.

After all had made this solemn pledge, the Bishop donned his ceremonial robes and, with the miter on his head and the espiscopal staff in his hand, proceded to the center of the sanctuary and up the altar steps. He removed the miter and handed the staff to an altar boy. With his back to the congregation and flanked by two priests, he recited the preliminary prayers. Then, turning around, he sat upon the chair at the top of the altar steps, which had previously been used by the Pastor. The boys came up to be confirmed two at a time, followed by their sponsors, who were adult males. These latter stood behind the youngsters, with their right hands on the boys' right shoulders, while they were being confirmed. Two men were confirmed after the boys had finished. Then the girls and their sponsors came up in the same manner, after which seven adult women were confirmed.

When the chrism had been wiped from the forehead of the last person confirmed, all recited the Apostles' Creed, the Our Father, and the Hail Mary. The Bishop then congratulated the children and spoke to both them and their parents and guardians about the importance of finding their true vocation.[3] This fourteen-minute sermon was followed by Solemn Benediction celebrated by the Pastor and two visiting priests. The final hymn sung by the whole congregation was "Holy God, We Praise Thy Name." The ushers again formed the honor guard through which the Bishop and other clergy walked, followed by the Sisters and the children.

On the day following the confirmation ceremony all the children of the class received Holy Communion again. They assembled to attend the children's Mass at seven forty-five, but a funeral had been scheduled for that time. Children in the schoolyard were sent in by the Sisters to attend the funeral and pray for the dead, but their own

3. See chap. 10, p. 114, for a brief summary of this talk.

Mass did not start until eight-twenty. All the school children attended and recited the Rosary during Mass; the confirmed children had reserved pews in front of the church and were the only ones to receive Communion.

After the Mass the Pastor consecrated them to the Blessed Mother and enrolled them in the Scapular. He told them that this was not just an extra ceremony but is something approved and blessed by the Church. "The brown Scapular takes the place of the habit that the holy monks wear. If you wear this all the time, the Blessed Mother will take care of you and make sure that you go to heaven." After some further explanation, he called one boy and one girl to the altar railing to receive the Scapular. Meanwhile Scapulars had been distributed to the other children, and each one put it over his own shoulders when the priest placed them on their representatives.

The boys were then enrolled in the Junior Holy Name Society and the girls in the Children of Mary Sodality. These ceremonies took almost an hour, so that these children, who had the rest of the day as a holiday, did not get home for breakfast until after ten o'clock. This was no particular hardship, since they had become accustomed to the same delay when they received Communion at the nine o'clock Mass on Sundays.

The nine adults who received confirmation on this occasion constituted the smallest adult group to be confirmed in any year since the present Pastor took office. The parish records show that, over a twenty-year period, 369 adults had been confirmed in St. Mary's Church, an average of 18.4 per year. In part this reflects the number of converts (175) who had come into the Catholic Church in the parish during these twenty years. The remaining 194 are accounted for mainly by persons who had gone to public schools and who had not been sent to the children's confirmation classes by their parents.

Except for the annual announcement concerning confirmation and a public invitation for adults who had not yet been confirmed, the priests of the parish take no further steps to have all their parishioners confirmed. According to the census information, there are 105 persons above the age of eleven years who have not yet been confirmed. Sixty-nine of these are above the age of eighteen. This is the measure of the parish's failure to live up to the sacramental ideal in which all persons above the age of eleven should be confirmed.

During the twenty-year period in St. Mary's Parish there were 4,426 infant baptisms, 2,976 First Communions, and 2,679 children's confirmations. The comparison among these three figures indicates a steady decrease in the numbers who receive the sacraments as they get older. This rough conclusion is strengthened when we select a certain age cohort and follow them through the three sacramental steps. The infant baptisms in the five-year period 1932–36 numbered 914. This same group of children who should have received their First Holy Communion in the years 1940–44 had dwindled to 655. By the time they were to receive the sacrament of confirmation, 1944–48, there were only 465 (see Fig. 20). The census figures for the age group 12–16 showed 476 persons.

If this age cohort may be used as a sample for the whole parish, it means that only 71.66 per cent of the infants baptized there later

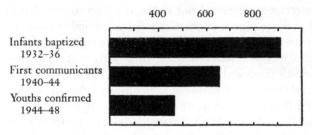

Fig. 20.—Comparison of the numbers who were baptized, received First Communion, and were confirmed, according to the succession of a five-year age cohort.

receive their First Communion and that only 50.87 per cent are confirmed as children. This startling decrease cannot be accounted for either by child mortality or by mobility from the parish. A small percentage of the decrease may be taken up by those persons who receive the sacraments of Communion and confirmation at other parishes. Some, as we have seen above, simply neglect to be confirmed, although they remain otherwise conscientious parishioners. But the great majority are those who have become dormant Catholics since their infant baptism.

Viewed only from the single aspect of the reception of the sacrament of confirmation, the parish may be said to have a fairly acceptable record. There are 4,984 actual parishioners of twelve years of age and more. Only 2.11 per cent of these are not yet confirmed. Considering the fact that confirmation is not an absolute requirement for membership in the Catholic Church and that there is no grave sanction on unconfirmed persons, we may conclude that St. Mary's Parish is somewhat above normal in this respect.

Chapter Nine

The Sacrament of Matrimony

THE marriage problem of our modern urban society has infiltrated into and become a part of the Catholic parochial system. In spite of the strict laws of the Catholic Church and the rigid controls of bishops and priests, this problem has come to absorb more and more of the parish priest's time and energy. St. Mary's Parish is no exception to this general trend. The Pastor is a member of the diocesan matrimonial court; hence he is more than ordinarily involved in matrimonial questions. Both he and his assistants are occupied in instructions for marriage and in counseling for marital problems.

The Catholic value system in marriage is clearly stated in the laws and doctrines of the Church at large and specifically outlined for the diocese itself. The ideal situation is that in which two Catholics living in the state of grace receive the sacrament of matrimony at a Nuptial Mass in their own parish church with the intention of preserving a permanent, monogamous, fruitful union. Any deviation from that situation must be considered a deviation from the ideal proposed by the Catholic religion. In varying degrees, therefore, the following actions fall short of the ideal pattern: afternoon weddings, mixed marriages, civil or religious unions "outside the Church," separation, divorce, adultery, birth control, and abortion.

In order to understand the total situation in this regard in St. Mary's Parish, we shall attempt to answer two questions: (a) What program of action is followed in the parish to promote the ideal and to offset deviations from it? (b) To what extent does the parish fail, or fulfil, the ideal? The first question is answered for the most part by the participant-observation through the year of the survey, while the second is answered mainly from the statistical data gathered in the detailed census.

96

a) What means are taken in St. Mary's Parish to prevent the abuses of marriage and to promote the Catholic ideal? The most general and long-term medium is that of instruction, which is of three kinds: the catechism for school children, sermons from the pulpit, and the immediate course of instructions given to all prospective brides and grooms.

We have already seen that the preparation of children for First Communion and confirmation emphasizes knowledge about all the sacraments. The essential doctrines concerning marriage are learned there. All Catholic school children know the precepts of the Church on marriage. They learn the catechism answers about monogamy, the sanctity and indissolubility of marriage, the degrees of kinship, the place and times of marriage. Of course, the individuals who attend Catholic high school and college learn this doctrine in greater detail, but that is a function outside the parochial orbit.

Occasionally during the year there is a sermon on the sacrament of marriage. During the mission given by the Lazarist Fathers, one evening was set aside for a sermon on matrimony. This was exclusively for married women, and the single women were asked to go to the school auditorium for their talk. In speaking to the married women, Father O'Hallohan was very clear cut and definite concerning their obligations and rights. "Marriage is God-made and is not a mere human creation. The laws that govern marriage are the laws of God, not the laws of man. The great and exclusive privilege of married women is the generation of human beings. This bespeaks an unutterable co-operation with God, who creates the human soul at conception. Husband and wife co-operate with each other and in so doing co-operate with God in the formation of a new being."

The missioner then explained in detail the kinds of actions which were sinful in marriage and those which are not only permitted but virtuous. He spoke of the abuse of the marriage act and of abortion and the sanction of excommunication which accompanies it. The reaction to this sermon was expressed by one lady who said, "I've been married fourteen years, and he embarrassed me with that sermon—he was too frank." Another said, "He didn't leave anything out; he couldn't have been more frank."

In the men's mission the following week, Father O'Hallohan gave almost the same sermon on matrimony, but he stressed the husband's duties in marriage. Toward the end of the sermon he spoke of the high vocation of fatherhood and particularly of the power of example in speech and behavior. Furthermore, he said, "you do not have the right to decide that your children go to the public school. Justice demands that they learn their religion, and in the parochial school. You do more harm to your child by depriving him of his religious education than you would if you cut off his hand. He can get to heaven without a hand, but without religion he will go to hell."

The diocesan weekly also contributes its educational share in preserving and furthering the ideals of Catholic marriage. In an editorial on Family Life Day, we read: "Anything that is done to make our people more conscious of the dignity of marriage, the sanctity of the marital bond and the importance of married life for the family, will help offset the tragic and degrading effects of movies with their romanticising claptrap built around broken marriages, infidelity and giddy and irresponsible characters, who have neither sense nor moral stamina to live up to the serious duties of married life."[1]

Some pastors of urban parishes act on the principle that a parochially sponsored social program will encourage young Catholic men and women to associate with each other and thus lead to marriages between members of the parish. This is intended to preserve and foster parochial loyalty and especially to prevent mixed marriages. In another section of this study we shall discuss the functioning of youth organizations in St. Mary's Parish. There was only a limited opportunity to bring young parishioners together during the year of the survey, and some small attempts were made in that direction.

Why are there so many mixed marriages, and what can be done to decrease them? The Pastor has stated frequently that nothing can be done once the couple comes in to make arrangements for their wedding. They cannot be expected to "fall out of love again." He maintains that, if parents insisted that their sons and daughters date only Catholics, the number of mixed marriages could be decreased by 50 per cent. If the Bishop were less lenient in granting dispensations for mixed marriages, and the priests more reluctant in asking for these dispensations, the number would probably decrease. All these factors must be added to proximity of residence in attempting to answer this question.

The instructions given in immediate preparation for marriage are ordered by the bishops in most of the dioceses in the United States. These are in the nature of a general refresher course in the Catholic religion with special emphasis on the duties and privileges of the marital state. As given in St. Mary's by the three priests, they are almost exclusively theological, with occasional psychological and eco-

1. *Diocesan Weekly*, February 26, 1949.

nomic advice drawn from the counseling experience of the priest. These are not sex instructions except in so far as they deal with the morality of sex relations. Although six is the average number of instructions, the Pastor frequently extends them, particularly in the case of mixed marriages, until he is satisfied that the couple realizes its responsibilities and intends to fulfil them.

The climax of these premarital lessons comes when each prospective spouse under oath answers the diocesan marriage schedule. They separately and solemnly swear with their hand on the Bible that they are free to marry and, not being coerced in any way, that they will not practice birth control, etc. In the case of mixed marriages there is an additional signed statement by the non-Catholic promising that the children will be reared as Catholics and that there will be no interference of any kind in the practice of the Catholic spouse's religion.

For three Sundays previous to the date of the wedding the banns are announced at all the Masses, to which is added the reminder that "if anyone knows of an impediment to these marriages he is obliged to inform the pastor." This is not done in the case of mixed marriages, a fact which puzzles some Catholics. One individual wrote to the "question and answer" column of the diocesan weekly asking why the banns were not read for mixed marriages. The answer was as follows: "The law of the Church forbids a Catholic to marry a person not of the Faith, because of the danger to one's own Faith and that of the children. A person, then, who chooses to marry someone from outside of the Church is acting contrary to the laws and the mind of the Church. Publication of the banns would publicize in church the fact that the Catholic party was acting contrary to the law of the Church, and the Church does not intend to encourage mixed marriages."[2]

The purpose of the banns is to uncover any impediments or previous binding obligations of either party in the proposed marriage. In no instance in the memory of the present Pastor has anyone ever informed the priests of an impediment to announced marriages. One prospective bride, however, after the announcement of her banns, received an anonymous letter informing her that her future husband "has colored blood." Three days before the scheduled wedding she and her mother came indignantly and tearfully to the Pastor, saying that the man denied the charge. Since the state laws forbid miscegenation, Father Urban advised them to postpone the wedding and seek proof. When this proof was forthcoming from upcountry, the girl returned to see the Pastor, relieved but still indignant. She declared:

2. *Ibid.*, April 15, 1948.

"If I had married him and become pregnant, I would have had an abortion—Church law or no Church law!" Both of the parties to this intended wedding were Catholics and could hardly be excused for misunderstanding the Church's clear teaching about miscegenation.

Some individuals sincerely prefer a quiet, unostentatious wedding. One man, whose father had died several weeks previously, was married at an afternoon ceremony. One woman in her thirties requested the same, because she did not want to distract from the public celebration of her brother's first Mass, who was to be ordained two months later. Others who feel that greater numbers of their friends are able to attend late weddings transfer the social ostentation from the church to the country club or the private dining-room of a downtown hotel. Still others tell the priest that they want an afternoon ceremony because they "cannot afford a Mass." To this the Fathers invariably reply that "the stipend is the same for both."

It must be noted that the external display at weddings is not a reliable indication of either the Catholicism or the social status of the persons and families involved in them. One of the wealthiest girls in the parish had a simple church wedding with four attendants. On the other hand, a family of the lower middle class provided the most lavish wedding of the year for their only daughter. All four families involved in these two marriages are known as "good Catholics" in the Riverside community. They are generally parochial-minded, well known to the priests, and active in the affairs of both parish and diocese. If a scale were constructed to show the gradations from most simple to most ostentatious weddings, there would be found both nominal Catholics and very active Catholics at almost every point on the scale.

The altar boys have their own criterion for judging weddings, which is the size of the tip they receive from the groom or the best man. They vie with one another for the opportunity to serve at Nuptial Masses, but they have no way of knowing beforehand which will be the most lucrative.[3] They dislike one wedding because the principals have their young relatives from another parish serve the Mass. Another they call a "cheap wedding" because they each receive a tip of only twenty-five cents. Another was "pretty good" because they received the normal tip of one dollar each. Still another was

3. The altar boys are not quite so enthusiastic about serving at funerals in the late afternoon or on Saturday mornings. Usually there is no tip involved, but there is an inducement in the fact that they are excused from school while accompanying the priest in the religious service at the church and at the cemetery.

"swell," said one of the three altar boys; "I got a dollar from the usher and five bucks from the groom."

Again the economic criterion based on the amount of the stipend given at the weddings during the year was not a reliable index of either the degree of Catholicism or the social status. The usual stipend is thirty-five dollars, but there were many exceptions above and below this norm.[4] Generally, it may be said that the more active Catholics tend to give above this amount. The most simple wedding at a Nuptial Mass may be accompanied by a check for two hundred dollars, while it is not unusual that a donation of less than a hundred dollars is given at a very lavish ceremony. During the year of observation and study none of the persons married was actually in the upper class of Riverside or city society. Most of them were people who have no pretensions to social climbing. In only one case was the bride the daughter of a lady who is desperately and unsuccessfully trying to "break into society."

There is an apparent lack of concern on the part of the priests for afternoon weddings. The following occurrence, while not typical, is an indication of this unconcern. On a Sunday afternoon in February our observer was present for the baptism of infants. He reports: "Father Paul seemed to be in a hurry with these baptisms, and I soon discovered the reason why. A funeral came into the church at two twenty-five, and while the baptisms were being completed, Father Dominic conducted the funeral services up at the altar rail. Before this was over and while the body was still in the church, I noticed the Pastor in an excited argument with a woman of about fifty at the side door of the church. I asked Father Paul what was the matter, and he said, 'We've got a wedding at three and another funeral at three-thirty.'

"When Father Dominic had gone with the funeral party, the lady in question came back to argue with Father Paul. She was tearful and belligerent and very loud. 'You priests make me sick. You always turn people away. I'm not going to have my daughter married at a

4. The Pastor, who is generous and thoughtful about financial affairs, follows a strict rule concerning stipends for marriages. He maintains that a "whole lot of money is spent foolishly at weddings, and any man ought to be able to give a few dollars to the Church when he gets married." If this detail is overlooked by the groom, the Pastor holds the marriage license at the rectory until the city recorder inquires from the married couple where their document is. Of course, they rush to the Pastor, who tells them suavely that "the wedding hasn't really been completed yet." He remarks privately, "How can a man buy food and clothes for his wife if he can't afford five or ten dollars for his wedding? Of course," he adds, "I make an exception if someone is in trouble and has to get married."

Carl A. Rudisill Library
LENOIR RHYNE COLLEGE

funeral. Why don't you take that black cloth off the altar and get ready for the wedding?' Father Paul quietly replied, 'It's not my fault, Madame; don't bawl me out.' She continued to cry and said, 'Father Urban is going to apologize to me for this.'

"Meanwhile, as I learned later, the Pastor had gone over to the rectory to phone the undertaker and request that the second funeral be advanced to three o'clock. Father Paul remarked as he was leaving, 'Whoever set up that schedule shouldn't have put things so close together.' The bride and her attendant sat in the last pew with her mother. They were all dressed in conservative suits and were not conspicuous except for their bouquets. The groom and his attendants were also there, and everybody was excited and talking at once. They had decided to wait until after the second funeral. The mother of the bride said, 'I told Father Urban he'd better have it at three o'clock, or he'll hear some more from me.' The bride then said, 'Why don't you call up the Bishop and tell him about it?' To which her mother answered, 'I'm going to call him up tomorrow.'

"The second funeral cortege arrived at the church at three-thirty as scheduled. Father Paul conducted the ceremony for this one in about twenty minutes, after which he left to accompany the body to the cemetery. After he had gone, the altar boys worked hard to eliminate all traces of the funeral by removing the black antependium and the candlesticks and by putting all the flowers they could find in the sacristy on the altar. While this was going on, the Pastor came over and asked the bride and groom to come to the rectory. He told me later that he apologized to the couple and said that this was one of those slip-ups that shouldn't happen and that he was sorry if he brought disturbance and sorrow to them on their wedding day. He apparently persuaded them very successfully. They were both smiling cheerfully when they came back to the church for their wedding. The Pastor himself officiated in a very gracious manner and seemed to spend an uncommonly long time speaking with the couple at the end of the ceremony before they signed the marriage certificates."

While display is discouraged and restricted at late weddings, it is permitted and even encouraged at the marriages which take place at Mass. The Pastor has frequently said, "I want to give my people all the music and beauty possible when they receive the sacrament of marriage." Of course, each bride has her own long-developed plans for her wedding day, and the Pastor allows her, within limits, to have the final decision concerning the decoration of the church, the number of attendants, hymns to be sung, etc. A rehearsal takes place, usually the day before the wedding, at which the officiating priest gives last-minute instructions for the ceremony. Occasionally a bride believes in the superstition that it is "hard luck" to take part in the rehearsal and appoints a "stand-in." The priests are adamant in refusing to allow this superstition, and they have almost succeeded in stamping it out among the parishioners.

In the opinion of "society people" and those who are working toward upward mobility in the community structure, the genuinely upper-class parish church of the city is St. Michael's, the one adjoining St. Mary's Parish. Catholics who wish to be married in another parish must obtain the permission of their own pastor. Although canon law permits the marriage to take place at the church of either bride or groom, tradition has more or less santified the custom of marriage in the bride's parish church. Father Urban expresses great annoyance when his own parishioners come to ask permission to be married elsewhere. Usually he refused to grant it unless they have a reason of some weight. He blames other priests, particularly those at St. Michael's, for encouraging this "disloyalty to the parish."

Occasionally, a girl who is determined to have a "fashionable" wedding moves to St. Michael's Parish and establishes a quasi-domicile there, thus coming under the parochial jurisdiction of the other pastor. After she has lived there for six weeks, she can apply as a parishioner to be married there. This practice has caused some irritation among the pastors of the city, and Father Urban has tried to have the Bishop make a ruling against it. While it seems an evasion and an abuse, it is a right protected by the canon law, even in its strictest interpretation.

The same is true of weddings in a private residence. This, too, is considered a fashionable procedure by some parishioners, and it is possible to obtain the permission of the Bishop. The Pastor refuses to ask this permission of the Bishop or to perform weddings in the homes of his parishioners. One incident will serve to illustrate the complications attendant on such arrangements. A young lady of the parish came with her fiancé to discuss plans for her wedding. Her future husband was a non-Catholic, and she planned to marry him in the garden of his father's palatial home in the country. The Pastor informed her that the Bishop would not grant permission for "garden weddings."

The girl thereupon moved to St. Michael's Parish, being certain that the Fathers there would understand her desire to be married in a garden and could obtain the Bishop's permission. The priest at St.

Michael's told her that, if she obtained the approval of the pastor of the parish where the paternal estate was located, the wedding could be performed *inside* the residence, while the reception could be held in the garden. The girl's mother, an Episcopalian, became impatient of all these technicalities and asked her own minister to perform the ceremony. Over the protests of her Catholic father, the girl finally had her fashionable garden wedding—but without benefit of Catholic clergy.

Father Urban seized upon this incident as a demonstration of several practical parochial theses which he holds. He was disturbed that it had happened and blamed it partially on "interference from other priests" and mostly on the fact that the girl was the child of a mixed marriage and had never attended a Catholic school. She simply "didn't know any better." Another case, however, was much more discouraging. The girl had attended both a parochial school and a Catholic high school. She was a senior in a Catholic girls' college when she eloped after a party one night to marry a Catholic young man before a county justice of the peace. The next day she was expelled from college, and her parents, tearful and ashamed, came for advice to their old friend, the Pastor. The latter called the young couple to his office when they returned to town and talked to them for more than two hours. They agreed to live separately for a few months but insisted that they were in love and would eventually get married. The girl showed her ring to all her friends and declared that she was "engaged to be married."

The census schedules show that there are 130 widows or widowers in the parish, and 1,795 marriages in which both husband and wife are still living. There were 44 divorced persons and 36 separated persons. Of these combined marriages, 1,925 in number, 1,698 (or 88.21 per cent) had been validly contracted according to the laws of the Church, while 227 (or 11.79 per cent) were invalid. Table 14 and Figure 21 give the general picture of the marital status of St. Mary's Parish.

The most obvious departure from the ideal of Catholic marriage is that of divorce with intention to remarry. There are instances, however, of divorce from a marriage in which one of the spouses has been treated so unjustly and unbearably that his or her safety and well-being are threatened. When all other means of reconciliation have failed, the Bishop may consent to legal separation, or even civil divorce, with the understanding that the persons are still validly married and may not remarry before the death of one spouse. Assuming

that the forty-four divorces and the thirty-six separations have occurred with the dispensation and consent of the Bishop, how does
St. Mary's compare to the larger community? The city[5] in which St.
Mary's Parish is located had a divorce percentage of 2.31, while the
nation as a whole had 2.66 per cent as compared to the parish's 2.29
per cent.

Actually, however, 35 per cent of these marriages had been invalid
from the start. In other words, twenty-eight of the eighty marriages

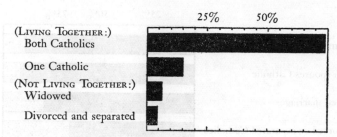

FIG. 21.—Comparative percentages of 1,925 marriages in St. Mary's Parish according to Catholic and mixed marriages and those not living with spouse.

TABLE 14

	No.	Per Cent
All marriages reported	1,925	100.00
Living together:		
Both spouses Catholic	1,424	74.03
One spouse Catholic	291	15.06
Not living together:		
Widowed	130	6.75
Divorced	44	2.29
Separated	36	1.87

which ended in separation or divorce were not true marriages according to the laws of the Catholic Church. Hence, there was no
need for consulting the Bishop and obtaining his consent for a separation. In fact, when Catholics are partners to invalid marriages, they
are living in sin, and they cannot receive the sacraments as practical
Catholics until they do separate or become validly married.

Thus, the criterion of validity of marital status is more satisfactory
than that of divorce and separation in judging the internal adherence
of Catholics to the Church's ideal. The person who contracts an invalid marriage cuts himself off from the sacramental vitality of the

5. The percentages for the city and nation do not include the large number
of remarriages after divorce.

parish, and, while he may attend Mass and participate in other parochial functions, he cannot be considered a practicing Catholic. Figure 22 gives the percentages for validity in three categories: marriages in which both spouses are Catholics, mixed marriages in which one is a Catholic, and Catholics who are divorced or separated. These percentages show an important relation between validity of marriage and its permanency and between validity of marriage and the religion of the spouses. It is quite obvious that divorce and separation should

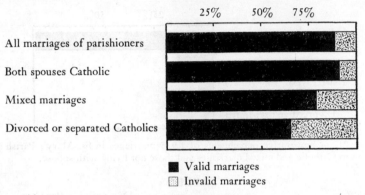

Fig. 22.—Percentage comparison of valid and invalid marriages in all marriages of parishioners and in three types of marital status.

be relatively frequent among Catholics who contracted their marriage without the blessing of the Church. Even ill-instructed Catholics are aware of the fact that the Church laws concerning marriage are definite and rigid, and they are conscious that they can no longer belong to the Church unless they dissolve their union or validate it.

While the percentage of Catholics who contract their union outside the Church is high, it is more than twice as high for Catholics who marry non-Catholics. More than 20 per cent of all mixed marriages in the parish are invalid. This difference is to be expected, since in many instances the person who allows himself to fall in love with the intention of marrying a non-Catholic is already lacking complete agreement with the doctrines and practices of the Church. The ecclesiastical law explicitly states that Catholics may not marry non-Catholics and that the marriage must be contracted before a duly authorized priest. One who thinks lightly of the first prescription is not likely to hesitate over an infraction of the second.

While the criterion of invalidity is the most serious one in showing complete defection from the value system of the Church, the criterion of mixed marriages may be used to show a partial withdrawal from those values. There were 291 mixed marriages in the parish, which represents approximately 15 per cent of all marriages. Since more than one-fifth of these are invalid, we know that at least that number of spouses in the mixed marriages cannot make their annual Easter duties or receive Holy Communion at other times of the year. There exists

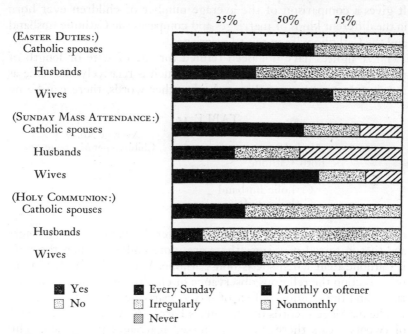

Fig. 23.—Percentage comparisons of religious observance by Catholic spouses in mixed marriages, showing the differences between husbands and wives in three kinds of observance.

a relation between the fact of mixed marriage and the religious observances of the Catholic spouse in the marriage. Of the 291 mixed marriages, there are 78 Catholic husbands and 213 Catholic wives. Figure 23 shows their degree of fidelity to the practice of Catholicism.

Almost two-fifths of all the persons involved in mixed marriages do not make their Easter duties. In this, as in all other measures of faithful observance, Catholic women have a better record than Catholic men. But the fact is that both sexes show a distinctly poorer record of observance than those who have married Catholics. Of course, we cannot say whether their beliefs, ideals, and behavior are affected by the fact of their mixed marriage, or whether the reverse is the case.

Apparently, there is a mutual influence of both factors. Less than 60 per cent of these persons go to Mass every Sunday and less than one-third receive Communion monthly.

There was no way of obtaining information about the practice of birth control by Catholics in mixed marriages. Table 15, however, may be cautiously employed as a partial indication in that direction. It gives a comparison of the average number of children ever born in the different kinds of marriages and compares the Catholic husband and the Catholic wife in mixed marriages.

These figures have not been refined for age of wife or length of marriage, but they give a comparison which is relatively the same as that in other sections of this study. In other words, there can be no

TABLE 15

Marital Status	Average No. of Children per Marriage
Both Catholic	2.25
Mixed marriages	1.92
Catholic husband	1.54
Catholic wife	2.10

doubt that Catholic marriages are more fertile than mixed marriages and that in mixed marriages there are more children when the wife is Catholic than when she is non-Catholic. We shall consider in another section the religious observance of children born to mixed marriages and the religious effect of mixed marriage on family life.

The marriage records of St. Mary's Parish show that over a period of twenty years there were 515 mixed marriages performed. This represents 29.15 per cent of all marriages during these two decades. The lowest proportion, 16.67 per cent, occurred in 1938, and the highest, 42.50 per cent, in 1932. The period 1941–46 showed that each year had a higher-than-average percentage of mixed marriages, a fact which may in some way be connected with the social problems of the war years. In the years before the war the yearly percentages were more frequently below the average than above it.

Over the whole twenty-year period, however, there seems to be no discernible trend either toward more or toward fewer mixed marriages in the parish. The popular theory among urban pastors is that mixed marriages are on the increase. This may be true in absolute numbers, since the population is increasing and more of our people are getting married, but it does not seem to be true in proportion to all marriages contracted.

St. Mary's Parish, like almost every urban parish, has a higher-than-average percentage of mixed marriages. The whole diocese, which is predominantly rural, had only 23.86 per cent mixed marriages over the twenty-year period, as compared to 29.15 per cent for St. Mary's. The neighboring parish of St. Michael's, an "upper-class" church, had a percentage of 34.51 over the same period of years. Although sufficient comparative statistics have not been obtained, it is generally supposed that urban parishes have more mixed marriages than rural parishes and that in the city the churches with the more wealthy, better-educated, and more socially mobile parishioners have the higher percentage of mixed marriages.

An interesting commentary may be made on the religious aspect of mixed marriages when we compare the findings of the parish census with those of the parish records. In the latter we see that 1,767 marriages have been contracted during twenty years, of which 29.15 per cent were mixed marriages. On the other hand, we find that, among the actual parishioners, 16.96 per cent of the spouses living together are in mixed marriages. Why does this large difference exist? If over a long period of time, approximately 30 per cent of the marriages performed at St. Mary's Church are mixed marriages, then approximately 30 per cent (instead of about 17 per cent) of all the married people in the parish ought to be in mixed marriages. In other words, there ought to be about five hundred mixed marriages in the parish instead of less than three hundred. The most likely conclusion seems to be that the difference between these two figures represents defections from the Church as a direct or indirect result of mixed marriage.

The need for validation of marriages is a negative criterion of the way in which Catholics of a parish live up to the sacramental ideals of Catholic marriage. "Validation" is simply the name for the marriage ceremony performed for those who have been invalidly married "outside the Church." During the course of two decades 209 marriages have been validated. Sixty (28.7 per cent) of these marriages have been between a Catholic and a non-Catholic. The fact that about 30 per cent of all marriages in the last twenty years were mixed and that almost 30 per cent of the validations were of mixed marriages may lead to the erroneous conclusion that both Catholic and mixed marriages have approximately the same rate of invalidity. This comparison, however, must be used cautiously, because a greater proportion of the invalid marriages which still exist in the parish are mixed marriages. As we have seen above, 37.55 per cent of the invalid marriages are between a Catholic and a non-Catholic.

It was said above that the sacramental marriage at a Nuptial Mass is the outward visible ideal which pastors strive for in arranging marriages. During the course of instructions they urge Catholics to be married at Mass. The legislation of the Church does not allow mixed marriages, or validations of either Catholic or mixed marriages, to take place at Mass. The study of the 338 marriages performed in the three years 1946–48 shows that, of the 245 Catholic marriages performed, 213 (or 87.94 per cent) took place at a Nuptial Mass.[6] This appears to be a very good record, and the Pastor claims that it is a great improvement over the customs as they existed when he first took office.

To what extent could this record be improved, so that all who are eligible would have their marriages performed at Mass? Why do some Catholics insist upon being married in the afternoon or evening? It must be noted that fourteen of the thirty-two marriages occurred in Lent and Advent, periods in the liturgical year when the Church forbids the external solemnization of marriages. In all these cases there was sufficient reason for the marriage to be held at these times; for example, the groom could not get his vacation at any other time; he was being transferred to another location by his employer; etc.

Hence, there remain only eighteen marriages during these three years which were held in the afternoon or evening against the counsel of the Pastor and the known wish of the Bishop. The latter has made a regulation that no music may be played and no decorations placed in the church on these occasions. Two candles may be lit, and, if there are any bouquets remaining on the altar from the morning Mass, they need not be removed. These restrictions have successfully struck at the main reason why some parishioners desired afternoon and evening weddings. The social and glamorous aspect has been removed from the ceremony, so that the actual marriage is a cold, silent, and almost drab affair.[7]

6. During this same three-year period there were 23 Catholic and 93 mixed marriages which took place in the afternoon and evening. There were also validations of 25 Catholic and 9 mixed marriages which could not be performed at Mass.

7. It is to be noted for those interested in the "social aspects" of religious ceremonies that the proportion of morning funerals is much lower than that of weddings. A little more than 54 per cent of the funerals at St. Mary's Church are conducted in the afternoon.

Chapter Ten

Vocations in the Parish

ONE of the most significant criteria of a spiritually alert Catholic parish is the number and kind of spiritual vocations among the parishioners. The complete dedication of one's whole life and energies as a priest, Sister, or Brother is a signal characteristic of flourishing Catholicism. The person who so dedicated himself is certainly prompted by supernatural grace; he is said to have a special "calling" from God, a divine inspiration of some kind which manifests itself externally in the actual separation from lay people. The internal nature of a spiritual vocation is a question that belongs to the ascetical writer and the theologian and not to the sociologist.

Manifestly, however, persons who enter seminaries, convents, and novitiates are generally the product of a Catholic environment. There are exceptions, of course—persons who were brought up as Protestants, became converts to Catholicism, and eventually became priests or nuns. But the largest number appear to have nurtured their vocations in the midst of their pious Catholic families, who in turn are active members of their own parish.

By this yardstick of vocations, St. Mary's is a fairly good parish. At the present time there are twenty-two men and thirteen women from this parish who have entered the service of God.[1] Ten of the men are already ordained priests, and, of these, one is the chancellor of a diocese, two are pastors of city churches, and three are still assistant pastors in rural areas. Of the remaining four priests, two are Passionists, one is a Benedictine, and the fourth a Jesuit. Thus there are six diocesan priests and four priest-members of religious orders. Besides these priests there are two brothers of the same family who

1. There is no reliable record of vocations in the past history of the parish. There has never been an American-born pastor of St. Mary's, a fact which indicates that the Catholic Church in the southern United States is only barely out of the missionary stage of its development.

are members of the Christian Brothers' teaching Order. Ten others are preparing for the priesthood, five in the major seminary, three in the minor seminary, and two in the scholasticate of the Jesuit Order.

Whether or not this is a good percentage of male vocations for the parish cannot be ascertained until comparable statistics in other parishes are gathered and made available. The record is: twenty-two men from 1,806 families; twenty-two men out of 2,216 males seventeen years of age and older;[2] or, more specifically, twenty-two men in religion as compared to 501 unmarried laymen seventeen years of age and over who are in the parish at the present time.

Numerically and proportionately the women of the parish show a lower representation in the religious life than do the males. Of the thirteen nuns who have come from the parish, eight are professed, while five are still in their novitiate or training period. Seven of these women are members of the Benedictine Order, two are Dominican Sisters, and there is one each among the Sisters of Mercy, the Little Sisters of the Poor, the Sisters of Charity, and the Medical Missionaries.

Although the proportion of vocations among the women is not so large as that among the men, no reliable judgment can be formed until comparisons can be made with other parishes. The record is: thirteen women from 1,806 families in the parish; thirteen women out of 2,292 females seventeen years of age or older;[3] or thirteen women in religion as compared to 577 unmarried lay women seventeen years of age and older.

These thirty-five persons who are working exclusively for the service of God are the children of faithful Catholic parents. None of them comes from a mixed marriage; almost all of them are from large families. All of them had most of their education in St. Mary's Parochial School and attended the Catholic high schools of the city. Actually, they represent only thirty-two families, since three families each contributed two members to the religious life. The names of these families are most prominent in the active sacramental and organizational life of the parish, and it appears that the two elements react on each other. A pious Catholic family stimulates vocations,

2. This is a rate of 9.9 in every thousand, as compared to the proportion for the whole United States, which is 7.8 in every thousand, and for the diocese, which is 4.8 per thousand.

3. This is a rate of 5.6 in every thousand, as compared to the proportion for the whole United States, which is 15.09 in every thousand, and for the diocese, which is 9.5 per thousand.

while a vocation in the family stimulates the Catholic action of the other family members.

As far as influences and motivations can be observed, family life is not the sole factor in the development of religious vocations. Generally speaking, there has been a reaction in American Catholic life against so-called "persuasion" of young persons to enter the seminary or convent. This trend has developed almost a reticence on the part of adults, so that they try hard to avoid the impression that they are persuading any particular young person toward a dedicated life. Yet there are religious forces at work in the parish toward this end.

Every Sunday of the year, during the Holy Hour service, a special prayer is recited by the priest and people asking God to increase the number of vocations. The priest speaks the words of Holy Writ, "Why stand ye here all day idle? Go ye also into my vineyard." The people answer, "Pray ye therefore the Lord of the harvest, that He send forth laborers into His vineyard." The whole congregation then reads in unison from the Holy Hour booklet: "O God who dost not desire the death of the sinner, but rather that he be converted and live, grant we beseech Thee through the intercession of Blessed Mary ever Virgin and of all the saints, an increase of laborers for Thy holy Church who, co-operating with Christ, may give themselves and generously spend themselves for the salvation of souls. Through the same Christ Our Lord. Amen."

The appeal for vocations is made occasionally through the medium of mass propaganda. At St. Mary's Church several techniques are used toward this end. The first is by means of the pulpit. During both the men's and the women's mission, brief mention was made of vocations in the Tuesday-night sermon for single persons. The missioner said: "We all have some sort of vocation in life. In God's eyes there is a particular vocation for each one of us, and He gives special grace and help so that we are able to follow it. One vocation is that of a nun—a very good and happy life. If you feel that you are called to be a Sister, pray hard and consult your pastor. The single state is another vocation. Older single women are called 'old maids' as though they are 'left-overs,' but, if the whole story were known, they are probably single by choice and for a high motive. Finally, there is the vocation of marriage."[4]

The Bishop, too, both personally and by letter, made use of St.

4. For more about this sermon see chap. 9, pp. 97–98. The same ideas were presented to the young men on the following Tuesday night, with the appropriate changes.

Mary's pulpit for the promotion of spiritual vocations. After the confirmation ceremonies on Monday night, April 19, His Excellency gave a fourteen-minute sermon to the parents and guardians of the children. He said that both children and adults must ask God for spiritual strength and guidance to find the right vocation in life. If the child shows signs of a vocation to the religious life, he or she should not be discouraged from it. As a matter of fact, vocations seldom come automatically. They must be fostered and developed. The child learns his values mainly from parents, and, if he sees the parents concerned primarily with worldly matters, he too will put worldly things first. The Bishop then pointed out the Church's great need for more priests, Sisters, and Brothers and promised that God's special graces will come to parents whose children follow these spiritual callings.

On three occasions during the year the parish priests themselves preached briefly on the matter of vocations. These sermons were generally in relation to the collections made for the diocesan seminary, the propagation of the faith, and the foreign missions.

The annual appeal in support of the diocesan seminary was made on the Feast of St. Joseph. In the letter which he ordered to be read in all Catholic churches at the Sunday Masses, His Excellency asked for vocations as well as for funds. "May we also plead with you for your prayers and solicitude for an increase of vocations to the priesthood. We regret to state that we are falling far short of the number of vocations which are necessary to staff properly our churches and works of religion, to replace the priests who are called to their eternal reward, and to meet the growing need for new parishes and for more priests in the larger parishes and in the mission areas of the diocese. Our Catholic population is certainly large enough to furnish abundant vocations to the priesthood, but there is need of overcoming the worldly spirit which often prevents parents from co-operating with divine grace when God indicates a vocation in the immediate family circle; there is need of giving encouragement to well-qualified boys who would make excellent priests if they were given the opportunity for the necessary education and training. There is, therefore, need of prayer and still more prayer for God's grace in this important matter."

The Bishop returned to this theme in a letter read at all Masses on Sunday, May 2, when he commended to the faithful the annual Novena to the Holy Ghost. "Among the intentions which the Church has in mind for this novena, let us include the increase throughout the diocese of vocations to the holy priesthood and to the religious life.... Responsibility for the encouragement and development of these holy vocations rests not only with the Bishop, the priests, the Brothers, and the Sisters; all the members of the flock of Christ must be earnestly concerned in promoting these holy vocations. Every parish throughout the diocese should aim to present a series of boys and girls, of adolescent youths of both sexes, as candidates, respectively, for the priesthood and the religious life; it should also be the pious desire of many families to count among these their favorite sons and daughters."[5]

During Advent the diocesan major seminary celebrated its twenty-fifth anniversary. The chapel had been redecorated for the occasion. One of the new stained-glass windows was donated, at a cost of $2,000, by the Pastor of St. Mary's. The Bishop issued a public invitation to all Catholics to visit the seminary on the third and fourth Sundays of Advent. But the only persons from St. Mary's who accepted this invitation were the relatives and close friends of the seminarians. This was the first "open house" the seminary had had since its beginnings. Visitors were allowed to go all through the buildings and were able to see how the seminarians live.

The Bishop's invitation, read at all the Masses on the second Sunday of Advent, again contained a plea for vocations: "Jubilee celebrations urge us also to look forward into the years that lie ahead. Our seminary must continue to provide pious, well-instructed, and zealous priests for God's honor, for the progress of the Church, for the welfare of souls. The great need of the diocese is more vocations that will come right out of the homes, homes in our cities, homes in our countrysides. One hundred vocations a year for the diocesan and religious priesthood, the promise of a hundred priestly lives per year out of the more than a hundred thousand families in the diocese, would be a worthy goal of dedication in this Silver Jubilee year of our seminary.[6] These vocations will come in answer to our earnest

5. In this letter His Excellency also urges that "the faithful attend Holy Mass every morning during the Novena as well as the evening devotions arranged by the Reverend Pastor. If unable to attend church, recite at least the Rosary and the Litany of the Blessed Virgin every evening at home. Special prayers should also be recited in our schools during the Novena." (The Novena to the Holy Ghost starts the day after Ascension and ends on Saturday, May 15, the eve of Pentecost.)

6. St. Mary's contributes about 2 per cent of the marriages and more than 1½ per cent of the infant baptisms performed each year in the diocese. If one hundred young men entered the seminary each year, St. Mary's comparable contribution would be an average of almost two priest vocations *every year.*

prayers jointly with the co-operation with divine grace of God-loving parents. Let the exhortation of our Blessed Savior be our Jubilee watchword: 'The harvest indeed is ripe but the laborers are few. Pray therefore the Lord of the harvest to send laborers into His harvest.'"

Probably the most effective propaganda was employed by the teaching Sisters in the school. Three times during the year an "outsider" is permitted to come in and talk to the eighth-grade children. A Sister from another community of the order which teaches in the school talks to the girls about the life of the convent. A Brother talks to the boys about his own order, while a priest tells the boys about the religious and the diocesan priests. These talks are very simple, starting with the *cui bono* notion, "What doth it profit a man if he gain the whole world, and suffer the loss of his soul?" They are interspersed generously with stories of a semipious nature and always emphasize the recreational facilities and opportunities at the seminary or novitiate which the speaker represents.

It is a set policy after these "vocation talks" to distribute slips of paper on which the children are asked to write down what they want to be when they finish their schooling. (Incidentally, during this year no girl ever wrote "wife and mother," and no boy wrote "husband and father.") When the child indicated interest in a spiritual vocation, his or her "case" was discussed privately by the speaker, the Principal, and the child's teacher. If all three agree that the child may have a potential calling, the visitor contacts the parents of the child. This leads to varied and interesting results.

The reaction of the parents to these visits differs widely because of a number of factors: the habitual religious attitude of the parents, the number of children they have, the age and the sex of the child in question, the kind of vocation indicated. Generally, even devout Catholics prefer their sons to be priests than brothers, home missioners rather than foreign missioners, and are more reluctant to allow their daughters than their sons to follow a vocation. Although there are mothers and fathers who pray daily that one of their children will "have a vocation," all of them say that the child must make up his own mind.

On the other hand, there are parents who positively refuse to discuss the question of vocation. This is usually true when there is only one child, and even more noticeable when that child is a girl. One instance of this kind is illuminating. A visiting Brother had interested an eighth-grade boy in the brotherhood. The boy, an only child, told his mother that he wanted to attend a certain boarding high school operated by these Brothers in another city and eventually enter their novitiate. Both parents objected to the Brother and their son that the latter was "too young to know his own mind," that he should not leave home, and that he must attend a Catholic high school in the city. The Brother wisely agreed to this course of action, but the boy thought differently. He reluctantly attended the local Catholic high school for two weeks, came home one evening, slammed his books down, and declared he would deliberately flunk out if they kept him in that school. The parents thought that a strict boarding-school in another part of the South would distract him, and he was sent there. At Thanksgiving their son returned with another declaration of independence. This time his parents allowed him to go to the Brothers' school of his original choice, where he was accepted as a transfer student. Whether his determination will carry him through to the novitiate remains to be seen.

The Sisters in the parochial school have other indirect methods of interesting the children in a religious vocation. In reading classes they sometimes read stories about priests and nuns, and in the school play at the end of the year they usually enact some episode from the life of a religious hero or heroine. In September the centennial celebration with its pageant offered a golden opportunity for such propaganda. Six of the older girls were dressed as nuns, and several of the boys were able to play the part of previous pastors in the history of the parish.

The children's mission, which was conducted by the visiting missionaries during the school hours of the first three days of the women's mission week, gave these priests a chance to speak of vocations. There was no formal sermon on the subject, but it was mentioned several times as an ideal of the better life toward which all Catholic children should strive.

Near the end of the school year, Sister Berthold, who is in charge of the Children of Mary and interested in the Sodality, arranges a week-end retreat at a boarding-school conducted by her order. All five of the girls who entered the novitiate this year made this retreat, which seems to have been the deciding factor for them. They had undoubtedly been considering the step for some time previously and wanted these days of meditation in which to make up their minds. For many years past this annual retreat has never been productive of more than two vocations, and most of the times no one made the decision.

Annual retreats are conducted in every Catholic high school of the city, and these are undoubtedly influential in fostering vocations among St. Mary's boys and girls attending them. To some extent this may also be said of the men's and women's retreats conducted at near-by retreat houses several times during the year, but most of these are attended by parishioners who are over twenty years of age, and there is only a slight possibility that they have a direct bearing on religious vocations.

Boys and girls who aspire to the religious priesthood, sisterhood, and brotherhood leave their homes permanently and thus separate themselves from active membership in the parish. Three of the Sisters now teaching in St. Mary's Parochial School are an exception to this, for they have been assigned by their superiors to work in their home parish. They are subject to change to another community of their order at any time, and the general rule is that such persons are no longer part of parochial life.

This is not true, however, of seminarians, the eight young men of St. Mary's who are studying for the diocesan priesthood. They are sent back to the parish by the Bishop during the summer months, and, although they live at home with their parents, they are under the general spiritual supervision of Father Urban. The latter employs them in various ways, depending upon their age, experience, training, and other commitments they may have made. They served the six o'clock Mass on weekdays, conducted the summer catechism classes for children from the public schools, and helped in the office work at the rectory.

Announcements of the summer catechism school were made from the pulpit in the church for three Sundays before the school was to open. The school was planned from Wednesday, June 23, to Friday, July 23. The Pastor hoped that about ninety children would attend, thus giving each of the three instructor-seminarians about thirty pupils. Frank Boucher, Joseph Millet, and Henry Meunier, the seminarians in charge, arrived the first day to find only three children ready for classes.

They were quite discouraged after spending the morning with these children. They reasoned that two factors accounted for this small attendance: the first was that many of the families were out of town during the summer months; the second was the guess that perhaps the parents of children who attend public schools did not come regularly to Sunday Mass and thus had not heard the announcements. While they were bemoaning the situation, another seminarian, Michael Walsh, came in and asked them how the school was going.

"Mike" is one of the younger seminarians, not entirely in good favor with the Pastor, who considers him impetuously zealous. The boy is outspoken in criticism of many priests' attitude on labor, race relations, and other social questions and has the zeal, energy, and enthusiasm of a social reformer. When he heard that only three children showed up for catechism, he said, "I'll get those kids here." He went to the assistant pastors and got the list of public-school children who had been attending the regular classes of the Confraternity of Christian Doctrine during the year. Then he spent the afternoon at his home calling up all the mothers he could reach. Most of the women told him that they had heard nothing about the classes; three were sending their youngest children to the Lutheran summer school "where they learn Bible stories and play games and wouldn't lose their religion." Mike told us afterward that he suspected many of the women were glad to have someone take care of their children all morning.

The result of Mike's phoning was that thirty-six children showed up the following morning. That was the complete extent of his connection with the summer school. He attended Mass daily but seldom came into the rectory, knowing that he could not keep his opinions to himself and that these opinions differed sharply from those of the Pastor. He got a job doing ordinary laboring for almost six weeks and then returned to the seminary in September.

The three seminarians were with the children every day from nine until noon except on Saturday and Sunday. The second hour was a recreation period in the school yard, where the instructors supervised the play. They separated the whole group into three classes according to age and knowledge. The oldest children, approximately from ten to fourteen, were most advanced in their catechism and were almost ready for their Solemn Communion. The sixteen children in this group gradually dwindled down to eight by the end of the term. The second class, conducted by Joseph Millet, contained nineteen children ranging in age from seven to ten, and needed about a year of preparation for their reception of Communion. They, too, showed a record of irregular attendance, with only nine remaining for the entire course. The third class was a special daily session for a retarded child, a girl of ten years, who received instruction for a whole month from Henry Meunier.

Meanwhile the remaining seminarians of the parish engaged in various activities that would prepare them for their priestly ministry. They attended courses in sociology and economics during the summer session of a Catholic college. In their spare time they did street preaching in the Negro sections of the city (but not in Devil's Elbow and Pension Town in Riverside). Twice a week they went around a selected neighborhood during the day time telling the children they would show pictures that night. Then they brought a projector, asked at the nearest house to plug in the current, and proceeded to explain the slides on the life of Christ, the Church, and Catholic doctrines. Usually while one was talking, the others circulated among the people, answered questions, and arranged for personal instructions. Frequently they were invited into homes for a cup of coffee and a sandwich. Eating with Negroes was the "test" they always passed successfully, and they believed that this action gained them more prospective converts than the "pitch" itself and the pictures.

This Catholic evidence work was not parochial activity but was directed from the seminary itself. Father Urban took a dim view of the whole procedure, saying privately that it was a tremendous effort for meager results.[7] He was careful, however, not to discourage the young men, who had the encouragement and approbation of the Bishop in this work. When the seminarians enthusiastically related incidents of their experience, he listened with more than good-natured tolerance and almost always ended with the practical question, "How many of them are coming into the Church?" The accurate answer to that question cannot be given, for who, except God, knows when, where, and how the harvest of souls is reaped?

The two most active seminarians, Charles Whitcomb and Alfred Moreau, took an informal tour of ten days in the beginning of August, looking for examples of Catholic Action. They went by train to Cincinnati and spent four days at the Grailville school, where a week end in marriage and family study was going on. They were greatly impressed by the work and program of Catholic lay people, especially in their reports of Catholic Action on the parochial and family level. They then hitched a ride to South Bend, where the Notre Dame summer school was still in progress. The priest student-counselor there called a special Catholic Action meeting for their benefit, and

7. The Pastor is extremely generous with newly ordained priests of his parish. When Father Whitcomb celebrated his First Solemn Mass the following June, Father Urban gave him a chalice and paid all expenses for a dinner and reception in his honor. He also announced that the collection taken up at his Mass would be the parish's gift to the newly ordained priest.

for several hours they were greatly impressed by the positive, spiritual, "noneconomic" attitudes of these college students.

The two seminarians then "bummed a ride" to Chicago, where they spent two days at Friendship House, took part in discussions, washed dishes and swept floors, and attended Mass and other spiritual activities with the workers. Since they were from the South, they were the center of attention in this group of people who are practicing Christian race relations in their daily life. These southern seminarians came away with the belief that several of the Chicago Friendship House workers are too one-sided to understand the Negro question in the South. "They think of the whole of Catholic Action revolving around race relations, instead of considering the race problem as only a part, but a significant and integral part, of the whole structure of social action."

This brief description of seminarians' summer activity is an indication of the type of men who have come out of St. Mary's Parish and a preview of the kind of priests who will be serving southern parishes during the next half-century. Multitudinous influences are at work on these young men, some from their families and parochial associates, but most apparently from their professors at the seminary. If the parish priest is the center and initiator of the Catholic renaissance, these men promise well for the Church in the urban South.

There are two other features that must be mentioned in connection with vocations to the diocesan priesthood. These are diocesan organizations which cross-cut parochial lines and which have as their purpose the fostering of vocations and the support of seminarians. The Seminary Guild is operated from the major seminary, and its membership rolls are made up of all lay persons who contribute a dollar or more a year. Members share in spiritual benefits, the Masses of priests and the prayers of seminarians, and they are themselves expected to pray daily for the clerical apostolate. This association never has meetings or officers, engages in no formal or secular activities, and is not broken down into parochial units.

The St. Charles Co-operative Guild[8] is an active, formal organization which centers its attention on the needs of the minor seminarians. It is composed mainly of the parents and other relatives of seminarians and priests, although any other interested person is invited to co-operate. They are very active people, holding regular meetings on the fourth Friday of every month at one of the parish halls in the city. The average attendance at these meetings is about

8. Named after the minor seminary, St. Charles College, situated about sixty-five miles from the city.

ninety persons, 25 per cent of whom are men. During the summer the attendance dropped to as low as thirty-seven persons.

The members from St. Mary's Parish play a prominent part in this Co-operative Guild. Three of them, Mrs. Millet, Mrs. Whitcomb, and Mrs. Tureaux, who are also active in parochial organizations, have been officers of this diocesan group. The meetings start on time, end promptly at nine o'clock, and are conducted very efficiently. A typical meeting opens with a prayer by the reverend diocesan director, minutes of the last meeting are read and passed, the treasurer's report is made, unfinished business is discussed, and then new business is taken up. The president closes the meeting with a brief recapitulation of things done, says a word of encouragement, mentions the theme of the next meeting, and asks the director to say the closing prayer. The members from St. Mary's show an efficiency and ability here which is not notable in most of the meetings held by organizations back in the parish.

At the time of the study the Co-operative Guild had been in existence for eight years. During that period it had completed one major physical project, the building of a swimming pool at the minor seminary, and has now raised almost enough money to finance a new gymnasium. Besides these general projects, the members take a personal interest in individual seminarians, finding summer jobs for them, financing their vacations, and also bearing the main expenses for the street preaching and evidence work by the major seminarians. Money is raised through two large social functions each year. During the study these consisted of a minstrel show which netted more than sixteen hundred dollars[9] and a lotto party which brought in more than a thousand dollars. The ubiquitous chance books accompanied both of these affairs; they were peddled all over the diocese and accounted for more than half of the income.

The Pastor has no official status in this formal diocesan organization, but his interest on behalf of both the major and the minor seminaries is shown in an extremely favorable attitude toward these activities. He encourages the persons from his parish who are members and tries to get others to co-operate in the work. Logically enough, the assistant priests are also keenly aware of the importance of the work and maintain cordial relations with the faculty of their alma mater as well as with their classmates and other alumni throughout the diocese.

9. Objections voiced by some of the seminarians against black-faced travesties have been heeded, and the minstrels are now being replaced by other types of musical entertainment.

Chapter Eleven

The Sick and the Dead

U SHERING a parishioner out of this life into the next world is one of the important functions of the parish priest. Both priests and people realize the need of spiritual comfort in the crucial experience of death. The last rites of the Catholic Church are administered at this time. These sacraments are given by the priest when he is called to the side of a dying person, and they are usually three in number: penance, Holy Viaticum, and extreme unction.

There is a noticeable difference of attitude toward the "last sacraments" on the part of practicing and dormant Catholics. Practicing Catholics are well aware of their supernatural importance. They have heard the priests at St. Mary's speak at least once during the year concerning the importance of extreme unction. They are warned not to wait until the patient is unconscious before they call the priest. Many of them have "sick-call outfits" in their homes ready for the day when they will need the priest.

On Thursday night of the parish mission Father Carter, the visiting Lazarist, gave a brief description of the manner in which parishioners should prepare for the priest's sick call. After quoting St. James,[1] he told them to send an adult personally to the rectory who could reveal the seriousness of the sickness and whether or not the sick person will receive Holy Viaticum and who could accompany the priest to the sick person. "But in case of real necessity and haste, phone for the priest." He instructed them on the preparation of the sickroom. "Have the face and feet of the sick person clean, and the room well aired. Prepare a table with a white cloth on it to serve as an altar. On it place a crucifix, with a candle on either side, a glass of water

1. St. James says: "Is any man sick among you? Let him bring in the priests of the Church, and let them pray over him, anointing him with oil in the name of the Lord" (5:14).

123

and a spoon, a little dish for the priest to use in washing his hands, and a napkin for a Communion cloth."

"Send for the priest as soon as there is probable danger of death; do not wait until a person is at death's door. Being ahead of time is better for the priest and the patient and for yourself. The patient will be able to make an easier confession and may also have a better chance of recovery. You will be better off too. Then you will never have cause to reproach yourself as you would if the person died without the last sacraments."

Dormant Catholics who do not attend church services have never heard this sound priestly advice. They have in most cases enjoyed little Catholic instruction, and they entertain the common superstition that the appearance of the priest is the sure sign of approaching death. They are unwilling to "frighten the patient" by calling the priest, a fear which is still prevalent among poorly instructed Catholics as well as among dormant Catholics. This reluctance on the part of some parishioners and their own practical experience are the main reasons why the parish priest feels the necessity for preaching about the sacrament of extreme unction.

Incidences in their own experiences during the year will indicate how far the parishioners are from the "ideal situation" encouraged in the mission by Father Carter. Father Urban was just finishing the midday meal on the second Sunday in May when a phone call came saying that a man was dying. Our observer reports: "I pulled out my watch. It was one twenty-five. Father got the oils and the Viaticum while I dashed to the garage and backed out the car. Within three minutes of the call we were at the residence, about six blocks from the rectory. Father was greeted at the door by a weeping daughter, son, and daughter-in-law. He went to the sickroom immediately but found the man dead and gave him conditional absolution and extreme unction."

This fifty-six-year-old man had not been feeling well and had not attended Mass that morning. ("He hasn't been to church since one night of the mission," remarked the Pastor later.) He suffered a heart attack at about twelve-fifteen. His son called a doctor, who pronounced him dead just before one o'clock. Then almost a half-hour elapsed before someone in the family thought about calling the priest. "The Pastor was very much disturbed about this neglect but, since he was carrying the Blessed Sacrament, said nothing about it until returning to the rectory."

One Saturday night in September at almost eleven o'clock Father

Dominic took a phone call from a lady who said her husband had been unconscious for almost thirty hours. Father took the holy oils and went immediately to the residence, where the doctor was hard at work trying to bring the man back to consciousness. The doctor assured him that this forty-eight-year-old patient was not in danger of death. He had been sick in bed for several weeks and seemed to be losing his memory. On the previous day this forgetfulness had caused him to take his regular dose of sleeping pills three times.

"Help me wake him up, Father," said the doctor. Father Dominic shook the patient vigorously but was reluctant to "slap him hard" as the doctor advised and demonstrated. After about a half-hour's work they were able to revive him sufficiently, so that the priest could hear his confession and the doctor could make him take some food and drink.

In neither of the above cases was there any preparation made for the visit of the priest, according to the advice given in the mission instruction. As a matter of fact, this lack of preparation was characteristic of most of the calls made by the priests to dying persons throughout the year.[2] It is quite probable that the mental and nervous excitement present in members of the family when they realize that death is near causes them to forget the details of preparation. This seems to be true in every case where there was hope of eventual recovery or where the doctors refused to reveal the seriousness or the nature of the illness. On the other hand, persons who had been seriously ill during the year and had enjoyed visits from the priest on different occasions were almost always ready for the "last visit" and the last sacraments.

A distinction must be made here among three kinds of sick calls. Those which are made for a dying person are answered promptly by the priest on duty at any hour of the day or night. These are emergencies, and, while the priest knows exactly what to do, the people in question are too distressed to think clearly and to act promptly. Almost a hundred of these emergency calls were made during the year by the priests of the parish. Some of the patients later recovered, and some were already dead. Several calls were made outside the parish.[3] At any rate, the priests of St. Mary's lived up to the ideal of prompt and ready service to the dying, even though

2. Except in the Catholic hospital, where the Sisters and nurses are experienced in these matters.

3. Hence the figures for funerals and final sick calls do not coincide.

the great mass of parishioners seems to fail in the obligations expected of them.

The second kind of sick call is that made to parishioners who are too ill to come to the church for Mass and the sacraments and who request that the priest visit them for confession and Communion. There is no question here of the administration of the sacrament of extreme unction. These calls are made in the morning immediately after Mass, and they average in number a little more than three each week during the whole year. Most of them are made on the First Friday or on a day near that time. The Church permits the reception of Communion for bedridden persons and in some circumstances allows the privilege without fasting. In danger of death, when the Viaticum is given, the fast is never necessary.

The third type of sick call is simply a friendly visit of consolation to a sick parishioner. It is on this level where the priests of St. Mary's show the least activity. They will, upon request, visit persons whom they know intimately through parochial participation, but otherwise they seem hesitant "to intrude" in people's homes. At the time of the census, numerous parishioners complained that the priests never visit their homes. One lady said she had lived in the parish for thirty-five years and that no priest visited even when her husband died. Another said that her teen-age daughter was sick in bed for several months, that she phoned the rectory, but that no priest came. Others had similar complaints, and some remarked bitterly that "the only time you see them is when they want money."

In extenuation, and in answer to these statements, Father Urban remarks: "We can't read minds. People move in and out of this parish and never make themselves known at the rectory. We don't know who they are, and we can't visit them if we don't even know they are sick." The Pastor also feels that he is not well enough to make frequent visits to parishioners' homes and that his assistants should take this responsibility.

In general, there is no organized plan or method for discovering the sick in the parish. The Blessed Virgin's League, a small group of fervent women parishioners, occasionally finds a sick person in need of spiritual care and informs the Pastor. No other lay group has systematic responsibility for the whole parish, or any section of it, through whom such information could be obtained. Some years ago the Pastor had assigned "captains" in various parts of the parish, women from the Parents' Club who were to keep him informed about all Catholics and especially of their needs in time of sickness and death. "It didn't work out," he said. "People just don't want to take the trouble."

More and more sick persons in this urban parish are sent to hospitals, and, since the latter have regular visiting Catholic chaplains, the parochial curates are relieved of some of their obligation in this regard. But even here there are difficulties. One lady complained that Father Dominic passed her door three times to visit another sick person but never stopped to see her. She was "hurt" at this neglect, but Father Dominic later said, "How was I to know she was there?" Several times during the year Father Urban commented on the favorable circumstances of the sickroom for bringing people back to the sacraments. "You can get people to think about God and their own souls when they have so much idle time, simply lying on their back."

During the year of the study there were eighty-five funerals conducted at St. Mary's Church. Seventy-nine of these persons had been visited by the parish priest and had received the last sacraments before their death. Of the remaining six, one was an infant, two had been killed in accidents, and the others died unexpectedly after only a short illness. Since no records were kept in previous years, it is impossible to judge whether this is a high percentage. In comparison with the verbal reports of priests in other parishes it appears to be a commendable record. With the qualifications made on the previous pages, it indicates that both the priests and the people of St. Mary's are zealous and alert to the spiritual needs of the dying.

During the course of the year the Pastor had to refuse Christian burial services to seven other persons. These were former Catholics who committed suicide, or belonged to secret forbidden societies, or had in some other way cut themselves off from membership in the Church. Usually a Catholic member of the deceased person's family telephoned to the rectory in the vain hope that the body could "pass through the church." None of these had asked for the parish priests before their death, and they are presumed to have been unwilling to return to the practice and belief of their religion.

Two of these deaths occurred during the second week in June. Mrs. Moran, who was not known to the priests, killed herself. She was fifty-three years old, apparently in her right mind, and had not been attending Mass for many years. Arthur Catonese, a leading politician in the state machine, was a member of the Masonic order. He died suddenly of a heart attack while at the state capitol. Neither of these persons was a parishioner, but their families called themselves Catholic. Without mentioning their names, the Pastor took occasion on the following Sunday to speak of the importance of living and dying "like a good Catholic." He continued: "Please do not ask us to have a funeral Mass or other services for people who die outside the Church. We would be going against their will, since they did not want to be Catholics."

The funeral Mass in the Catholic liturgy is composed of special prayers appropriate for the dead. The Christian belief in eternal life and Christian hope even in the midst of sorrow and loss are notable in the preface for the Requiem Mass. "Life is not taken away from thy faithful, O Lord; it is but changed; for when their dwelling place in this earthly exile has been destroyed, there awaiteth them an ever-lasting home in heaven." The Epistle, Gospel, and other parts of the Mass are especially selected by the Church and are used only at the so-called "burial Mass," as distinguished from other commemorative Requiem Masses.

The complete acceptance of Catholic life and worship in the parish would be approximated if all baptized Catholics who died in River-side were "buried from Mass." We have already seen that those dormant Catholics who die alienated from the Church cannot have this privilege. The ideal would be more nearly realized also if all of the eighty-five parishioners who died during the year were buried after a funeral Mass. Actually, only thirty-nine of them were thus buried, while the remaining forty-six funerals were conducted in the afternoon. There are several elements to be considered here in the explanation of this apparently low percentage of funeral Masses.

In this warm climate the traditional practice had been to bury the corpse on the day of death. This was necessitated in the years before embalming had become legally mandatory and particularly during the epidemics of yellow fever. While such haste is no longer required, the habit has carried into the present generation at least to the extent that quick burials occur. The funeral is seldom delayed more than twenty-four hours from the time of embalming.

A second consideration, besides the difficulty of changing long-standing custom, is the fact that people think of a funeral Mass as "more expensive" than an afternoon funeral. While there is no set stipend expected for a funeral Mass, there is generally a donation of fifteen to twenty-five dollars. In many instances the bereaved persons neglect to give a stipend, but they are never reminded of this neglect by the Pastor.[4] The latter, however, has many hundreds of dollars "on the books" from these cases and has suggested to the Bishop that

4. The Pastor follows a very different pattern at weddings (see chap. 9, p. 101).

undertakers include the Mass stipend in their general service charges and remit it to the pastor.

Finally, a funeral is surrounded with certain social expectations and obligations. People want honor shown to their dead, and they realize that a congregation can gather more easily in the late afternoon than in the morning. This is indicated in the comparison between morning and evening funerals. Funeral Masses at nine o'clock in the morning had an average attendance of thirty-five, while funerals at four o'clock in the afternoon had fifty-three. Generally speaking, the family of higher status in the community prefers an afternoon funeral and a longer delay between death and burial. Thus, more friends of the family are able to pay their respects to the dead. The exception to this generalization is always the family of high Catholic ideals and of parochial activity, regardless of social status.

This same consideration of social status extends to the choice of mortician and the selection of caskets and other funeral appointments. Although the difference between a simple funeral service and an elaborate display is not always a reliable index of the difference of social status, there are certain behavioral expectations which cannot be ignored. The expense of mortician's services varies considerably, and a relatively large percentage of families in the parish "spend beyond their means" in doing "decent honor" to their dead. As far as church services are concerned, there is merely the difference between the Low Mass and the High Mass, with occasionally a professional singer in the choir loft.

Except when the dead person is a child, the funeral Mass is celebrated in black vestments, and the altar is draped in black. The actual burial service is conducted after the Mass, and the priest blesses the coffin in the center aisle near the altar rail. He then accompanies the body to the cemetery, taking with him four altar boys in one of the undertaker's limousines. Appropriate prayers and further blessings are said at the grave, whence the priest returns to the church still attired in cassock, surplice, and biretta. This same procedure is followed at the afternoon funerals.

As soon as the priests learn of a death, they phone to the family of the bereaved, give them consolation, and ask about funeral arrangements. Frequently they will learn of the death from the undertaker.[5]

5. Henninger, the only undertaker in Riverside, maintains cordial relations with the priests at St. Mary's. He sends them expensive gifts at Christmas and frequently invites Father Dominic to visit his home. The House of Florsheim, prominent undertakers in the city, is getting an increasing percentage of the parish business.

If the deceased person was a member of a parochial organization, the priest informs one of the officers and asks that the group be present at the funeral home for the recitation of the Rosary. Whether or not the dead person was an organization member, one of the priests visits with the family and recites the Rosary while kneeling on the *prie-dieu* before the coffin. He then speaks a few words of consolation with members of the family before taking his departure.

The practice of offering Masses for the dead is in strong favor in St. Mary's Parish. These Masses fall into three categories: (*a*) Requiem High Masses, (*b*) Requiem Low Masses, and (*c*) non-Requiem Masses for the repose of the souls of departed parishioners. It has been the custom at St. Mary's Church to announce publicly each Sunday the High Mass intentions for the following week. The date, time, and intention are announced so that any parishioner who wishes to join in the Sacrifice of the Mass for the specific intention may do so. Only High Masses, for which a stipend of five dollars or more is offered, are announced from the pulpit. Other Masses, for which the stipend is usually one dollar, are not mentioned.

During the course of the year, 243 High Masses were thus publicized, and 219 of these were for the repose of the souls of departed parishioners. The others were Masses of petition and thanksgiving. On only one occasion, in connection with the centennial celebration in September, was a Solemn High Mass of Requiem celebrated for all dead persons in the history of the parish. These High Masses require the services of the parish organist, Miss Koehl, who usually sings all the responses and the choir parts of the Mass by herself. The priest is obliged to sing this Mass on the date and time for which the stipend is given.

In analyzing the names of the deceased persons for whom High Masses of Requiem were offered during the year, we find generally those families which are at the center of parochial activities. Consciousness of the importance of praying for the souls in purgatory and a devotion to the traditional Catholic liturgy may be said to be the primary motivation. Two other less worthy factors, however, must be realistically noticed: first is that not every parishioner is willing and able to offer the stipend for a High Mass; and the second is that some parishioners may appreciate the prestige of having the family name mentioned in the pulpit at the Sunday Masses. These two latter motives may partially account for the names of families on the list who are not at all notable for their Catholicism.

On the other hand, the absence of family names from the list of announced Requiem High Masses does not mean that these families are not active and devout parishioners. Some of the persons at the center of the parish life have not had a death in the family for many years. The names most frequently mentioned during the year were: Frank Boucher, Sr., Carl Tacit, Mr. and Mrs. Patrick Neil, and Agnes Pathe and family. All these were prominent in the parish before their death, and their families continue as devout parishioners. Requiem High Masses for these four intentions combined a total of forty-nine,

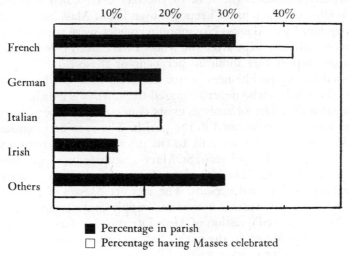

Fig. 24.—Percentage comparison of parishioners of various national backgrounds having Masses celebrated in St. Mary's Church.

or 22.37 per cent of all the Requiem High Masses announced from the pulpit.

We were interested in discovering whether ethnic and national background had any influence on devotion to the souls in purgatory as exhibited by the list of Requiem High Masses. Figure 24 compares the percentages of the parishioners according to their nationality background with the percentage who had Requiem High Masses celebrated.

Requiem Low Masses celebrated in the parish during the course of the year did not lend themselves to the same kind of analysis. There are only certain days of the year, those which have the rank of semi-double or less, on which the Requiem Low Mass may be celebrated. These numbered fifty-one days. Ordinarily, the Requiem High Masses (except anniversary Masses) would be restricted also to these days, but the diocese in which St. Mary's is located has a privilege dating back to 1829, according to which these High Masses may be sung on feast days ranking as "doubles."

Since the Requiem Mass is specifically designated by the Church for the commemoration of the dead, and since it is also shorter than the ordinary Mass of the day, the priests of St. Mary's prefer to celebrate this type of Mass whenever the liturgy of the Church permits it. The only exception is Father Paul, the youngest of the priests, who occasionally celebrates the feast of the day even when a memorial Mass is allowed. Each priest keeps his own list of Mass intentions for the Requiem Low Masses. No announcements were made of these, and no records are kept after the Masses have been celebrated. But the priests report that about 20 per cent of these Low Masses are requested by nonparishioners or are celebrated for the intention of deceased Catholics who never belonged to St. Mary's Parish.

The same difficulty of analysis exists concerning the non-Requiem Masses which are celebrated in the parish. The specific intention of each Mass is usually known only to the priest and to the person who offers the stipend. The priests of St. Mary's estimate that approximately 90 per cent of the Mass intentions they receive are for the repose of the souls of departed persons. The rest are Masses of petition or thanksgiving. If the secular notion of "supply and demand" may be applied to the sacred question of Mass intentions, it may be said that the demand for Masses in the parish has outrun the "supply" during the last eight or nine years.

There is an interesting correlation between times of prosperity and war, on the one hand, and the number of Mass stipends offered by the parishioners, on the other. Economic well-being has some influence on the increased expression of the parishioners' devotion to the souls in purgatory. Every priest reports that the number of Mass intentions he received reached a low ebb during the depression thirties. During the year of the study the reverse was the case. The priests of St. Mary's received more Mass intentions than they could possibly fulfil, and they sent the surplus stipends to foreign and domestic missioners and to European priests who do not receive sufficient Mass stipends. Some of the parishioners did likewise. They sent their Mass intentions for the dead to missionary societies or to priests they knew in other places.

For all these reasons mentioned above it is a practical impossibility to discover accurately the full extent of prayerful commemoration and devotion to their dead practiced by the parishioners of St. Mary's.

A rough conclusion, however, would indicate that there are grades of devotion to the dead among the parishioners which are similar to the various categories already mentioned. The best Catholics pray for their dead. The marginal Catholics and dormant Catholics tend to ignore them. More than half of the eighty-five persons who died during the year were not mentioned in the list of Requiem High Masses. About one-quarter of them, as far as could be ascertained, had no Masses celebrated for them at St. Mary's Church after their burial.

We have said in a previous chapter that any estimate of the growth or decline of St. Mary's Parish must take into consideration the number of deaths.[6] During the last twenty-year period there were 4,601 baptisms (including adult converts) and 1,790 funerals at St. Mary's. All else being equal, these figures would show an increase of 2,811 parishioners in these two decades. In a stable, rural Catholic parish these statistics would have some significance, but in an urban parish the mobility of families and the defection of individuals from the Church make them almost meaningless.

The crude birth and death rates, however, may be compared for the year of the study in order to obtain a rough estimate of the rate of natural increase of the parish. Judged only from the baptismal and funeral records, the former is 24.1 and the latter is 12.6. Theoretically, without the consideration of any other factor, this would indicate a natural increase rate of 11.5 persons per thousand per year. To some extent, a problem similar to that which faced us in the baptismal records confronts us here in the funeral records. The baptismal records had to be refined for the parochial birth rate because they contained the names of many children who had no further contact with the Church. The crude death rate of 12.6, taken from the funeral records, is likely to be close to the true death rate, because the Pastor excludes notorious nonparishioners and former Catholics from Christian burial service.

Father Urban does not exclude infants from the sacrament of baptism as long as the parents claim they are Catholics (even though they may not be practicing parishioners). But he can and does exclude deceased persons from the Catholic funeral service when he knows that they have publicly repudiated the Catholic faith. The death rate of 12.6 is slightly higher than may be expected in a relatively young population like that of St. Mary's Parish; and it lends itself to the

6. See chap. 4 above.

suspicion that some of the dormant Catholics of Riverside were permitted Catholic burial through the Pastor's oversight or charity.

Another question may be asked at this point. How dependable is the assumption that every practicing Catholic is "buried from the Church"? Although the expected stipend is low in comparison to other expenses incurred at a funeral, and the Pastor never asks for payment, it is quite possible that some Catholics may feel that they cannot bear the added expense of a church funeral. The parish records

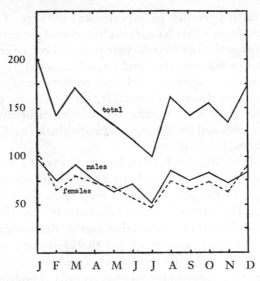

Fig. 25.—Monthly variation in the number of funerals by sex over a twenty-year period in St. Mary's Church.

show that during several years of the depression the number of funerals was below the twenty-year average. But the same can be said of 1942, when there were only seventy-three funerals, the lowest number during the period. The priests of St. Mary's have never made economic demands in regard to funerals, and it is quite unlikely that in normal times the contemplated expense of a church funeral has prevented parishioners from asking for this service.

Over a period of twenty years there were 1,790 funerals in St. Mary's Church, an average of 89.5 per year. In three widely separated years the number was a hundred or more; and in four years it was eighty or less. It is interesting to note that males had sixty-four funerals more than females during this twenty-year period. Thus males have an average of three more deaths every year than females.

This seems extraordinary, since there are actually more females in the parish than males. The census shows us 3,381 females of all ages to 3,346 males, or a sex ratio of 98.96. The age distribution of the parish, however, is relatively low. The parish population is young by ordinary urban standards. This, together with the fact that females have a longer life-expectancy, probably accounts for the sex differential in funerals.

Figure 25 shows that the greatest number of deaths, for both male and female, occur in January (203). The month with the lowest number for both sexes is July, when there were approximately half as many as in the worst month. With the exception of February, there is almost a steady decline in the number of funerals between January and July. While it is true that February has two days less than January or March, this would hardly account for the sudden dip in the statistics for that month. The months from August to December show an irregular increase in the number of funerals. January, May, and December are the only months in which there are more deaths for females than for males. All these data are interesting, but there seems to be no satisfactory theoretical explanation for the differences.

In summary, it may be observed that the priests are more prompt to respond to the needs of the dying than the parishioners are to ask for the last sacraments. On the other hand, there is some dissatisfaction among the parishioners who complain that the priests fail to visit the chronically ill and the temporarily bedridden members of the parish. Only 45.88 per cent of the funerals are conducted at Mass. Devotion to the souls in purgatory, as measured by the Masses offered for them, is exhibited consistently by the inner circles of participating parishioners.

Chapter Twelve

Mass on Sundays

THE central act of worship of the Catholic Church is the Sacrifice of the Mass. It is the re-enactment of the sacrifice of Calvary, which was the act of redemption and the means of salvation experienced by Christ for the benefit of the whole human race. The parish church is designed and built so that the congregation may participate in this mystery. The Mass takes place on the altar, at the center of which is the tabernacle containing the Real Presence of the Divine Christ.

Even the dormant Catholic has some realization that God is the focus of this most important worship of the Church and that God is really present on the altar when the change takes place from bread and wine to the Body and Blood of the Savior. This act of worship is of such great value that the Church orders all Catholics, under pain of mortal sin, to attend Mass on Sundays and certain holy days throughout the year. Even poorly instructed Catholics are aware of this command, and "going to Mass" is accepted as one of the identifiable characteristics of Catholic behavior.

From the point of view of the casual observer, Mass attendance may be accepted as the minimum external criterion of Catholicism. It is not, of course, an exact psychological measure of the intensity or duration of spirituality in the congregation, but it can serve to some extent as an external index of internal spirituality. We must be satisfied with generalized answers in this area of investigation. What patterns of conduct are observable in Mass attendance? What kinds of persons attend Mass? When do they go? How do they behave?

In the first place, it may be said that the behavior and attendance of Catholics at Mass differ according to age and sex. There are other diversities and many exceptions, but the patterns of conduct are most consistent and noticeable when viewed from these two aspects. Good Catholic parents sometimes carry their infants to Mass, point out the statues of Jesus and Mary, show them the attitudes of prayer, and try to keep them quiet during the services. The Pastor encourages this practice and never objects to the crying of infants in church, although the parents seem embarrassed when it occurs. The parish has no arrangements for baby-sitters to take care of the youngest children during Mass. Several years ago the girls in the Sodality offered their services, and this offer was announced from the pulpit, but the plan was never actually put into practice.

At all except the earliest Masses on Sunday mornings there are a half-dozen preschool youngsters sitting in the pews or squirming about playing with rosaries and prayer-books. One little boy came regularly with his parents to the ten o'clock Mass and amused himself with a stack of nickels and a pair of miniature dice. Usually, parents with small children find a pew near the rear of the church. Some scold the youngsters and want them to be piously attentive; others allow the child to play quietly by himself.

Most of the youth of high-school and college age attend Mass with a friend or two of the same sex. Girls tend to do this more than boys, and they occupy pews farther toward the front than the boys. They also seem to be more recollected and pious in their attitudes while at Mass, although an exception was one trio of high-school girls who regularly occupied the second last pew. All during the Mass, except at the Consecration, they exchanged the various contents of their purses with one another, but their conversation was more in glances and signs than in whispered words. The young men of the parish come late for Mass more often than the girls, and, even when they are early, they tend to lounge in front of the church until Mass starts. The boys of high-school age like to go up in the choir loft and to sit on the steps leading to the choir at those Masses when the choir does not sing. The Pastor effectively stopped this practice about halfway through the survey.

Another practice which irritated the Pastor was that of standing in the rear of the church. Several times during the year he mentioned this at the ushers' meetings, and once in the pulpit, after reading the Gospel, he invited all the standees to find seats. Usually, only the children's Mass and the last Mass on Sundays are so crowded that no empty seats remain. Our study shows, however, that every Sunday Mass has its percentage of standees. The average for the six Masses amounts to 12.4 per cent of the congregation. The people who come late prefer frequently to remain in the rear of the church. They seem embarrassed to walk up the aisle, even when an usher finds an empty pew and beckons them forward.

The Sunday obligation, as taught by the Church, requires Catholics to attend the whole Mass, from the time the priest comes to the altar until he leaves. A measure of the parishioners' devotion to the Mass and of their fulfilment of this obligation is seen in the numbers who arrive late and who leave early. By actual count it was noted that, at all the Sunday Masses, 8.37 per cent of the congregation arrived after Mass had started and that 6.35 per cent left before it was completed. If we combine these percentages, we find that 14.72 per cent of the attendance did not fulfil their obligation to the letter of the Church precept. Although we have no accurate count, we have noticed that many of these persons are duplicated in both categories. In other words, those who come late also tend to leave early.

Here again there is an age-sex distinction. The younger males constitute the majority of those who omit part of the Mass, while the older females make up the majority of those who arrive in church well in advance of the Mass. On the other hand, there are also those Catholics who remain in their pews or go up to the altar rail to pray after the Mass ends. Except after the Pastor's Mass there was almost always an interval of about ten minutes before the next Mass started on Sundays. By actual count we observed that 3.44 per cent of the congregation followed this custom of remaining to pray. Some of them went to the vigil-light stands before the various statues, deposited their coin, lit a candle, and prayed for their intention there. These individuals presented no particular pattern but were persons of all ages and both sexes. Seven of these vigil-light stands are located at either end of the Communion rail.

Another pattern of conduct that has noticeably increased in recent years is the use of the Sunday missal. By actual count, 35.08 per cent of the congregation read the missal all during the Mass, while another 22.08 per cent read some sort of prayer-book while following the priest's reading of the Gospel. The younger members of the congregation use their missals and prayer-books much more than the older persons. The latter, either because of poor eyesight or of inadequate lighting in the church or because they had not been trained in their younger years to follow the Mass, make up the bulk of the 21 per cent of the congregation who use the rosary all during Mass. The remaining persons simply stare off into space, although several men in the last pews sometimes read a copy of *Our Sunday Visitor* during Mass.

The action and personality of the priest who is celebrating the Mass have some influence on the behavior of the congregation. Father Paul is deliberately slow and methodical in his manner of saying Mass. His sermons are always brief and well prepared. He is popular with the people. Father Dominic is much more rapid in his actions and finds his popularity mainly among the younger people, while some of the older persons think that he is too fast. The parishioners tend to complain about the Pastor, and this mainly because of his long, rambling talks at Sunday Mass. Occasionally during these sermons individuals in the congregation turn to look at the clock, which is placed at the front of the choir loft. Others read their prayer-books or patiently say the Rosary.

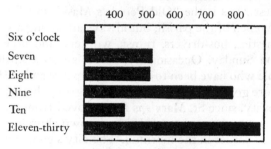

Fig. 26.—Average attendance at the various Sunday Masses in St. Mary's Church for the year.

In recapitulation, we may say that the great majority of St. Mary's parishioners conduct themselves with becoming gravity and propriety at Mass. Some come into the church, dip their right hand in the holy-water font, and make a vague motion toward their neck. This is presumably the sign of the cross. Usually the same persons make a genuflection by a slight bending of the knee toward the floor or by bending of the left knee. A few pious souls always stop at the statue of St. Anthony at the rear of the church and place their hand on his foot while saying a short prayer. The ultimate test of devoted Mass behavior, however, comes at the time of the Consecration of the Mass. After the warning bell is rung by the altar boy at the "Hanc igitur," a complete silence engulfs the congregation. They are almost motionless as they watch the priest elevate the Sacred Host and the chalice, and then bow in adoration of Christ really present on the altar. This is the moment when any observer must be convinced that these people have a deep realization of the central mystery of Catholic worship.

St. Mary's Church follows a regular schedule of Sunday Masses throughout the year. Masses are celebrated hourly every Sunday morning from six until ten o'clock, and a final Mass is celebrated at eleven-thirty. The only time when this schedule was changed was on Easter Day, when a "Sunrise Mass" was held at five-thirty in place of the usual six o'clock Mass. This time regularity enables us to follow each of the six Masses through the year and to comment upon the group of people who attend at the different hours.

Figure 26 gives a brief view of the average attendance at the different Sunday Masses throughout the year. It shows that the Masses most crowded are the children's Mass and the last one, which is largely attended by marginal Catholics. The earliest Mass and the High Mass are the most poorly attended.

The earliest Mass is the "Old People's Mass," usually heavily attended by women of the parish, but always attracting a sprinkling of nurses, domestics, bus-drivers, transit workers, and others who are employed on Sunday. Occasionally, there is also a small group of young people who have been to an all-night party and wish to "catch a Mass" before going home to bed. This last group, however, is something of a rarity, since St. Mary's is far removed from the city's club and theater area and since one of the downtown churches has a "Fisherman's Mass" earlier in the morning. The city's gambling houses are situated in the county just outside the parish boundaries. They close at five o'clock in the morning, and sometimes a few of the patrons and the croupiers who live in the parish attend the six o'clock Mass.

The congregation at this Mass through the whole year averaged 73.47 per cent female and 26.53 per cent male, and it averaged 92.70 per cent adults and 7.03 per cent children. The number of those who receive Holy Communion is not so high at this Mass as it is at the seven o'clock Mass, 21.31 per cent of the congregation doing so; but a higher percentage of those receiving are females (82.91 per cent) than males (17.09). The proportion of the congregation performing this spiritual act is higher than at any Mass except the seven o'clock Mass.

Attendance at the six o'clock Mass follows a definite seasonal pattern. In the winter months—November, December, January, and February—the average number of people at this early Mass is quite low. From the lowest (180) in February, the number gradually climbs to its peak of 510 in June, and then drops gradually again through July, August, September, and October (Fig. 27).

These fluctuations are explained by several factors, of which the main one is the weather. At that hour during the winter months it is dark and relatively cold even in this southern city. In the spring and early summer this condition changes, and the possibility of outdoor activities becomes greater. People who plan Sunday picnics and outings begin to attend the six and seven o'clock Masses rather than the later Masses. While the numbers do not remain so high in relation to the other Sundays of the year, their proportion is high in relation to the attendance at the later Masses on the hottest Sundays of the summer.

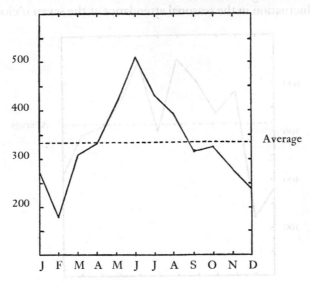

Fig. 27.—Average Sunday attendance at the six o'clock Mass for each month and for the year.

For want of a better name, the seven o'clock Mass might be called the "Women's Mass," and the women in this group are noticeably young mothers of families. The typical Catholic family with small children has the Sunday-morning problem of attending Mass "in shifts." While the husband stays at home with the baby, the wife will usually attend the earlier Mass with her other preschool children, who do not attend the nine o'clock Mass. This gives her an opportunity to get the housework finished and the Sunday dinner started while her husband and other members of the family are at church.

The average for the seven o'clock Mass shows 77.05 per cent females to only 22.95 per cent males, while the age composition shows that there are 76.62 per cent adults as compared to 23.48 per cent children. This is the largest ratio of children at any Mass with the exception of the nine o'clock Mass. Except for young mothers with children, no other group is regularly and noticeably present in appreciable numbers at this Mass. It must be noted, however, that those men who do attend this Mass receive the Sacrament in greater proportions than they do at any other Mass, 35.36 per cent of the communicants being males. The same is true of children attending this Mass, 49.06 per cent of the communicants being children. This is a higher ratio of children to adults receiving Communion than at any other Mass.

The fluctuation in the seasonal attendance at the seven o'clock Mass

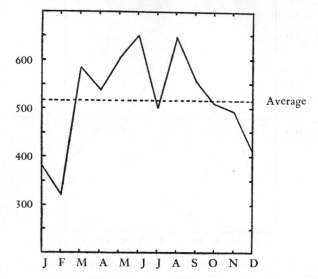

FIG. 28.—Average Sunday attendance at the seven o'clock Mass for each month and for the year.

is not so marked as that of the six o'clock Mass. The highest average attendance is 664 in August, after which there is a steady and gradual decline each month until the low of 321 is reached in February. An abrupt jump to 582 in March may be accounted for by the fact of Lent. The high average of 610 in May and 649 in June may be explained by both the fine weather and the special devotions peculiar to those months. However, the drop to 501 in July, between the two peaks of June and August, is inexplicable (Fig. 28).

The eight o'clock Mass is known as the "Organization Mass," so called because the parochial organizations usually schedule their monthly Mass and Communion at this time. In previous times when there were more diversified groups within the parish, each Sunday was designated for a particular one. The first Sunday is now reserved for the Children of Mary and the Young Ladies' Sodality; the second Sunday of the month is traditionally in all parishes the day for the Holy Name Society. The third and fourth Sundays in St. Mary's Parish are no longer specifically reserved, although occasionally the St. Anthony Guild or the Parish Council of Catholic Women is expected to utilize them. These organizations always gather in the schoolyard or the school hall before the Mass, march into church behind the society's banner, and occupy the pews off the front-center aisle on the right side.

In the over-all average the sex composition of this Mass is approximately the same as that of the seven o'clock Mass, being 76.63 per cent female and 23.37 per cent male. There are usually very few children at this Mass, constituting 10.67 per cent of the congregation, while adults make up the remaining 89.33 per cent. The children, however, account for 27.94 per cent of the Communions distributed, compared to 72.94 per cent for the adults.

The fluctuation in attendance at the eight o'clock Mass shows an interesting variation in that the lowest and the highest months are side by side, February and March. Except for the fact that January and February are usually inclement months, this cannot be accounted for by reasons of weather. From the peak of 595 in March there is an almost unbroken decline to the number of 442 in October. Another peak (531) appears in November, and then the attendance declines in successive months to the low of 408 in February (Fig. 29).

The nine o'clock Mass is always the "Children's Mass," set aside for the pupils of the parochial school. This Mass is frequently late in starting, because the Pastor, who celebrates the previous Mass, is slow, gives a relatively lengthy sermon, and distributes many Communions. The children begin to assemble in the schoolyard as early as eight-thirty, where they run around and play until the bell warns them to form ranks for the procession into the church. The children are lined up according to sex and school grade under the watchful eye of their teachers, and they are permitted to talk until the second bell rings.

This pre-Mass scene in the schoolyard is an interesting sociological study in itself. The smallest children in the kindergarten and first grade are often accompanied by an older brother or sister or by a parent, usually the mother, who thus has an opportunity to talk with her child's teachers. When mothers are not engaging the attention of the nuns, there are usually small groups of children clustered around their teachers. The size of the group is a partial index of the Sister's popularity, but it is also an index of the age group. The youngest children are less inhibited and often hold the teacher's hand or her cincture.

The children in the seventh and eighth grades think that this whole procedure of lining up in the schoolyard is "kid stuff." Many of the girls in these two grades have become physically mature. They wear makeup and adult dresses and appear to be somewhat self-conscious. As a result, only about half of these girls enter the line; the rest stand on the sidewalk in front of the church, as do all the boys in the

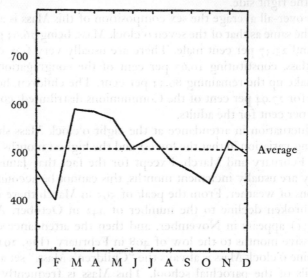

Fig. 29.—Average Sunday attendance at the eight o'clock Mass for each month and for the year.

seventh and eighth grades. They then fall into line as the group enters the church and goes up the main aisle. In the beginning of the school year the Sisters charged these older children with an absence from Mass and kept them in school on Monday afternoon as a punishment. The culprits were so numerous, however, that the Principal relented and now checks the attendance of the seventh and eighth grades after they have entered the church and taken their places.

The youngest grades present another kind of behavioral problem. They talk and play, skip and jump, while in the yard and going into the church. One of the ushers has assigned himself to help the Sisters maintain order with these youngsters. He lines them up when the bell rings, walks along with them to their pews, keeps them from over-crowding the pews, and ranges back and forth across the front of the church all during Mass, correcting noisy children and reprimanding those who talk. The nuns, each of whom occupies a pew directly behind her class, also assist in this corrective process but do so much less obtrusively. Occasionally they will leave their place to warn a child and on rare occasions may make the child kneel in the aisle.[1]

The boys are the first to enter the church, and they take their places on the Gospel side of the main aisle. The girls, in similar class rankings from the smallest to the largest, occupy the other side of the church. No adults are permitted to take a pew until all the children are placed. Although the whole school body has never been in attendance at one time, those who do come occupy about two-thirds of the pews. The adults who attend this nine o'clock Mass are usually the parents or older brothers and sisters of the school children. In spite of the crowded conditions, this seems to be a fairly popular time of the morning for adults to attend Mass. During the school year there are worshipers standing in the back and along the side walls of the church, so that this is the most crowded of any of the four Masses discussed thus far.

Except for the High Masses which are sung by the adult choir on Sundays from October to May, the children's Mass is the only one which has music and singing. Miss Koehl, the organist, practices with a group of seventh- and eighth-grade girls once a week in the school auditorium. The boys consider this a "sissy" pastime and will have nothing to do with it. These girls number about twenty, shepherded by a Sister, and they take their places in the choir loft at the nine o'clock Mass, where they lead the whole congregation of school children in singing hymns. Small hymnals are distributed to the children of the four higher grades, three to each pew. Both boys and girls sing as loudly as they can and seem to enjoy the hymns. Their repertory is limited to less than a dozen selections. Occasionally, the organist selects a hymn which the children have not sufficiently practiced, whereupon the girls in the choir, assisted by the nun and the organist, attempt to sing it themselves.

Since the children must report their absence to the Sisters in the school on Monday mornings, there is a wide divergence in the attendance in the summertime and during the school year. Unlike the other early Masses, the highest attendance is during the winter months, and

1. Sisters are most unwilling to embarrass the child in this way at a Sunday Mass when many adults are present. They use this punishment more frequently at the weekday Masses when the children are trained how to attend Mass with the proper exterior composure.

the lowest in the summer months. The worst time is the first vacation month, June, when an average of 501 persons attend the nine o'clock Mass. July and August are somewhat better with 602 and 597, respectively. September shows a large increase to 946 during which the pupils are being newly taught the obligation of Sunday Mass, while October is the peak of the year (1,020) for this Mass. Between No-

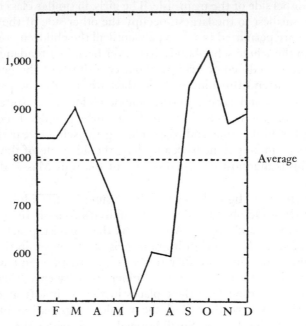

Fig. 30.—Average Sunday attendance at the nine o'clock Mass for each month and for the year.

vember and March the average shifts between eight and nine hundred, while the months of April and May decline to around seven hundred (Fig. 30).

In spite of the fact that the sex ratio for the children in the school is only slightly in favor of the girls, there is a continued disproportionate number of females, as at the other Masses. This may be explained by the fact that boys "play hooky" from Mass more than do girls or that parents do not insist upon their boys' attendance at Mass as much as on their daughters'. At any rate, on Monday mornings the Sisters in the school always have more boys' absences to check than girls'.

Although the Pastor and the Sisters are much concerned about the attendance of public-school children at the Sunday Mass, they have not succeeded in bringing them into the parochial school group for the nine o'clock Mass. When the release-time program is in operation, the teachers question their pupils each Tuesday afternoon concerning their attendance at Sunday Mass. Most of these children seem to attend other Masses. At any rate, the teacher must depend upon the

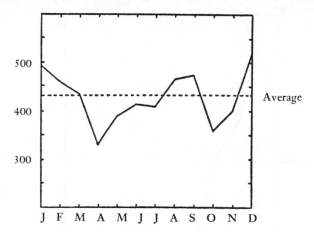

Fig. 31.—Average Sunday attendance at the ten o'clock Mass for each month and for the year.

honesty of the child to admit his absence. When he does so, his name is given to the members of the Blessed Virgin's League, who phone or visit the parents to inquire about their child's religious observance.

The ten o'clock Mass, with the exception of the earliest Mass at six o'clock, is the most poorly attended Mass at St. Mary's Church. This is the High Mass, which involves the singing of the parish choir and is supposed by the parishioners to consume more time than any other Mass. Actually, this is a false impression, for the eight o'clock Mass, celebrated by the Pastor every Sunday, requires as much time, and often more time, than this High Mass. Furthermore, the Mass is not sung during the summer months, but even then the attendance stays at a low level. Whatever the reason, the parishioners of St. Mary's have formed the habit of avoiding this High Mass and generally give as their reason that "it takes too long."

The congregation at this Mass is an older group, not so old as at the earliest Mass, but noticeably different from the seven, eight, and nine o'clock Masses. There is always a notable proportion of married couples who appear to have reached middle age and completed their families. Very few children attend this Mass, the proportion being 8.07 per cent to 91.93 per cent for adults.

In some parishes this High Mass is the "Music Lovers' Mass," but St. Mary's Choir is a distinctly amateur aggregation of talent. Hence, those who appreciate the solemn singing of the Mass are attracted to other churches in the city which boast professional talent and which

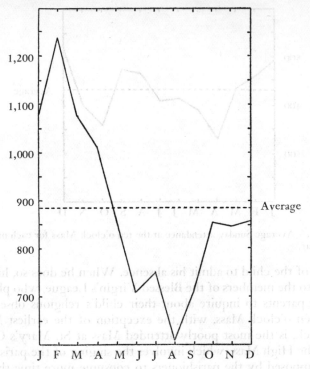

FIG. 32.—Average Sunday attendance at the eleven-thirty o'clock Mass for each month and for the year.

adhere closely to all the liturgical demands of the function. Frequently during the year the choir simply sings hymns instead of the regular Mass music. This is, of course, a Low Mass, but people are apparently deceived into believing otherwise by the peculiar custom of having always the "Asperges Me" or the "Vidi Aquam," by which the celebrant opens the Mass with the sprinkling of the congregation.

The largest congregation at this ten o'clock Mass came in December, when the Sunday average was 518. From that time there was a gradual monthly decline to the lowest figure of 331 in April. From

May until November, the monthly average never went below 388 or above 468. The fluctuations show no uniformity or design and appear to be impossible of useful analysis (Fig. 31).

The most popular Mass at St. Mary's, as at all churches where it is

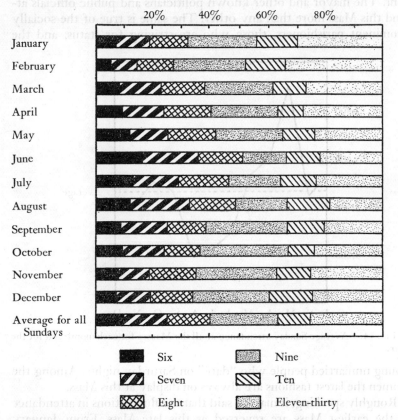

FIG. 33.—Percentage distribution of the average Sunday attendance at the various Masses for each month and for the year.

not a High Mass, is the last Mass. This is the one best attended by the marginal Catholics, those who attempt to fulfil their obligation with the least trouble and in the shortest time. During the winter months the church is so crowded that folding chairs must be placed in the sanctuary, and people are standing not only along the wall on both sides but in the vestibules and even on the outside steps in front of the church. Unattached boys and girls of high-school and college age who arrive late consistently tend to congregate at the entrance.

The congregation at the late Mass contains a larger proportion of males than any other Mass. Females, of course, still predominate, as they do at all church and religious functions, but at this Mass they represent only 59.42 per cent, while the males represent 40.58 per cent. The mayor and other known politicians and public officials attend this Mass more than any other. The same is true of the socially prominent parishioners, those who are striving for status, and the

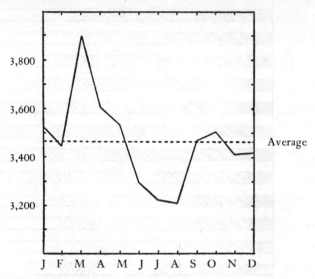

Fig. 34.—Average Sunday attendance at all the Masses for each month and for the year.

young unmarried people who "date" on Saturday nights. Among the women the latest fashions are always on display at this Mass.

Roughly speaking, it may be said that the fluctuations in attendance at the earliest Mass are reversed at this late Mass. From January through April the average Sunday attendance is over one thousand, with the highest month being February (1,237). In the months of May, October, November, and December it is between eight and nine hundred. During the remaining four months, from June through September, the number never passes 750, the lowest month being August, with 607. Thus, it may be seen that the late Mass is crowded in the cold weather more than during the summer months (Fig. 32).

The analysis so far given has been of the six different Sunday Masses celebrated at St. Mary's, with the composition of the congregation and the fluctuations of attendance throughout the year. This picture may be filled in by a discussion of the Sunday averages for all the six Masses combined. During the fifty-three Sundays when the count was taken at all the Masses, there were certain wide variations noted by the observers. The average Sunday attendance at all the Masses throughout the year was 3,465 persons. During the months of June, July, and August the Sunday attendance was somewhat over thirty-two hundred persons. During the other months of the year it was consistently higher, with March showing up exceptionally well with 3,904. This last number, of course, includes Easter Sunday (Fig. 33).

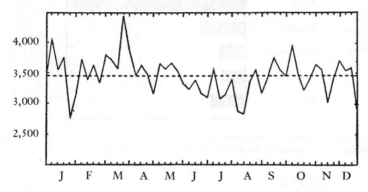

Fig. 35.—Total attendance at all the Masses on each Sunday and the average attendance for the year.

The difference of several hundred in church attendance between the summer and winter months is mainly explained by the fact that many families "go away" for a vacation during the summertime. This usually means a short stay with relatives in the country, although some of the families rent summer camps or "shacks" in certain resort towns within a hundred miles of the city. They usually speak of "going across the lake" or "out to the country." The pastors in these resort places always report a large attendance at their Sunday Masses as compared to the attendance during the winter months. Hence it cannot be said with certitude that the people of St. Mary's are lax in their religious observance during the summer. An exception must be made to this statement in the case of some children who know that the Sister will not check up and report to their parents (Fig. 34).

Considered separately, the fifty-three Sundays on which the count was taken show some interesting variations. The smallest number in attendance at Mass on any Sunday of the year was on the last Sunday in January, when 2,758 persons were counted. This was a bitterly

cold day for this southern city, and the 140 people going to the six
o'clock Mass saw icicles hanging from the trees reflected in their
automobile headlights. On the Sunday between Christmas and New
Year's Day, the cold weather was most responsible for a small attendance of only 2,818 persons. The third lowest attendance of the year
was on the third Sunday in August, which coincided with the Feast of
the Assumption, when 2,878 people came to Mass (Fig. 35).

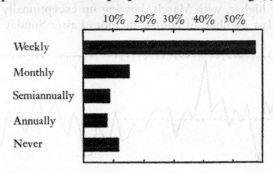

FIG. 36.—Percentage distribution of the parishioners (seven years of age and older)
according to the estimated frequency of Sunday Mass attendance.

TABLE 16

Classification of Sunday Mass Attendance	No. of Parishioners	Per Cent
Weekly	3,033	57.43
Monthly	778	14.73
Semiannually	452	8.56
Annually	410	7.77
Never	608	11.51
Total	5,281	100.00

What, finally, can be said of the people of St. Mary's Parish when
they are judged by their observance of the precept of Sunday Mass
attendance? We noted above that Mass attendance may be accepted
as the principal external criterion of Catholicism. If a person goes to
Mass on Sunday, he is at least giving outward adherence to the Catholic Church. There are in the parish 5,281 persons of seven years of age
and older, who are bound by the obligation of attending Mass. On no
Sunday during the year were that many people at Mass in St. Mary's
Church. The largest number ever to attend Mass was 4,468, on Easter
Sunday. The smallest number ever to attend was on the last Sunday
in January, when 2,758 were there. The average for all the Sundays
of the year was 3,465.

In Table 16 and Figure 36 an attempt is made to classify the parish-

ioners according to their fidelity to Sunday Mass. It is a rough estimate based on the information provided in the census schedules by the
people themselves and on the actual count taken at all Sunday Masses
through the year. An estimated 10 per cent has been added to the lowest Sunday attendance for the year (2,758) to account for those who
fulfil their obligation at other churches and for those who may have
legitimate excuses.

The monthly attendance estimate of 778 is the difference between
the adjusted lowest attendance and the adjusted average attendance.
The last figure (608) is probably an underenumeration. It is taken
from the census schedules and represents those who admitted that
they never attend Mass. The comparison between the census returns
and the actual count at Sunday Masses indicates that the former are
not completely reliable. Of persons seven years of age and older, 4,293
(81.29 per cent) claim that they go to Mass every Sunday; 380 (7.20
per cent) admit that they attend irregularly; and 608 (11.51 per cent)
say that they never attend. The actual count taken at all the Masses on
every Sunday of the year, together with information from the Sisters
concerning the absence of school children from Mass, shows that the
first figure must be revised downward and the others upward.

Two comparisons may be used to evaluate St. Mary's parishioners'
fidelity to the obligation of Sunday Mass. The first is made above,
where we have estimated that only 57.43 per cent of those who ought
to go to Sunday Mass actually do so. This seems a very low percentage even when we realize that we are considering only parishioners.
It would be much lower if we considered also the thousands of baptized but dormant Catholics of Riverside.

The second comparison, that between the parishioners of St. Mary's
and the white Catholics of all the parishes in the city, shows that St.
Mary's is better than average. A count taken in all the Catholic
churches of the city on the same Sunday showed that only 46.09 per
cent of white Catholics seven years of age and over actually attended
Mass on that Sunday. The count was taken on the first Sunday in
May, on which date 3,186 (or 60.32 per cent) of St. Mary's parishioners were at Mass in St. Mary's Church. Thus, if the criterion of
"what-ought-to-be" is used, the parishioners show themselves relatively poor Catholics in their Sunday Mass attendance. If the criterion
of actual Mass attendance by other white Catholics is used,[2] St. Mary's
parishioners may be called better-than-average Catholics.

2. This comparison must be used cautiously, since the estimated number of
Catholics in the whole city is not accurate and probably includes many dormant
Catholics.

Chapter Thirteen

The Mass Goes On

THE parishioners of St. Mary's may be divided into two general categories: those who do not even fulfil the minimum external observance of Sunday Mass attendance and those who do comply with this obligation. This second group of parishioners may be further refined. A person's training and sense of duty may stop at this point, with the result that he comes to be known as a "Sunday Catholic." Parishioners who tend to become marginal Catholics are usually of this state of mind. Any further manifestation of religious affiliation or observance is deemed unnecessary by them. After all, they are not "out to be saints."

The fact is, however, that the Catholic's obligation to attend Mass on the six designated holy days is just as serious as it is for Sundays. Attendance at the regular daily Mass and on the First Friday of each month does not carry this obligation, and parishioners who are present at Mass on these occasions are likely to be most devoted and enthusiastic Catholics. The demands of the urban occupational system and the distractions of our secular culture seem to minimize the importance of "weekday religion."

SPECIAL FEAST DAYS

Certainly, in our modern economy, where great emphasis is placed upon one's occupational status, it is much more difficult for an employed person to attend Mass on a weekday than on a Sunday. Valid excuses for missing Mass on these days are therefore quite numerous, and we expect that the numbers will be much lower. Whatever the explanation may be, there is one group which is conspicuous by its absence from church on the special feast days of the year; they are the standees of the eleven-thirty o'clock Sunday Mass.[1]

1. It is quite possible that many of these attend the noonday Mass in the downtown churches which are located near their places of business.

There are six holy days of obligation in the parish which Catholics are to consider the same as Sundays, that is, they must hear Mass and refrain from servile work just as on the Lord's Day. These are Christmas and New Year's Day and the feasts of the Ascension, the Assumption, All Saints, and the Immaculate Conception. During the year of the study at St. Mary's one of these feasts occurred on Sunday, the Feast of the Assumption on August 15; hence it did not serve for purposes of distinction and had to be included in the account of Sunday Masses. On that day the attendance of 2,878 at the Masses was one of the lowest for the year, although the proportion of those receiving Communion (537) was appreciably higher than usual.

At the beginning of the study we assumed that the most important day on the Catholic calendar was Christmas and that the second most important was Easter. We thought, therefore, that the largest attendance at Mass and the greatest number of communicants would be recorded for the Nativity of Christ and that the Feast of the Resurrection might almost equal it.

The facts were quite different. On Christmas, 3,505 persons attended Mass, as compared to 4,468 on Easter. Easter is always on a Sunday and therefore is not included in the list of special holy days of obligation, as the term is currently employed. The largest number ever to attend Mass on any one day was 4,468, while 1,415 persons received Communion. Thus, Easter Sunday was the peak of the year in the outward expression of Catholicism in St. Mary's Parish.

The Pastor knew from experience that this Sunday would bring crowds of people to the church, but he also thought that in previous years the Protestants had drawn many of his Catholic parishioners to a "sunrise service" in one of the city parks. In order to offset this leakage of people who become religious once a year and who think that any service is better than none, he decided to have a Solemn High Mass at five-thirty o'clock in the morning. The weather was cool, hence women wore winter coats over their Easter finery, and only a few wore new hats. Like the earliest Mass on Sundays, this one was the least attended of the day and was made up predominantly of women. There were 458 persons present, of whom 319 received Holy Communion. Since the reception of Communion indicates to some degree the true Catholic spirit, it is doubtful whether the Pastor succeeded in attracting those Catholics who planned on going to the Protestant sunrise service.

The large total attendance for Easter Sunday seems to show a shift of the regular churchgoers from the three later Masses to the three earlier Masses so that they could receive Holy Communion, their places being taken at the three later Masses by many Catholics who apparently go to church only on Easter Sunday. In other words, the first three Masses had a total of 2,014 persons attending, of whom 1,088 received Communion. In both attendance and reception of the Sacrament this is a larger total than that of the first three Masses on any other day of the year. On the other hand, the last three Masses had in attendance 2,454 persons, a figure which was surpassed on numerous ordinary Sundays throughout the year. However, the number who received Communion (327) was about twice as large as the average Sunday communicants at the last three Masses (Fig. 37).

In attempting to analyze the factors behind the large Easter attendance, and especially the unexpected popularity of Easter over Christmas as a religious feast, we have not discovered any satisfactory hypothesis. In the popular American mind is the religious importance of Easter greater than that of Christmas? Among Catholics, does the Lenten preparation, especially the emphasis on Holy Thursday and Good Friday, bring out the religious significance of Easter as compared to the lack of liturgical preparation for Christmas? Finally, the suggestion was made by the female observers on the study that the traditional "Easter clothes" motive was an important factor. It has become an American folkway to exhibit one's new spring clothing in church on Easter Day. The so-called "Easter Parade" began as the walk from services to home on this day and has now expanded to an autonomous activity. Perhaps a combination of all these factors must be considered the explanation for the large Easter crowds.

Ascension Thursday came during the first week in May, a time when everything is ordinarily propitious for large church attendance. Neither the weather nor vacation time could be used as excuses for the poor attendance of only 2,458 at all the Masses on this holy day of obligation. The children's Mass and the two late Masses were poorly attended as compared with the previous and succeeding Sundays. The absence of the children is probably accounted for by the attitudes of many parents who are themselves lax; while the absences at the late Masses are a reflection of the fact that holy days are also business days, and many employed persons simply missed Mass (Fig. 38).

The next holy day, the Feast of the Assumption, fell on a very warm Sunday in the month of August. The attendance of 2,878 was one of the lowest for the whole year, although the number of Communions (537) was proportionately better on most Sundays. The fact that the day was a Sunday and the month a vacation period makes

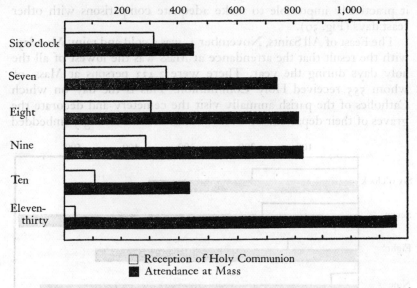

Fig. 37.—Comparison of the numbers who received Communion and attended Mass at the various Masses on Easter Sunday.

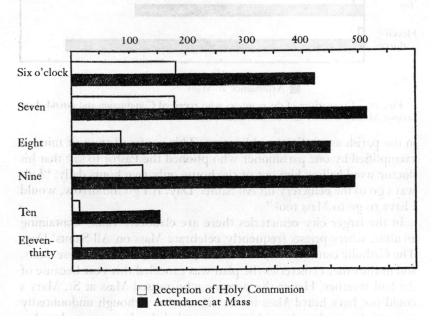

Fig. 38.—Comparison of the numbers who received Communion and attended Mass at the various Masses on Ascension Thursday.

it practically impossible to make adequate comparisons with other feast days (Fig. 39).

The Feast of All Saints, November 1, was a cold and rainy Monday, with the result that the attendance at Mass was the lowest of all the holy days during the year. There were 2,433 persons at Mass, of whom 555 received Holy Communion. This is the day on which Catholics of the parish annually visit the cemetery and decorate the graves of their departed. This custom has become strongly imbedded

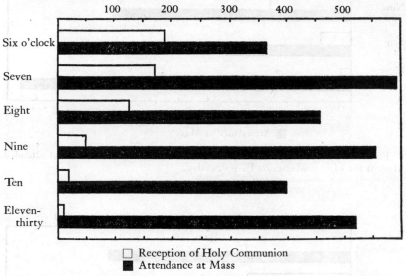

☐ Reception of Holy Communion
■ Attendance at Mass

Fig. 39.—Comparison of the numbers who received Communion and attended the various Masses on the Feast of the Assumption.

in the parish as a religious obligation. This confused state of mind is exemplified by one parishioner who phoned the Pastor to say that his doctor would allow him out of the house only two hours daily. "I always go to the cemetery on All Saints' Day. If I go tomorrow, would I have to go to Mass too?"

In the larger city cemeteries there are elaborate vaults containing an altar, where priests frequently celebrate Mass on All Saints' Day. The Catholic cemetery in Riverside does not have one of these altars, and in the other cemeteries the plan was canceled this year because of the bad weather. Hence the persons who missed Mass at St. Mary's could not have heard Mass in the cemeteries, although undoubtedly some of the employed parishioners attended the downtown churches (Fig. 40).

The Feast of the Immaculate Conception, December 8, was on a Wednesday, and although weather conditions were ideal for church-going, the number attending all the Masses was only 2,667, of whom 573 received Communion. This feast was marked by a large attend-ance at the children's Mass at nine o'clock. Since the parish itself is under the patronage of the Blessed Mother, the nuns made a special effort to induce all the school children to attend Mass. Rain and cold make a great difference in children's attendance, but on this day this

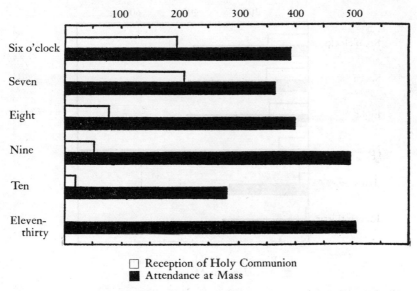

Fig. 40.—Comparison of the numbers who received Communion and attended the various Masses on the Feast of All Saints.

obstacle was not present. Hence the onus of missing Mass was on the adult parishioners. The Feast of the Immaculate Conception occurred between the second and third Sundays of Advent, which saw 3,707 and 3,542 attending, respectively (Fig. 41).

The two remaining holy days of obligation were Christmas and the Feast of the Circumcision, both of which fell on Saturdays. On Christ-mas there was an additional Mass at midnight, a fact which should ordinarily have increased the total number of churchgoers over any other day of the year. Actually, however, the total number fell short of many ordinary Sundays during the year. The midnight Mass was crowded with almost twelve hundred persons, but all the other Masses had less than the average of most Sunday Masses. The cold rain of the early morning probably kept down the attendance from the six o'clock to the nine o'clock Mass. When the weather cleared for the ten o'clock Mass, 497 persons came to church, a number higher than the parallel Mass on Easter. But the eleven-thirty Mass was heard by only 718 persons. Thus, it seems that the bad early-morning weather shifted the regular Mass goers to the later Masses, while the marginal Catholics, who usually go to the last Mass on Sundays, went to the midnight Mass on Christmas.

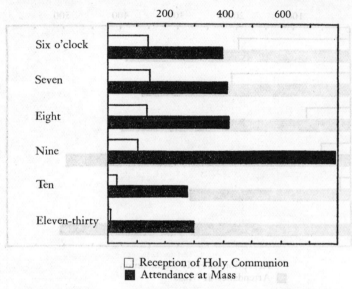

☐ Reception of Holy Communion
■ Attendance at Mass

FIG. 41.—Comparison of the numbers who received Communion and attended the various Masses on the Feast of the Immaculate Conception.

A noticeable phenomenon of the midnight Mass was that people came in groups. This was especially true of the younger persons of high-school and college age. Small groups of boys were identifiable in the back of the church; girl friends who came together were in various parts of the congregation. An exceptional number of "date couples" were observed, and, upon questioning, it was discovered that many of these had been to a show or party before coming to Mass. As at Easter, social custom had become important in the question of the midnight Mass. This Mass is crowded at all the city churches; and to some Protestants and most marginal Catholics it has become a religious spectacle "worth seeing." In spite of this apparent secular attitude, however, approximately one-third of the congregation re-

ceived Holy Communion at this Mass. A similar high proportion of
the attendance received Communion at the Masses on Christmas Day,
with the usual exception of the ten and eleven-thirty o'clock Masses
(Fig. 42).

It may be noted in passing that on the day after Christmas, a Sunday, the attendance dropped to 2,818, all the Masses having smaller
congregations than the corresponding Masses on the other Sundays of

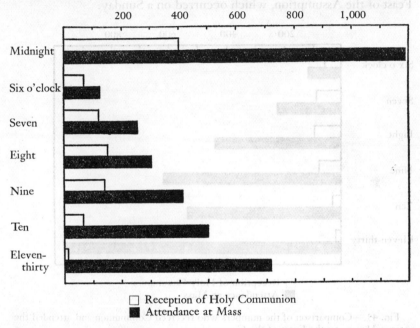

□ Reception of Holy Communion
■ Attendance at Mass

FIG. 42.—Comparison of the numbers who received Communion and attended the
various Masses on Christmas.

December. The cold weather may have been partially responsible for
this poor showing.

One week later, on Saturday, January 1, the Feast of the Circumcision of Our Lord was celebrated. Except for the two early Masses
when the weather was very cold, all the Masses were better attended
than on Christmas Day. Since there was no midnight Mass, however,
the total attendance was down to 2,902 for the day, of whom 357
received Holy Communion. New Year's Eve celebrations are clearly
reflected in this small proportion of communicants, as well as in the
general lack of attendance at the Masses. On the day following the
Feast of the Circumcision, there were almost five hundred more

people at Mass. This is quite the reverse of Christmas and the succeeding day. It probably indicates that, while many Catholics consider Christmas a more important day than any Sunday, they also consider Sunday a more important day than the Feast of the Circumcision.

Figure 44 gives a brief summary of the attendance at Mass and the reception of the Sacrament on the holy days of obligation. This is the actual count taken at all the Masses on those days, including the Feast of the Assumption, which occurred on a Sunday.

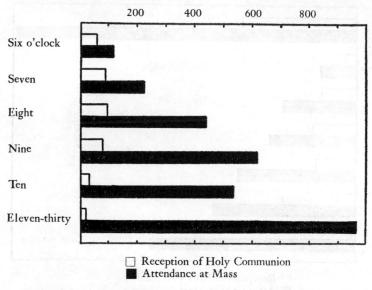

☐ Reception of Holy Communion
■ Attendance at Mass

Fig. 43.—Comparison of the numbers who received Communion and attended the various Masses on the Feast of the Circumcision.

These figures show that an average of 2,807 persons fulfilled their obligation of attending Mass on those feast days appointed by the Church as the most important of the liturgical year. This average is considerably lower than the average Sunday Masses (3,465). If we use the lowest number of the year, 2,433 persons who went to Mass on All Saints' Day, as an indication of those Catholics who fulfil their obligations in spite of difficulties, we may establish still another category of parishioners. Adding an estimated 10 per cent for those who may have been excused or who went to other parish churches, we find that 2,676 fulfil the holy-day obligations. These are "conscientious" Catholics, and their number is appreciably smaller than the estimated 3,033 persons who regularly attend Sunday Mass.

FIRST FRIDAYS

A further index of the external manifestation of Catholicism among the parishioners of St. Mary's Church may be found in their attendance at Mass on the First Fridays of each month. This practice is entirely voluntary and differs specifically from Mass attendance on Sundays and holy days, which is obligatory. We may safely conclude that those who go to church on First Fridays are more thoroughly Catholic than those who attend only when they have the obligation to do so.[2]

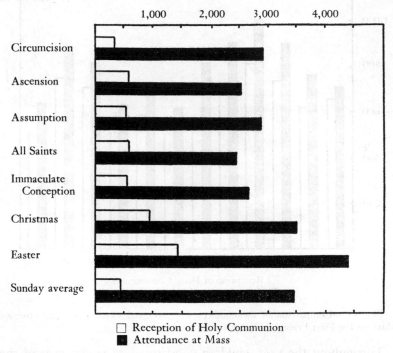

Fig. 44.—Comparison of the numbers who received Communion and attended Mass on the various feast days and on Easter Sunday and the Sunday average for the year.

This average of 783 Catholics who attended Mass on the First Fridays of the month throughout the year may be placed in a separate classification. Only those who attend daily Mass could be considered as better and more observant Catholics. We must remember, however, that the greater proportion of those who go to Mass on First

2. The custom of this Friday Mass attendance is in devotion to the Sacred Heart of Jesus (see chap. 6, pp. 49–51).

Fridays are children from the parochial school. This is the only individual school day of the month (besides holy days) when the children are expected to attend Mass. The Sisters prepare them on the day before when the priests hear confessions, but attendance is expected only of the children in the five upper grades. The children's Mass at seven o'clock is too early for the smallest children; hence they are excused.

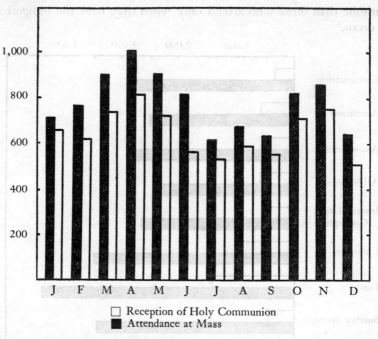

FIG. 45.—Comparison of the numbers who received Communion and attended Mass on the First Fridays of the year.

Throughout the year, children constituted 57.23 per cent of the attendance. If we subtract this number (448) from the average (783), we find that there are only 335 adult parishioners who attend First Friday Masses. Of these, 273 are women and 62 are men. It must be noted, however, that this is not a true picture of the adult devotion to the Sacred Heart in St. Mary's Parish, because a relatively large number of those who are employed in the city attend Mass and receive Communion at downtown churches on First Fridays. It is probably safe to add an estimated 10 per cent for these parishioners (Fig. 45).

The decline in attendance at First Friday Masses during the summer months is largely accounted for by the absence of children. The decline in the numbers of adults was not so sharp during this period. The lower attendance on December 3 was due to the inclement weather, when many children were kept at home. March, April, and May were the highest months of the year, and this is most probably because March was in Lent, the First Friday of April was in Easter Week, and May is the month of devotion to the Blessed Mother.

DAILY MASS

As in the case of First Fridays, there is no obligation to attend Mass at St. Mary's Church on weekdays. The school children are expected to go to Mass every day during Lent and in the months of May and October. Here, again, the youngest children do not have this obligation imposed by the Sisters and the Pastor. Actually, the "obligation" is an encouragement without sanction and is fulfilled carefully and religiously mainly by those children whose parents are most interested in their spiritual welfare. Unlike the First Friday Mass for children, which is at seven o'clock, the daily Mass during these periods is at seven forty-five. Since the children cannot easily obtain breakfast before going to school, the proportionate number of Communions at this Mass is considerably lower than at the earlier Masses.

Figure 46 gives the average daily attendance at each of the three daily Masses at St. Mary's Church. It shows also how these Masses were attended in the different months of the year. These figures therefore reveal that an average of 193 persons attend daily Mass at St. Mary's Church. These statistics exclude the figures already given above for holy days of obligation and First Fridays. Here again the greater proportion of those attending daily Mass are women. Although the children outnumber adults at the seven forty-five o'clock Mass during Lent, May, and October, they are in the minority at the two earlier Masses and at other times of the year. The abnormally high attendance in March is due to the women's mission, when hundreds of women went to Mass every day. A more accurate picture of daily Mass attendance could be obtained if the statistics for Lent (February and March) and for May and October were subtracted from the rest of the year. This would bring down the average daily attendance to 154.5 persons.

We are now able to review all our data on Mass attendance and reclassify the parishioners of St. Mary's in accordance with their external adherence to this central act of Catholic worship. At the beginning of this chapter we pointed out the two general groupings of parishioners: those who attend Sunday Mass regularly and those who do not. In Figure 47 both of these groups are further refined. The

3,033 who attend Mass each Sunday contain also those who go to Mass more frequently. Each of these four groups is estimated by adding 10 per cent to the lowest average attendance.

The bottom four categories in Figure 47 are of parishioners who are not fulfilling their obligation to hear Sunday Mass regularly. They number 2,248 parishioners, or 42.57 per cent of all persons seven years of age and over. They are to be distinguished sharply from all other classifications which contain the "minimum" practicing Catholics of the parish. The first four categories contain 57.43 per cent of the parishioners obliged to attend Mass, and they are scaled upward from

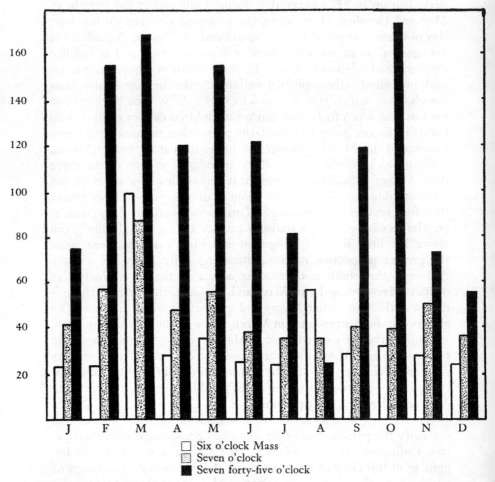

☐ Six o'clock Mass
▨ Seven o'clock
■ Seven forty-five o'clock

Fig. 46.—Comparison of the average attendance at the three weekday Masses for each month of the year.

the whole group which hears Mass at least on Sunday to the small number of persons who hear Mass on every weekday of the year.

Since there are no similarly detailed and comparable statistics for other Catholic urban parishes, it is difficult to estimate whether St. Mary's parishioners have a better general record than others for Mass attendance. If we use as a criterion complete fidelity, or 100 per cent attendance at Mass on Sundays and holy days, we must admit that St. Mary's Parish falls far short of perfection. Approximately one-half (50.67 per cent)[3] of the parishioners seven years of age and older

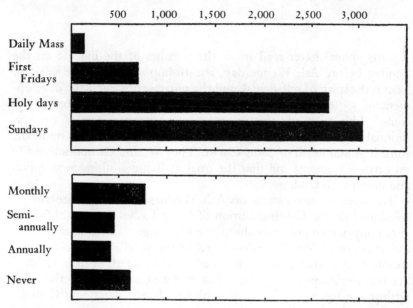

FIG. 47.—Distribution of the parishioners (seven years of age and older) according to the estimated frequency of Mass attendance.

follow this minimum obligation imposed by the Church under pain of mortal sin.

The whole question of this large failure to comply with the regulations of the Church concerning Mass attendance cannot be taken up at this time. What are the factors which explain this drift away from minimum obligations by parishioners in an urban area? Generalized conclusions to this question are attempted in various parts of this study. Here we have been constrained to present only the statistical facts drawn from careful observation and enumeration.

3. This percentage refers to the 2,676 parishioners who fulfilled the holy-day obligation.

Chapter Fourteen

The Observance of Lent

In his annual letter read in all the parishes of the diocese on the Sunday before Ash Wednesday, the Bishop said that "the spirit of Lent is the spirit of self-denial, and the purpose of Lent is the development of self-control that will lead to the ultimate salvation of our souls." This spirit and this purpose are an integral part of the traditional Christian observance of Lent in that they recall to mind the sufferings and death of Jesus Christ. They remind Catholics that life on earth is transient and that the goal of living is ultimate salvation and union with God.

The Lenten season starts on Ash Wednesday with a forceful reminder of death. The distribution of blessed ashes to the faithful is a ceremony which contrasts sharply with the gay and uninhibited social functions which have flourished in the pre-Lenten season. "Remember, man, that thou art dust, and unto dust thou shalt return," are the words spoken by the priest in Latin as he presses the ashes against the forehead of each parishioner. Every practicing Catholic is aware of this custom, and apparently many who do not attend services regularly also come to church to receive the ashes.

On the morning of Ash Wednesday there were celebrated the three regular parochial Masses at six o'clock, seven, and seven forty-five. Ashes were distributed to 265 persons who attended these Masses. This was only 20 persons more than the average Mass attendance for the week. However, 147 persons received Communion, which was more than twice the average number for the week. The last Mass was over about eight-twenty. At this time the parochial school children, who had been told to come to the schoolyard at eight o'clock, began to come into the church. They entered the side door in orderly ranks, approached the altar rail, received ashes, and then formed ranks down the center aisle. The three priests ranged along the altar rail giving the ashes quite rapidly as the children came and went in some confusion. It required almost an hour (until nine-fifteen) for 612 parochial school children to receive the blessed ashes.

At three o'clock in the afternoon Father Dominic again distributed ashes to the children who were not present in the morning and also to any adults who wished to receive them. At this time 74 children and 121 adults appeared; and the priest remained at the altar rail for about ten minutes waiting for others to come forward. Again, after the services on Wednesday night the whole congregation of 295 persons came up to the Communion rail for the ashes. The total number to receive this sacramental was 1,367 persons, which represents 25.88 per cent of the parishioners of St. Mary's Church seven years of age and older. This figure, however, is an undercount, since large numbers of employed parishioners visited the downtown church during the business day, where ashes were distributed every half-hour. Hence, it cannot be reliably employed as a criterion of the spirit of Lent in the parish.

A more dependable measure is that of attendance at Mass and reception of the Sacrament. On the Sunday before Lent the people had been urged to go to Mass and receive Communion daily during Lent. To discover whether this advice was followed in the parish, we compared the weekday Mass attendance and reception of Communion in the first three weeks of Lent with those of the three previous weeks. There were seventeen days in each period. Before Lent the average daily attendance at Mass was 185, with 64 Communions; after Lent had started, the average daily attendance was 248, with 91 Communions. It must be noted, however, that this increase was accounted for mainly by school children who went to Mass under the supervision of the nuns during Lent. The difference in the Sunday Masses and Communions is not so marked. The Mass attendance increased on Sundays, but the number of Communions decreased. The average Sunday Mass attendance for the three Sundays before Lent was 3,208, while the average for the first three Sundays of Lent was 3,459. On the other hand, the average number of Communions per Sunday was 413 before Lent and only 395 after Lent started.

Figure 48 shows the attendance at Mass and Communion averaged for all the Sundays of Lent (February 15 through March 21), excluding Easter. These compare favorably with the average for all Sundays in the year, but the difference is not sufficient to indicate that there is a large increase in religious devotion at this penitential period of the year.

In making comparisons with other periods of the year, we must remember that two of the Sundays of Lent witnessed the conclusion of the missions preached by the Lazarist Fathers. There were more persons receiving Communion and probably more attending Mass after these missions than would normally do so. If these factors are given adequate weight, we might well conclude that the spirit of Lent had practically no effect in increasing the external religious observances of the parishioners of St. Mary's.

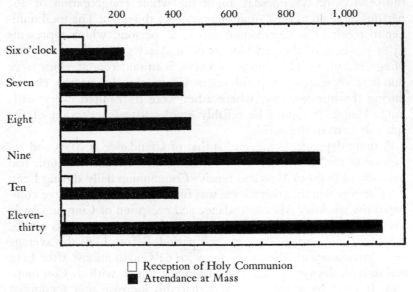

FIG. 48.—Average numbers who received Communion and attended Mass on all the Sundays of Lent (excluding Easter).

There are, however, other external criteria that may be used to measure this observance. Each week during Lent there are special church services on Wednesday and Friday nights, but this program was interrupted by the parish missions. Hence, we have a partial but indicative study on which to base our conclusions.

The Wednesday-night services consisted of the group recitation of the Rosary, a sermon, and Benediction of the Blessed Sacrament. The services started at seven-thirty, and for the most part the congregation was on time. Women predominated in the congregation even to a greater percentage than they do at other services and Masses in the church. Figure 49 gives the percentage present at Lenten services on the four Wednesday nights.

The Pastor himself delivered the sermon on Ash Wednesday after Father Dominic had led the congregation in the Rosary. His topic was the importance of a careful observance of Lent. He told the parishioners that the ashes distributed to the faithful on this day were symbolic of their mortality. "This should make us think about why we are here, and that we won't be here a long time. We must work in the vineyard of the Master for our salvation. . . . God is calling you to work for Him, and He will repay you what is just." The need for good work, as well as for faith, was stressed by the Pastor, and at this point he mentioned that "Luther was jealous of the Church and he gained a following by giving them something easy to do. . . . Salvation is not easy. . . . We must work for it. . . . If faith alone were enough, there would not be a hell." He concluded by stressing the mercy and

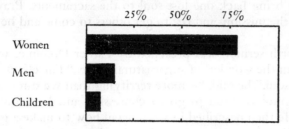

Fig. 49.—Percentage distribution of women, men, and children who attended the four Wednesday-night services in Lent.

forgiveness of God and urging the people to take advantage of the Lenten period.

The effect of this sermon seemed to be spoiled somewhat in that the people became restless toward the end. Father Urban spoke for almost forty minutes. Several persons in the rear of the church sighed audibly when the sermon was over.

On the second Wednesday in Lent, Father Dominic delivered a twenty-minute sermon which appeared to be well received by the congregation. He began by praising Mahatma Gandhi, who had just recently died, and declared that he had been a naturally good man, while the Catholic must be a supernaturally good man. Father Dominic uses supernatural grace as one of his frequent topics in the pulpit, and on this night he described the various effects of grace on the human soul. "The salvation of your immortal soul cannot be accomplished without grace. Your salvation is God's prime reason for putting you on earth. Therefore, during Lent, resolve to stay in the state of grace; for, if you die without it, your whole life will have been lived in vain." Three men slept through this sermon, but the rest of the people paid relatively good attention.

Father Paul gave the sermon on the third Wednesday of Lent, and he preached about the sacraments. He outlined the sacramental life of a Catholic in the order in which he receives and needs the various sacraments. Hence there was a brief definition of each of the sacraments and a few words of exhortation concerning the importance of each. "The sacraments are the means of obtaining grace, and we all need grace to reach heaven. Therefore, we must use the means to grace, and we should receive the sacraments frequently." He reminded them that a mission would be preached soon in St. Mary's Church and that a wonderful apostolic work would be to encourage people to make the mission. "It will be a very successful Lent for you if you can bring back one lost soul to the sacraments. Pray for the success of the mission, and try to get others to come and be reunited to God."

The fourth sermon was preached by Father Dominic, who again talked about the wonders of supernatural grace. "The effect of mortal sin on the soul," he said, "is more terrifying than we can realize. We need the grace of God to go to confession and have our sins removed." He then described in some detail how to make a good confession. Like the other priests, he also once more advertised the coming mission. "We should take time out and see what the score is. ... The mission will be a good opportunity for this time. ... Satan still prowls around to ensnare many from God into his kingdom of fire. ... So, make the mission and encourage your friends to do so. Advertise the mission and pray for its success."

All these Wednesday-night sermons were preceded by the Rosary and followed by Benediction. When Father Paul preached the sermon, Father Dominic led the Rosary and gave Benediction. The congregation's responses to the prayers of the Rosary were always crisp and loud, but there was one woman in the church who consistently prayed louder and longer than the others. This was a source of amusement to the younger people, especially girls, who knelt in the rear of the church and made signs to one another. Approximately 25 per cent of the people did not have rosaries, and some of them were seen counting the prayers on their fingers. Between the fourth and fifth decades the priest and people stood to sing a hymn in honor of the Blessed Mother.

Toward the end of the sermon the altar boys came out to light the rest of the candles in preparation for Benediction. On every occasion there were some persons distracted from the sermon by this action. They seemed fascinated by the movement of the taper in the hands of the invisible server behind the altar. As soon as the sermon ended, the priest and altar boys came into the sanctuary to begin Benediction. This was the signal for the four ushers to go up the center aisle, genuflect, and start the collection. They never were able to complete this task before the Blessed Sacrament was exposed in the monstrance, and this too seemed a distraction to the younger people in the rear of the church.

During Lent the closing hymn of the Benediction is the "Parce Domine," which very few of the congregation know. The organist and girls in the choir sing it while the priest stands at the foot of the altar steps. As soon as he genuflects to leave, the people begin to do the same, even though the hymn has not yet been ended.

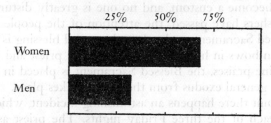

Fig. 50.—Percentage distribution of women and men who attended the three Friday-night services in Lent.

There was another regular Lenten service, the Way of the Cross, on Friday nights at seven-thirty. This is a shorter service than that on Wednesday nights, since there is no sermon and the Rosary is not recited. Benediction is celebrated after the Way of the Cross, and there follows immediately the regular weekly Novena in honor of Our Lady of Sorrows. Because of the missions there were only four scheduled Friday-night services. However, only three of these were held. On Friday, March 5, a downpour of rain flooded the streets and held up traffic. No one appeared for the services,[1] and the sexton did not even open the church doors.

Figure 50 shows the breakdown of attendance on the first three Friday nights of Lent. Approximately 10 per cent of these people come late to the services on these nights. A little more than 75 per

1. Except our observer, who removed his shoes and socks and waded the last two blocks to the church. He stopped at the rectory and asked Father Dominic why the church was closed. The latter laughed and said, "It's hard enough to get these Catholics out to night services, much less in weather like this."

cent use the booklets which contain the prayers for the Way of the Cross and which are distributed in the pews by the altar boys before the services start.

The services begin when the priest comes out of the sacristy preceded by an altar boy carrying the crucifix and two others bearing lighted candles. They kneel on the first step of the altar and say the opening prayer and then go down the middle aisle and stop before each of the fourteen Stations to say the customary prayers. There is a pause after every second Station while the choir and people sing a verse of the "Stabat Mater" hymn. After the fourteenth Station the priest returns to the altar and there says the concluding prayer. The other priest then comes out of the sacristy to give the Benediction.

As at the Wednesday-night services, the ushers take up the collection at the beginning of Benediction. This slight distraction has apparently become a custom, and no one is greatly disturbed by it. After the ushers have passed, the attention of the people is focused on the Blessed Sacrament, and, when the actual blessing is given, the congregation bows in hushed immobility. The priest and people recite the divine praises, the Blessed Sacrament is placed in the tabernacle, and a general exodus from the church takes place.

At this point there happens an astonishing incident, which was repeated on each of the three Friday nights. The priest ascends the pulpit even before his confrere has reached the sacristy; and the prayers for the Novena[2] are started. The middle aisle is crowded with people who are leaving the church and thus have their backs turned to the pulpit and the altar. They came for the Way of the Cross, which lasts approximately one half-hour, and had no interest whatever in remaining for the Novena, which would require about another half-hour. On the three successive Friday nights forty-six, sixty-six, and sixty-five persons stayed for the Novena. On the average for the three nights this represents only 15.69 per cent of the congregation who had been present for the Way of the Cross.

Why did an average of 317 persons leave the church rather than attend the Novena services? While this action may seem disedifying, it helps us to learn something about the influence of Lent upon the religious behavior of the parishioners of St. Mary's. It draws a sharp distinction between those who faithfully attend Novenas all during the year and those who come to church specifically because it is Lent and for the traditional Stations of the Cross. Thus we may definitely

2. This Novena in honor of the Blessed Mother is described in chap. 15, pp. 188-94.

say that there are at least 317 adults in the parish who are affected by the Lenten spirit to the extent that they will come to night services once a week.

There was no way of learning how many of these persons also attend the Wednesday-night sermon during Lent. The average attendance at the latter was 301 persons, many of whom were probably at church on both Wednesday and Friday nights. This was undoubtedly true of the girls of high-school age, who were thus permitted an extra night out per week by their parents. These young people were the least attentive at services, especially at the sermon, and, since this was noticeable by our observers, we frequently tried to find the reason why they came to church. We could get no satisfactory direct answer. We noticed that they went to one of the drugstores for a "coke" after services and were able to spend an extra half-hour with their girl friends before going home.

There were hardly ever any young men of high-school and college age at the evening Lenten services. Ten or twelve youths worked out with the boxing team in the gymnasium or ran "laps" around the schoolyard during services. Another group was frequently in the gymnasium playing basketball or practicing softball. When the Pastor became aware of this, he ordered the gym closed until after services. This did not bring the young men into the church; they practiced either before or after services.

Among the more devout Catholic families of the parish, especially those with young children, the parents alternated at the services, one remaining at home with the children on Wednesday nights and the other on Friday nights. Not only is this fact known from questioning parishioners but it may be inferred also from the number of older married couples who attended the services together. Unlike the older women in the congregation, a middle-aged man was seldom seen alone in the church.

The sex differential at the two night services is an interesting one. The percentage of men who attended the Way of the Cross (30.85) was always higher than that which attended the sermon (15.19). The male sense of duty for the Lenten religious observance seemed satisfied by the less lengthy and less tiresome Friday-night service. Furthermore, as might be expected, the percentage of males who attended these night sermons was lower than that of the Sunday Mass attendance (28.35).

The age differential at the Lenten evening services is a noticeable one. At the Wednesday-night sermons only 7.30 per cent of the congregation was made up of children, while on Friday nights the percentage was even lower (1.86). On Friday, February 20, the only children of grammar-school age present were the three altar boys. This small attendance of children seems to be accounted for by several factors. On Wednesday nights they are expected to stay at home to "do their lessons" for the next day. On Friday afternoons at three o'clock the Stations of the Cross are held for the children of the parochial school, and Friday night is "kid's" night in the neighborhood picture shows of Riverside.

The assistant pastors alternated in conducting the Way of the Cross on Friday afternoons. It was the same service as at night, and it included Benediction of the Blessed Sacrament. All the children of the parochial school, except those in the kindergarten, marched by grades from the school to the church. They took their pews exactly as they did at Sunday Mass, with the younger ones in the front and the older to the rear, and a teacher in back of each group.

Since the children came directly from the school under the supervision of the nuns, the attendance was higher than at Sunday Mass or at the obligatory weekday Masses. There were always a half-dozen excused absences, but there were less than twenty reported cases of "playing hooky" throughout the whole of Lent. An average of thirty-six women was in attendance at each of these afternoon services, most of them being mothers who came to bring their children home from school; a few were women too old and infirm to go out at night. Only six men were counted at this afternoon service during the whole of Lent.

The ceremonies of Palm Sunday, which commemorate the triumphal entrance of Jesus into Jerusalem, seem a departure from the penitential spirit of Lent. It appears to be a joyous occasion and is to some extent celebrated in this spirit among St. Mary's parishioners. Because this Sunday was also the closing of the men's mission, it is difficult to determine how many were attracted merely by the Palm Sunday services. The Passion of Our Lord is read, and the Mass would thus ordinarily be very lengthy; but this was not noticeable, since the missioners ascended the pulpit, read the announcements and the Bishop's letter for the seminary appeal, and preached a sermon—all while the celebrant of the Mass continued the Latin reading of the Passion at the altar.

On Palm Sunday there were 3,598 persons in attendance at the six Masses, of whom 609 received Holy Communion. This shows an increase of less than one-half of 1 per cent in attendance and 10.53 per cent in Communions over the average for the Sundays of Lent. These Palm Sunday figures, however, are 3.70 per cent lower in attendance and 49.26 per cent lower in Communions than the previous Sunday, the closing of the women's mission. From these comparisons we may surmise that the celebration of Palm Sunday does not seem of high importance to the parishioners of St. Mary's.

The blessed palm leaves are not distributed to the faithful as they are in many other parishes. On Friday and Saturday schoolboys go through the neighborhood selling palmetto branches, which they sometimes steal from bushes in the yards and lawns of the area. On Sunday morning they stand on the street in front of the church hawking their wares for ten and fifteen cents, depending on the size and beauty of the branch.[3] The actual blessing of the palms took place by the Pastor, who celebrated the ten o'clock Mass on this Sunday.

A great deal of confusion was caused by this arrangement. Every child had brought a palm to the nine o'clock Mass with the intention of waiting for the blessing at the beginning of the next Mass. The younger children played with them a great deal, waving them back and forth, occasionally touching the head of the child in front of them. The Sisters and ushers seemed grieved and annoyed at such fooling and remonstrated with the children numerous times. After the Mass, the children crowded forward in almost complete disorder, holding the palms high in the air. Meanwhile the congregation for the ten o'clock Mass began crowding into the church, some of them carrying as many as six palm branches. The ushers had placed a chain across the middle aisle at the rear of the church to keep the aisle empty for the procession. The people had to enter the pews from the side aisles, and several women complained unsuccessfully to the ushers about such inconvenience.

The ceremony of the blessing of the palms occupied a full half-hour, with the whole congregation of over twelve hundred people from the two Masses standing in the pews and aisles. All held the palms in the air, the boys with the largest palms trying to outreach one another in the air. The ceremony started at ten o'clock when the cross-bearer, flanked by two acolytes and followed by the thurifer and an altar boy carrying the incense boat, came out of the sacristy. Nine smaller altar boys followed them and lined up across the sanc-

3. Five Negro boys were selling palm branches in front of St. Mary's all morning. By ten o'clock one of them had earned over two dollars, and said he was trying to make enough to buy his Easter shoes.

tuary. Then Father Urban, wearing the purple cope, and Father Paul, dressed in cassock and surplice, came to the main altar. After the usual "Asperges," the Pastor ascended the altar and read the Collect, Epistle, Gospel, and Preface before proceeding to the actual blessing of the palms.

There was a stack of about fifty palm branches on the table near the altar. The Pastor sprinkled them with holy water and also incensed them during the prayers and blessings. After the final prayer he presented a palm to Father Paul, who kissed his hand when taking it, as did all the servers who came to the altar in turn. A pocession of the altar boys and two priests then proceeded down the middle aisle to the vestibule where the outer church doors had been closed. Crowded into this space was also half the choir, which began to sing alternate verses of the hymn "Gloria, Laus et Honor," while the rest of the choir sang the other verses outside the vestibule. At the end of the hymn the cross-bearer struck the door with the foot of the cross; the doors were opened, and the procession returned to the sanctuary.

During this whole procedure less than 10 per cent of the people followed the ritual in their missals. Most of the adults craned their necks, some standing on the kneelers for a better view of what was going on in the vestibule. The crowded conditions and the antics of the children up front seemed to cause much of the whispering and restlessness evidenced in the adult congregation. The majority of the people immediately pushed toward exits when the procession was over at ten-thirty, and even after the Mass proper had started at the altar there was much confusion between those leaving the church and those trying to find seats.

The services of Holy Week have already been partially reported in the section on the Eucharist, where the Holy Thursday adoration of the Blessed Sacrament was described.[4] Since there were so many persons going to confession on Wednesday in preparation for the following day, there were no services on Wednesday night. The attendance at the Masses of Monday, Tuesday, and Wednesday and the reception of Communion were somewhat above the average for the rest of Lent. There remains, then, the observance of Good Friday, the most solemn and tragic day on the Catholic calendar.

There are a number of superstitious practices current in the parish on Good Friday, and a few may be recounted here. Apparently good luck is to be expected if one follows these customs. If sweet basil is planted near the front entrance of the home of an adult unmarried

4. Cf. chap. 7, pp. 77–80.

girl on this day, it is certain to attract a husband for the girl at some time during the year. People who have vegetable gardens know that, if parsley and similar plants are put down on this day, they will be protected from going to seed. The most popular superstition is that fish always bite best on Good Friday. Some men may come for adoration of the Blessed Sacrament at three or four o'clock in the morning and then go out and spend hours catching crawfish and crabs. Since there is no obligation to attend Mass, others will fish all morning and try to get back for the Stations of the Cross at two-thirty in the afternoon. Strangely enough, professional fishermen in the parish hold exactly the opposite superstition. They fish on any other day of the year including Sundays and holy days of obligation, but they refuse to work on Good Friday because it is "bad luck."

When the men's all-night vigil before the Blessed Sacrament ended at six o'clock in the morning, the church doors were opened in preparation for the Mass of the Presanctified. Over three hundred persons were present when the services started at seven o'clock. A procession, headed by the cross-bearer and two acolytes, was made up of thirty-two altar boys, the subdeacon, deacon, and celebrant. Because the Pastor was sick in bed, Father Dominic conducted the services, assisted by Father Paul and Father Bruno. Since the tabernacle was empty and the altar bare, no one genuflected.

After the Prostration the Mass of the Catechumens was said and the supplications made, with the sixteen choir girls singing the responses. "The choir girls were talking and laughing during the entire course of the Mass. The only function which they perform is the necessary singing. They do not seem to notice or enter into the Mass in any other way. There was a lot of talking, coughing, and shifting around while the priest was reading the Mass book at the altar. These girls were in contrast to the twelve nuns in the first two rows on the Gospel side of the church. They always made the first move at times when the congregation was supposed to stand or kneel and were imitated first by the people directly behind them and then by the others."

After the cross had been unveiled on three successive steps of the altar, it was placed on a purple pillow at the foot of the altar. The three priests then removed their shoes, and, after genuflecting three times on both knees, they kissed the wounds on the feet, hands, and side of the corpus on the crucifix. Two by two, all the altar boys made the same veneration of the crucifix. While this was going on, the priests put their shoes on again. Each received from an altar boy a smaller crucifix and a piece of white cloth. They proceeded to the altar rail, where the faithful surged forward to venerate the crucifix. After each one kissed the cross, the priest wiped it with the cloth, which was soon noticeably stained with lipstick.

By this time there were 391 persons in the church, many of whom had come in late. Our reporter remarks: "I have never seen anything like the stampede to the Communion rail for the veneration of the cross. The people all rushed toward the middle aisle and formed such a thick solid mass that those who were trying to leave the Communion rail could hardly fight their way through." In this group there were 11 children, 49 men, and 331 women. After completing the veneration of the cross, the people returned to their pews, and thereafter most of them (72 per cent) followed in their missals the Mass of the Presanctified.

Since no consecration takes place in this Mass, the priest went to the Repository, where the Blessed Host was reserved from the Mass on Holy Thursday. The procession of all the altar-servers led the priests out of the sanctuary to the altar of repose, where Father Dominic started to go up for the Host. He stopped, turned back, received the censer from Father Paul, and incensed the Host. The humeral veil was placed about his shoulders. He then ascended the altar, removed the Blessed Sacrament, covered it with the front of the veil, and followed the procession back to the main altar.

Meanwhile the crucifix had been removed from the pillow at the altar steps and placed upright in front of the empty tabernacle. Father Dominic incensed the altar, the crucifix, and the Blessed Sacrament. The altar-servers had to be reminded to bring water so that he could wash his hands at the Epistle side of the altar. He sang the "Pater Noster," which the choir answered. Since no bells could be rung between the Mass of Holy Thursday and that of Holy Saturday, the wooden clappers announced the elevation of the Host and the "Domine, Non Sum Dignus" of the celebrant. The congregation was silent and attentive when he consumed the sacred Host. This finished the Mass, and the whole procession filed out of the sanctuary in the same order in which it had entered. The service had lasted one hour.

Good Friday is the only day of the year on which Christ is not physically present in St. Mary's Church, and on which the sanctuary lamp is extinguished. It is the traditional custom of Catholics to visit the church on this day in order to venerate the cross. In the city itself this has become a ritual of walking to nine churches and to pay this homage in each parish church with the hope of obtaining a special favor from God. As far as could be learned, about thirty parishioners of St. Mary's made this "pilgrimage" on Good Friday.

After the Mass of the Presanctified, Sister Berthold, the sacristan, came into the sanctuary with the purple pillow and a crucifix. An altar boy carried a small table which he placed in the middle aisle just outside the Communion rail and covered with a white cloth. On this was placed the pillow and on it the crucifix. Two lighted candles stood on the Communion rail. A chair was placed on either side of the table, where two altar boys sat with small white cloths in their hands. Immediately, the people who had not been present for the earlier veneration of the cross came up the aisle, genuflected, and stooped to kiss the cross. An altar boy reached over and wiped the cross after each one. The people put silver coins on the table; and soon Sister Berthold came with a large silver dish to receive these coins.[5]

During the first hour after the Mass forty-four persons venerated the cross, eleven of whom stayed in the church to make the Stations of the Cross privately. Most of them, however, stayed in the church for only five or ten minutes. The flowers and the lighted candles still remained at the altar of the Repository, where a large crucifix, about four feet high, had been placed by an altar boy under the direction of the Sister-sacristan. Most of the worshipers, after kissing the cross in the center aisle and depositing their donation, went to the pews in front of this large crucifix and knelt for a while in prayer. Some of them may have thought that the Blessed Sacrament was still there.

During the next five hours, from nine in the morning until two in the afternoon, our observers noted that 645 persons came into the church to venerate the cross. There were 383 women and 135 children. The men numbered 127, about half of them coming in their working clothes—bus- and truck-drivers, policemen, storekeepers and clerks, while the remaining half were more or less evenly divided between young men of high-school and college age and middle-aged men. Only three of these males made the Stations of the Cross privately as compared to twenty-nine women. Many of the downtown stores, banks, and offices close at noon on Good Friday in honor of the death of Christ. This allows large numbers of Catholics to attend the afternoon services in the various city churches.

St. Mary's Parish does not conduct the traditional "Tre Ore" serv-

5. This money is used exclusively for the decoration and maintenance of the sanctuary.

ices from noon until three. Parishioners who wish to attend this solemn memorial of the Crucifixion go to one of a half-dozen other city churches where it is held. In spite of this drain away from the parish, there were 664 persons present for the Stations of the Cross, conducted by Father Paul from two-thirty to three o'clock. They began to arrive in large numbers at two o'clock, and a steady stream of almost three hundred persons went up the main aisle, where they were able to kiss the crucifix before the services started. The rest of them remained to venerate the cross after the Stations had been made. The whole congregation was quiet and solemn at this time, in noticeable contrast to the pushing at the morning service.

Father Paul read the prayers for each Station at the microphone in the pulpit, while the cross-bearer and two acolytes stood in the main aisle at the appropriate Station. The service was announced by the wooden clapper, and verses of the "Stabat Mater" were sung at alternate stations by nineteen boys and girls from the seventh and eighth grades. These latter were in the choir loft, where they sang without accompaniment of the organ and under the supervision of a Sister. An usher had been selling booklets of prayers for the Way of the Cross, and these were used by 84 per cent of the congregation.

There were 141 men in the church for this service, a percentage larger than usual. There were 318 women and 205 children. The greater proportion of men at this service may be accounted for by several reasons. Many of them were free of employment on the afternoon of Good Friday and probably felt that their time should be utilized for the purpose for which it had been given. On the other hand, this larger percentage of men may be partially explained by the smaller number of women, because many of the female parishioners undoubtedly attended the longer "Tre Ore" service in other churches. The number of school children was much smaller on Good Friday than on the previous Friday afternoons of Lent, when they had been marched over after school by their teachers.

After the services, 67 persons remained to pray for periods of five to ten minutes. Soon newcomers began to arrive for the individual veneration of the cross, and during these four hours between three and seven o'clock the church at no time contained less than 40 people. The sex and age division of the worshipers was as follows: 112 men came into the church, the largest concentration being between five and six o'clock, apparently when they were on their way home from work; of the 413 women, the smallest numbers came between five and seven, the meal period when they are most needed at home; the 116 children were also there in much smaller numbers during the meal-time hours.

At seven o'clock the people began to arrive for the evening services, consisting of the Way of the Cross and a sermon. It had been announced on the previous Sunday that a priest from another city parish would give the sermon. Most likely this was not the main reason why 813 persons crowded into the church, for, as the Pastor remarked, "there is always a good crowd on Good Friday night, no matter who preaches." Only 223 of these persons went up the aisle to venerate the cross, which indicates the probability that the rest had been in the church for that purpose earlier in the day.

The Stations of the Cross were prayed in the usual manner, with Father Dominic leading the prayers in the pulpit and the altar boys proceeding around the church with crucifix and candles. The adult choir of twenty-six sang the verses of the "Stabat Mater." All the teaching Sisters from the convent were present for the service, sitting in their usual pews in the front. All during the day there had been one or more nuns in the church, although at times they were represented only by the Sacristan or her assistant working in the sanctuary.

The Way of the Cross, completed at eight o'clock, was followed by a half-hour sermon in commemoration of Christ's death. The priest, Father Bruno, spoke of the empty cross on the first Good Friday night. To it in the night there came three separate figures of history, Pilate, Judas, and Salome. They represented pride, greed, and sensuality, and each spoke a monologue trying to persuade himself that this dead Jesus could not be the Son of God. "If He really were," said Pilate, "I would have to humble myself, lose status, love everybody, even to these terrible Jews and the black Africans in the Roman Empire." As our observer reported: "At the mention of how it would be necessary for Pilate to love all men, even the 'black Africans,' a number of the congregation turned in their pews to get a better view of the preacher. Even the members of the choir settled a little in order to hear better."

The observance of Good Friday ended about fifteen minutes after the sermon, when the sexton went around closing windows and turning off the lights in the church. The last worshiper left at ten minutes to nine, and the church was closed for the night.

In summary, what can be said of the degree to which St. Mary's parishioners demonstrated their Catholicism on this most sad and solemn day of the year? By actual count, 2,608 persons paid homage to the crucified Christ by venerating the cross. This is an average of

186 per hour during the fourteen hours from seven in the morning until nine at night. If this figure can be accepted without qualification, it represents almost one-half of all the parishioners seven years of age and older. It must be realized, of course, that there is no obligation whatsoever for Catholics to go to church on Good Friday. Hence, this percentage seems to indicate a relatively high degree of active supererogatory spirituality on the part of St. Mary's parishioners. Several qualifications, however, appear to be necessary: (*a*) this figure may include some persons who venerated the cross more than once during the day and some Catholics from other parishes; (*b*) it definitely excludes those parishioners who went to other churches in the city; and (*c*), as the Pastor pointed out, it includes dormant Catho-

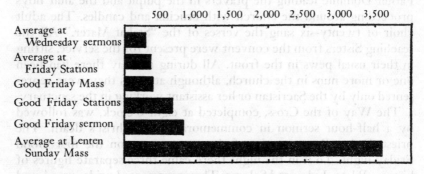

FIG. 51.—Comparison of the numbers who attended various services in St. Mary's Parish during Lent.

lics who come to church once a year—on Good Friday.

In recapitulation of the whole Lenten devotion of St. Mary's parishioners we may make comparisons among the various services of the season. The evening services on Wednesdays and Fridays attracted the smallest numbers. The Mass of the Presanctified had fewer present than the Mass on Holy Thursday, but neither of these approached the average Sunday Mass attendance during Lent. On Good Friday the Stations of the Cross in the afternoon and the sermon at night attracted more people than at any other time during Lent. (Fig. 51).

All of this, of course, falls far short of the ideal situation in which every member of the parish would participate completely in all of the Lenten services. When one hears that "Catholics flock to church" during Holy Week, he can get a realistic picture only if he realizes that there are 5,281 parishioners of seven years of age and older. Of this number, less than half venerated the cross on Good Friday, and about one-sixth listened to the sermon on the night of Our Lord's death.

Our discussion so far has treated mainly the external rituals of Lenten observance by the parishioners. In the Church's scheme for the observance of Lent, however, there are various other traditional and expected patterns of behavior for Catholics. It is a time of sacrifice, of self-denial and mortification. To what extent did the parishioners enter into this penitential spirit by curtailing their gratifications, by "giving up" legitimate pleasures during Lent?

In our modern environment the ancient severity of the Lenten fast and penance has been greatly tempered. The diocesan regulations are read from the pulpit each year on the Sunday before Ash Wednesday, but they admit such a latitude of interpretation that they seem to be observed more in breach than in the practice. "The law of fasting binds under pain of mortal sin all Catholics from their twenty-first birthday until their fifty-ninth birthday." There are, however, some valid excuses which exempt persons from the law. The exempted individuals fall into three categories: "(a) Persons performing severe and exhausting physical or mental labor. (b) The sick, convalescent, persons in delicate health, women in delicate condition, and mothers nursing infants. (c) In general, all persons whose health would be impaired by fasting or whom fasting would render unfit to perform their ordinary occupations."

Briefly, the law of fasting prescribes that only one full meal be taken throughout the day but permits a cup of coffee and piece of bread for breakfast and a light collation in the evening. The fact that so many parishioners were exempt by the law or dispensed by the Pastor influenced the priests to urge the practice of other good works and mortifications. This was the theme of short sermons which accompanied the Bishop's words: "The season of Lent should be one of self-denial and zeal for our sanctification. Therefore, we urge the faithful to practice mortification, almsgiving, and prayer; to abstain from intoxicating beverages, public amusements, the theater, the moving-picture shows, and dances."

To what degree did the parishioners of St. Mary's comply with this advice of the Bishop and the sermons of the priests? The children in the parochial school had been prepared for Lent by the Sisters, and all of them promised to "give up" either candy or dessert after meals. It became popular for the youngsters to say that they wanted to "give up school for Lent." To make the lesson of sacrifice practical, each Sister had in her classroom a small collection box for the foreign missions. The measure of this sacrifice is seen in the amount of $431.28 which was sent to the foreign missions at the end of Lent. On the other hand, the revenue of the cafeteria did not noticeably decrease, the children apparently buying more cakes and ice cream in place of candy.

In an attempt to discover whether the practice of self-denial increased during Lent, we surveyed the various stores, restaurants, bars, and movies immediately after Lent. The candy stores reported that the sale of candies decreased approximately 12 per cent during Lent but that the large volume of pre-Easter sales more than equalized this loss. The sale of salted peanuts rose by about 18 per cent, while that of cakes and pastries fell off almost 20 per cent. Drugstores and groceries reported a decrease of approximately 8 per cent in the sale of "cokes," while ice cream was sold in about the same volume as it was before Lent. Liquor stores, bars, and restaurants had a decrease of about 6 per cent in "hard" drinks but an actual increase of about 8 per cent in the consumption of beer.

The figures upon which these statements are based were obtained only after considerable difficulty because of the reluctance of businessmen to divulge such information. In some instances we met a flat refusal, and in all others we obtained answers only on the promise that they would not be divulged to competitors. It seems reasonable to assume that there is a negative margin of error because of the probable tendency on the part of businessmen to conceal any decline in their volume of sales. When we realize that the actual parishioners of St. Mary's Church constitute approximately one-third of the white population of Riverside, we must surmise that their self-denial in food and drink was quite remarkable. If we assume that non-Catholics and dormant Catholics were in no way responsible for the decrease in sales, we may estimate that the parishioners during Lent ate 36 per cent less candy and 60 per cent less cake and pastry and drank 24 per cent less "cokes" and 18 per cent less "hard" liquor than they did before and after Lent.[6]

The two moving-picture shows in Riverside have a combined weekly attendance of about 10,500 patrons during the winter season. The manager of the Strand, which is the larger of the two houses and the nearest to the church, claimed that there was no decrease in admissions during Lent, except in Holy Week, when it fell off by almost 15

6. This assumption cannot be taken too seriously in a city where many non-Catholics still observe the spirit of mortification based on supernatural motives.

per cent. He is a Catholic and pointed out that the children "pack the house" on Sunday afternoons and for the first show on Friday nights. The nine o'clock showing on Friday nights includes large numbers of people who have just come from the Way of the Cross at St. Mary's. The manager of the Tivoli, eight blocks from the church, said that the attendance dropped about 10 per cent during the first weeks of Lent and almost 50 per cent in Holy Week.

As far as could be discovered, the pictures shown at the Strand were more recent and of better quality generally than those at the Tivoli. Both are neighborhood show houses, and neither of them has first-run pictures. It is quite possible that persons who had resolved to go to the movies only once a week during Lent, instead of twice, decided to choose the better shows at the Strand. As far as the religious composition of Riverside is concerned, there are more Catholics concentrated in the neighborhood of the Strand than of the Tivoli. There were roughly four hundred fewer movie-goers per week during Lent in Riverside, but these figures do not take into account those who may patronize shows in other parts of the city, nor can they be said to apply exclusively to Catholics of the community.

In conclusion, it must be emphasized that the spirit of Lent, which the Bishop called the "spirit of self-denial," is an internal psychological and moral pattern. The description of Lenten observances by the parishioners cannot reach directly this internal state of soul. In so far as external manifestations can be a measurement of spiritual values, however, the parish of St. Mary's may be judged by the descriptions and statistics provided here. Whether or not St. Mary's parish is above the average in the spirit of Lent could be ascertained only by a comparison with other Catholic parishes in a similar urban environment.

Chapter Fifteen

Devotion to Our Lady

Any parish which is dedicated to Mary, the Mother of God, may be expected to conduct special services in her honor at various times in the liturgical year. St. Mary's Parish, for the last ten years, had been holding weekly Novena services in honor of Our Sorrowful Mother. In 1938 a great deal of publicity was given to this Novena in national magazines and the press in general. The Pastor remarks that "some of the parishioners said it would be a good thing if we could have the Novena here; and I thought so too because this is Our Lady's church. So I got in touch with them in Chicago, and they sent a lot of literature, statistics, and publicity spreads.

"I invited one of their Fathers to come down here and open the Novena. He was a big-timer all right but didn't do anything we couldn't have done. He came by plane on a Saturday, talked at all the Masses on Sunday, and then flew back. Then he flew down again on Thursday night and gave the Novena services three times the next day, at eight in the morning, three in the afternoon, and seven-thirty at night. The church was jammed each time. Thousands of people came from all over. Policemen had to be assigned to handle the traffic out in front of the church. The crowds kept up for nine weeks to finish the Novena, and then began to drop off. If they don't get the favor they ask within nine weeks, they just quit coming. You have to produce supernatural results for Novena crowds.

"The Chicago people wanted me to buy a thousand Novena booklets every week, but after a while I cut that down to five hundred; and then I told them to cancel my order completely. The crowds were getting smaller all the time. I was giving the booklets away; and the collection wasn't even enough to pay for them all. After two years I stopped the afternoon service, and after three more years I cut

out the morning service.[1] For the first few years we gave a short sermon at every service, but then we stopped that too. I don't give the
Novena myself any more. Maybe if my assistants would give a sermon
we could get more people."

Throughout the year of the survey the Friday-night Novenas had
an average attendance of a little over fifty-one persons. These were all
parishioners. The thousands in attendance in earlier years undoubtedly included many hundreds of people from other parishes. Still the
contrast between the earlier crowds and the present small group requires some explanation. Father Dominic is of the opinion that "Novenas are like fads and novelties. There's a type of Catholics you
might call 'Novena fans.' Of course, hard work, publicity, and promotion are necessary to bring in the crowds. But even then, after the
first nine weeks, you need a different twist, or angle. Get a new
preacher. Get a different saint. Use different prayers and new hymns.
The real Novena fans drift from one church to another in the city."

As far as we could discover, there are relatively few "Novena fans"
of this type in St. Mary's Parish who travel around the city attending
Novenas in various churches. The people who attend the weekly
Novena services at St. Mary's Church are exclusively members of the
parish and are in almost every instance the same individuals who
attend daily Mass during the week. Thus, just as we may use daily
Mass attendance as a criterion for a high degree of religious observance, so also may we use attendance at the Novena services. From
these two external criteria we may judge that this small group of
people constitutes the inner "core" of lay spirituality in the parish.

Of course, there was some shifting in the composition of this group.
A few came only for nine Fridays. Others who "broke" their Novena
by missing one service attended more frequently. A few came inter-
mittently. But the great majority were there practically every Friday
in the year when services were held. The largest number ever to attend was sixty-six, and the smallest number was thirty-one on September 3, when there was a heavy downpour of rain. The average was
51.5 on the forty-four Fridays. There was no Novena service on the
following eight occasions: the four Fridays of March, the first because of a torrential rain, the second and third were included in the
missions, the fourth was Good Friday; the other four Fridays were
September 17, when the Forty Hours' Devotion was held; October 1,

1. The bulletin board in the front vestibule of the parish church still adver-
tises "Novena Services Friday Morning after Mass."

which was part of the Holy Hour triduum; and Christmas Eve and
New Year's Eve, when confessions were heard.

Figure 52 shows the average attendance for each month, with the
proportions of women in each month. The children accounted for
less than 5 per cent of the attendance and are not shown on the graph.
The fluctuations in the average attendance at the Novena services do
not follow the usual pattern of St. Mary's Church devotions according
to which the summer months are the lowest and the winter months
are the highest. Actually, the months from September to December

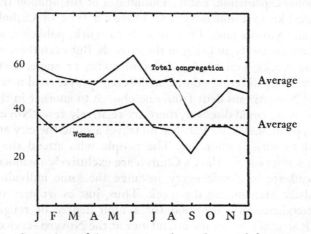

FIG. 52.—Comparison of the average total attendance and the average women's
attendance at the Friday-night Novena services for each month (except March, when
the Novena was not conducted).

show a consistently lower attendance than the other months of the
year. May, the month of Mary, had a higher than average attendance,
while October, the month of the Rosary, had the second lowest attendance of the year. June was the month with the highest number,
when an average of 62.2 persons attended. The fact that June is the
month dedicated to the Sacred Heart, and Friday is particularly dedicated to the devotion of the Sacred Heart, may be a partial influence
on the greater numbers who came to the Novena during that month.

The percentage distribution of the attendance at Novena services
shows that female parishioners constitute the bulk (66.33) of those
at the services. Men were 29.61 per cent and children 4.06 per cent.
This is generally in agreement with the observation of attendance at
all church functions. The children of the parish come to Friday-night
services in negligible numbers; there were thirteen occasions when

no children were present. Besides the lack of interest which they show in this type of church service, the fact that Friday night is the children's movie night in the neighborhood helps to account for their poor attendance. Frequently only one altar boy came, and on several occasions none appeared.

Friday night is also "date night" among the younger persons of the parish. The girls of high-school age particularly are allowed by their families to have one date a week, and this is preferably on Friday night, because there is no school or obligatory Mass on the following day. During the winter months some of the men of the parish use the gymnasium for "workouts" and for basketball practice. Furthermore, the Riverside Bowling League, some of the teams of which are composed of St. Mary's men, has its regular matches on Friday nights. All these factors are in the nature of "excuses," which may partially explain why Friday night is a poorly chosen night for church services. They are not, however, adequate factors to account for the poor attendance at the Novena. Other churches in the city hold successful Novenas on Friday nights, and in the early history of the Novena at St. Mary's the services were always crowded.

On two occasions, December 17 and January 21, the Parents Club held lotto parties in the school auditorium, but this did not seem to curtail the attendance at the Novena service. On the first date 66 attended the Novena and on the second date 51. The parties did not start until after the end of the Novena service; hence there was no interference from the point of time. But it does appear slightly incongruous that 521 persons were attracted to the games of chance on the first occasion, and 305 on the second. In other words, social gatherings in the school hall are seven times more attractive to parishioners than this religious service in the church.

The first Friday in November provided a test of the parishioners' interest in the Novena to Our Lady. This date marked the tenth anniversary of this weekly service in St. Mary's Parish. On the previous Sunday, the Feast of Christ the King, the following announcement was made at all the Masses: "This coming Friday is the tenth anniversary of the Novena of Our Lady of Sorrows in this parish. We invite you all to come and spend thirty minutes with the Mother of Christ on Friday night." On that Sunday 3,408 persons attended Mass and heard this invitation. The response on Friday night was made by sixteen men, thirty-three women, and three altar boys, almost the identical average group of regulars who came throughout the year.

It must be remembered that the statistics for the Novena services include the organist and sexton, who are obliged to be present, the two faithful ushers Moise and Bruns, two or three high-school girls who constitute the choir on these occasions, and one or two nuns. These latter "take turns" coming over to the church for this service, and they do it on a voluntary basis, since their regular spiritual duties preformed in the convent consume several hours every day.

If we search further for reasons why the Friday Novena to Our Lady is not popular in a parish dedicated to her, we may find internal evidence in the service itself. While no opinion poll was made among parishioners, the thought was expressed several times that the Novena is "too sad and solemn." It is indeed true that Our Sorrowful Mother is the theme and object of this Novena, which consists of the "*Via Matris*, six prayers culled from the ancient Servite Manual, two hymns to Our Blessed Mother, the 'Memorare,' and Benediction of the Most Blessed Sacrament." To these has been added a "blessing of the sick."

The service starts promptly at seven-thirty, when the priest, accompanied by an altar boy, comes out of the sacristy and kneels briefly at the lowest altar step. He then ascends the pulpit and while kneeling there speaks into the microphone the six official prayers of the Novena. The congregation also says the first prayer aloud, which is addressed to the "most blessed and afflicted Virgin, Queen of Martyrs," and in the middle of this prayer a pause is made so that each may silently make his particular request or ask a special favor of the Blessed Mother. The Hail Mary and the ejaculation, "Virgin Most Sorrowful, pray for us," are then repeated seven times. All then say together the prayer for a happy death.

The third prayer is a reconstruction of the Hail Mary, traditionally attributed to St. Bonaventure: "Hail Mary, full of sorrows, the Crucified is with thee; tearful art thou amongst women, and tearful is the fruit of thy womb, Jesus. Holy Mary, mother of the Crucified, give tears to us, crucifiers of thy Son, now and at the hour of our death. Amen." A prayer is then recited for sick relatives and friends and another prayer for "our beloved dead," each of these including a pause during which sick and dead persons' names might be recalled to mind. The sixth prayer is an act of consecration to Our Sorrowful Mother.

The whole congregation then stands to sing the hymn "Come, Holy Ghost," and kneels to say in unison a specially worded act of contrition. Meanwhile three altar boys, a cross-bearer and two acolytes, come out of the sanctuary and take their places in front of the first Station of the *Via Matris*. The "Way of the Sorrowful Mother" consists of seven Stations attached to the walls of the church, four on the Epistle side and three on the Gospel side.[2] These seven Stations are prints in color depicting the seven swords or sorrows of the Blessed Mother: (1) the prophecy of Simeon, (2) the flight into Egypt, (3) the loss of Jesus in the Temple, (4) the meeting by Mary of Jesus on the way to Calvary, (5) the death of Jesus on the Cross, (6) the receiving by Mary of the dead body of Jesus in her arms, and (7) the placing of Jesus in the tomb.

As the altar boy stops in front of each Station, the people stand and the priest slowly reads the appropriate meditation; then the congregation kneels to read together the appropriate prayer from the booklet. Finally, a Hail Mary and the ejaculation are recited, and the altar boys go on to the next Station. After the Stations have been completed and while the priest prepares for Benediction, the choir and congregation sing one of the twenty-one Marian hymns which appear in the Novena booklet. The most popular hymn and the one most frequently sung is "Mother Dear, O Pray for Me." Benediction is then celebrated in the usual manner, with the exception that the "Memorare" is recited after the hymn "O Salutaris Hostia."

It may be surmised that the whole sorrowful and penitential theme of the *Via Matris* is incongruous with the secular ethos of the American community. All seven Stations depict the most heart-rending experiences that occurred between the Mother and her Divine Son. Explicitly in the prayers these sorrows are shown to be the result of mankind's sins. To atone for them and to demonstrate their affection for Mary and Christ, the people must do penance. The very notion, much less the practice, of penitential sorrow seems to be almost foreign to our secular, materialistic, urban culture.

It seems reasonable to assume that, in so far as the spirit of penance and sorrow for sins has been accepted in the value system of the Catholics in the Riverside community, it has been associated only with the Lenten season. Even during Lent the actual expression of this penitential spirit has been narrowed down to one day: Good Friday. The public Stations of the Cross were not well attended on the Fridays of Lent. Making the Way of the Cross individually in the church was such a rarity that it was not observed more than twenty

2. Unlike the statuary which marks the fourteen Stations of the Cross, the *Via Matris* has small 12 × 12 color prints. These Stations must be canonically erected before the Novena can be officially conducted in any church.

times outside of Lent. During Lent five or six women made the Stations daily, and on Good Friday sixty-three persons were counted performing this devotion in private.

Of course, the same argument cannot be employed for the more joyful expressions of the parishioners' love of Mary. While the Novena in honor of the Mother of Sorrows was the principal continuous Marian devotion in the parish, there were other instances of this devotion. May is traditionally the month of Mary, and in this parish the school children attended Mass every day except Saturday. Special devotions to Our Lady consisted of the recitation of the Rosary and the Litany of Our Lady and Benediction of the Blessed Sacrament after the seven forty-five Mass. As a matter of fact, the Sisters have the children recite the Rosary during the Mass whenever the children attend Mass on weekdays during the year. The average attendance at the seven forty-five weekday Mass during May was 37 per cent higher than the average for the year.[3]

On the last Sunday in April the announcement was made at all Masses concerning these weekday devotions to the Blessed Mother, and the people were invited to come to church in her honor. They were asked also to listen to the "Rosary Broadcast" at six-thirty each evening over a local radio station and to recite their Rosary in company with the broadcasters. In a poll on radio-listening taken in the parish, 30.5 per cent of the families questioned said that this broadcast of the Rosary was one of their "favorite programs."

The first Sunday of May was chosen by the Bishop for the reading of a letter partially concerned with the Blessed Mother. It was the second annual appeal for funds toward the building of the national shrine in honor of the Immaculate Conception at Washington. "We regard it as a fitting testimonial of our love and devotion to the Immaculate Mother of our Divine Savior, who has been designated by His Holiness, Pope Pius IX, as the Patroness of the United States of America." The collection of funds was announced for the following Sunday, Mother's Day. The Bishop's letter continued: "As we venerate our earthly mothers and remember them affectionately on Mother's Day, we will also be mindful in loving gratitude of our heavenly Mother and of the tender solicitude with which she watches over us. What expression would be more appropriate than on Mother's Day to make a generous contribution toward the erection of our

3. Average attendance at this Mass was 119.6 in April, 155.08 in May, and 121.32 in June.

national shrine as the symbol of our confidence and a perpetual memorial of our faith and loyalty. . . . Let us endeavor to make this year's contribution even larger than last year's as a more worthy expression of our veneration and gratitude for many favors received through her intercession. *At least $1.00 per wage-earner or family would seem commendable.*"[4]

Mother's Day, the second Sunday in May, gave an opportunity for the priests to speak at all the Masses on devotion to the Mother of God. "On this day," said Father Urban, "let us turn our thoughts toward Mary, give her our love and attention, but never forgetting our own earthly mothers. Ask Mary to help your mother; if she is living, to help her live close to God; if she is dead, to bring her out of purgatory and to heaven as soon as possible. . . . Today the country and the world need spiritual help from Mary. Start your prayers today to Our Lady of Fatima, and perhaps, as she promised, Russia will be converted."

The most elaborate and best-attended parish function in honor of the Blessed Mother was the public Sodality "crowning" on Sunday, May 23. This affair started at four o'clock in the afternoon with a procession from the school auditorium. The Children of Mary, dressed in white and wearing white veils, led the procession, followed by fifteen members of the Sodality dressed in white dresses and skullcaps—"beanies." The children from the first to fifth grades also took part, the girls coming in before the boys. The members of the "court" of Mary were twelve girls in blue formal evening gowns, carrying bouquets of blue cornflowers and chrysanthemums. A small girl carried a crown of flowers on a white satin pillow. The last to enter the church was Catherine Doermer, the prefect of the Children of Mary.[5]

Crowds of people lined the sidewalk and the side aisles of the church while this procession passed. More than one thousand persons were in attendance, many of them the mothers of children in the procession. All the girls carried bouquets which they finally heaped around the statue of the Blessed Mother. When the members of the court had entered the sanctuary, they took seats arranged before the altar, six on each side with the prefect in the middle. The Pastor came

4. The italics were in the letter itself. The collection on the following Sunday amounted to $258.00. There are 1,806 families in the parish (average contribution $0.14). There are 2,482 wage-earners in the parish (average contribution $0.10).

5. She is now in the convent, studying to be a teaching Sister.

from the sacristy to the altar steps, where he led the Litany of the Blessed Mother. The congregation then sang the hymn "On This Day."

Father Urban's sermon lasted twenty-five minutes. In it he proclaimed Mary the Queen of the whole human race and showed that not only the Catholic countries but even the United States have accepted her as a Royal Person. "The world has seen the crowning of many queens, but never of one who rules over so universal a kingdom as the Blessed Mother. We honor Mary every day, but on this day we gather to do special homage to her. . . . I am happy to see the large number at this service, but do not let this be the end of your May devotion. Come to Mass and Communion to honor Mary for the rest of the month of May." He then gave a strong warning concerning the "state of the world," the problem of war and peace, and the need for heaven's assistance in our distress.

After the sermon, the movable microphone was brought over to the prefect, who read the Act of Consecration. All the maids in the court then gathered around the statue of the Blessed Mother, which had been set up on an improvised altar in the middle aisle. They and the rest of the congregation knelt while singing the hymn "Bring Flowers of the Rarest." The prefect stood before the statue with a wreath of flowers in her hands, and at the words "We crown Thee" she placed the wreath on the head of the statue. After this ceremony a procession started around the church and back to the statue, where each girl deposited her flowers and wreath as she passed. A large mound of flowers accumulated at the foot of the statue and along the altar rail. The children were supposed to return to their pews and wait until the end. But many of the mothers gathered up their children as soon as the flowers had been relinquished and left the church. The Pastor announced over the loud-speaker that the Holy Hour would begin immediately, but more than three-quarters of the people departed before the next service began.[6]

The Feast of the Assumption provided another opportunity for pulpit instruction concerning the Mother of God. At the first two Masses, celebrated by Father Paul, no sermon was delivered. At the other Masses the celebrants gave an account of the traditional Catholic belief that the body of Mary after her death was taken intact into heaven. The congregation listened carefully to the description of the death and burial of Mary, of the opening of the tomb to satisfy the

6. This is similar to the exodus before the Novena service on Friday nights in Lent (see chap. 14, pp. 174–75).

curiosity of St. Thomas, and of the discovery of fresh flowers in the place where she had lain. Each preacher made the point of Mary's great favor with God in heaven and the fact of her love and willingness to assist human beings.

There was no other celebration or service to mark the Feast of the Assumption. Later in the year, the month of October is dedicated to the devotion of Our Lady in her holy Rosary. At all the Masses on the last Sunday in September it was announced that devotions to Our Lady of the Rosary would be held each weekday at the seven forty-five Mass. These were the same as in May: the group recitation of the Rosary, the Litany of the Blessed Virgin led by the priest, and Benediction of the Blessed Sacrament after Mass. The average attendance at this weekday Mass during October was 174, the highest of the whole year. In September it was 119, and in November only 72.5. The October attendance was 54.21 per cent higher than the average for this Mass throughout the whole year.

On the first Sunday in October the Bishop's letter was read at all the Masses. In it he stressed the importance of prayer to the Mother of God, particularly through the use of her Rosary. The Pastor chose this day to speak at all the Masses concerning the drive for the new convent building. After this speech and the reading of the letter, he told the people about morning devotions. "Now, I know that some can't make it; but some don't have to go to work, and they can come. How edifying it is to see the children, trained in the school, coming by themselves every morning. How much more edifying it would be to see the mothers and fathers who don't have to work come with them. Friends, say the Rosary every day. Our Mother of Fatima has promised that Russia will be converted, and there will be peace in the world. Let us prolong the peace and not let them break it up. That's possible, you know. Only prayer can save the world—and, anyhow, don't you need the assistance of the Blessed Mother yourself? I know I do. Never tire of repeating 'Holy Mary, Mother of God, pray for us sinners.' Don't let a single day go by without those prayers. God bless you."

The full extent of the external devotion to the Blessed Mother in St. Mary's Parish cannot be understood without a consideration of the specific organizations which are dedicated to her service. The Children of Mary, the Sodality of the Blessed Mother, and the Blessed Virgin's League, all female groups, will be studied in a later volume. Their activities are varied, both spiritual and material, and some of them occur outside the actual parochial center, the church.

Chapter Sixteen

The Word of God

For many members of St. Mary's Parish the only contact they had with either the priests or the teaching of the Church occurred at the sermon time in Sunday Masses. The pulpit is used for an important function in the operation of the parish. It is the principal means of public communication whereby the priests announce parochial activities, invite participation by the faithful, and interpret the teachings of the Catholic Church and the Sacred Scriptures.

How was the function of the pulpit carried out in St. Mary's Church? In order to answer this question, we took notes on all utterances that were made during the course of the year. Some of these are included in other sections of this book, as in the mission preaching and the Lenten sermons. This section contains an account of the Sunday Masses only and attempts to analyze the content of the talks and sermons delivered at 318 Masses on fifty-three Sundays.

Letters from the Bishop of the diocese were read on twenty-two of these fifty-three Sundays. Sometimes the letter was so long that there was no time for a sermon; at other times a short sermon or some words of explanation were given by the priest. The reading of the Bishop's letter was omitted at some of the Masses at which it should have been read. These letters were read 112 times instead of 132 times, but they were at least summarized or commented upon. For purposes of study these episcopal letters fall into two neat divisions: those which asked for financial contributions and those which did not. The following is a list of causes for which appeals were made:

1. Negro and Indian Missions (Lenten regulations on same Sunday)
2. European Relief Fund
3. Support of Diocesan Seminary
4. National Shrine of Immaculate Conception
5. Peter's Pence (and Local College Drive)
6. Overseas Aid
7. Diocesan Bureau for Displaced Persons
8. Catholic Charities and Mission Fund

9. Propagation of the Faith
10. Catholic University of America

11. Anniversary of Diocesan Seminary

Thus, the Bishop "asked for money" eleven times during the year, but an analysis of these appeals suggests two necessary remarks. In the first place, every episcopal letter contained spiritual exhortations of a lofty nature. The Bishop explained the particular need, then urged the highest motivations for answering the need, and finally appealed for prayers and a generous donation. Second, all these requests for money from the parishioners were directed toward the social and moral improvement of human beings, and none was for the "selfish and individual profit of the clergy." The Bishop and priests were acting in their official capacity as dispensers of Christian alms, a function which the clergy has fulfilled in Christian society from apostolic times.

With the exception of the monument in honor of the Immaculate Conception at Washington, D.C., the Bishop's appeals fall into three general categories: helping persons in distress, extending the missionary activities of the Church, and supporting Catholic education. (a) In the first group there were three requests for the destitute people of Europe and only one for the work of the local organized Catholic charities. Thus the generous hand of St. Mary's parishioners was extended to suffering humanity beyond the parish and even beyond the diocese. (b) The duty of helping to bring the true faith to all peoples was followed in the collection for the Society for the Propagation of the Faith, the annual Peter's Pence, and for the Negro and Indian missions. In the latter appeal the Bishop took occasion to urge the earnest practice of interracial love and justice. (c) For educational work there were two seminary appeals, the second occasioned by the twenty-fifth anniversary of the diocesan seminary. Both mentioned the need for more vocations and for the support of persons in religious training. There was an appeal also on behalf of a local Catholic college drive, and the annual collection for the Catholic University of America. The following is a list of the other episcopal letters:

1. The Diocesan Weekly
2. Diocesan Pilgrimage to Rome
3. Catholic Literature
4. Prayers for Peace
5. Catholic Boy Scouts
6. Letter from Pope to Bishop and Diocese
7. Letter on four topics: (a) the National Council of Catholic Women; (b) Local Safety Campaign; (c) Catholic Education; (d) the Catholic Home
8. Labor Day Letter
9. Devotion to the Rosary
10. Catholic Education
11. The Legion of Decency

These remaining eleven letters from the Bishop contained instructions and exhortations of a moral and social nature. Two of them dealt with the important question of wholesome literature as published by the Catholic press. A third treated another type of recreation: the influence of the movies and the pledge of the Legion of Decency. Three might be placed in the general category of educational advice, praising and encouraging: the Boy Scout movement, the work of the Council of Catholic Women, and the Catholic system of parochial schools and colleges.

While all the episcopal letters were written on a high spiritual level, only two were exclusively concerned with the spiritual: the letter asking for prayers for universal peace and that which encouraged the devotion to the Blessed Mother by the recitation of the Rosary. Finally, the Labor Day letter exhibited the progressive social thinking of the Bishop, wherein he made a plea for social justice to all groups in the American economy. This communication is even more notable when read in the conservative social climate prevalent in the southern community of Riverside.

There were three letters in which the relationship between the Holy Father and the local parishioners was discussed. The Peter's Pence collection has already been mentioned. The announcement of a pilgrimage to Rome, to be led by the Bishop himself, explained the importance of filial devotion to the Holy See and invited the parishioners to make the proposed journey. A letter from the Holy Father to the Bishop and people of the diocese gave His Holiness' blessing to them and expressed deep thanks for the way in which they had responded to his appeals for prayers and funds.

At this point it may be well to discuss briefly the oft-heard complaint among churchgoers to the effect that "the priest talks money too much." It was said that in other years the parishioners of St. Mary's sometimes made this complaint about their Pastor, Father Urban. This objection has now practically died down in the face of the facts. What really are the facts?

Besides the eleven appeals for funds made at the order of the Bishop and through his letters, the following is a rough summary of the year's "money talk" at St. Mary's Church. On the second Sunday in January the Pastor gave a sermon on the "state of the parish" at all the Masses. This was primarily a spiritual report about the attendance at Mass and the sacraments, family life, and parochial education, but it did contain a brief financial statement pointing out that per capita contributions were falling off. During May the announcements contained a request for donations to a new bell system as a memorial to the dead of the parish. No sermons were preached on the subject. Finally, in October, the Pastor took the pulpit for all Masses on two successive Sundays and preached about the proposed new convent for the Sisters, who had been working for over seventy years in the parish. On three other Sundays he preached at his own Mass on this topic.

A building the size of a new convent is the sort of project that a parish may endeavor once in twenty years. Besides the relatively small bell memorial for the dead of the parish, this is all that the Pastor asked for during the year for the parish. By any standard of comparison, these financial appeals must be considered very modest and reasonable.

On two occasions, however, the Pastor asked the parishioners to hear the needy pleas of Catholic missionaries. On one Sunday in April, Father Urban invited the Brooklyn-born bishop of a Central American diocese to speak at all the Masses on behalf of his missions. On the third Sunday of January he allowed a missionary priest from rural Tennessee to ask the congregation at all the Masses for financial aid. These requests, like those of the espiscopal letters, offered opportunities for the expression of the virtues of generosity and almsgiving which are supposed to be characteristic of Christ's followers.

There is still another type of "money talk" which is really an advertisement and a stimulus rather than an effort to collect funds. This includes the various kinds of civic drives for which the churches of the city are used as sounding boards. St. Mary's Church, like other city churches, usually co-operates with community leaders who ask that a brief announcement be made about the Community Chest, Red Cross, tuberculosis, cancer, heart disease, and other campaigns. The Pastor feels that these numerous drives are multiplying too rapidly, but he always complies graciously by giving them brief notice in the Sunday announcements.

The Sunday sermons may be placed in a general category separate from the reading of the Bishop's letters, even though both sermon and letter were sometimes delivered on the same Sunday. Figure 53 gives the comparative numbers of the Masses celebrated and the sermons delivered by the various priests. There were 318 Masses but only 168 sermons on the fifty-three Sundays.

There were twenty-two Masses at which both sermon and letter were given, and eighty-four Masses at which only the episcopal letter was read. Thus, there were sixty-six Sunday Masses during the year when no instruction or preaching was given to the people. This is equivalent to all the Masses on eleven Sundays. From a negative point of view this may be called the parish's degree of failure in the full utilization of the pulpit. The Pastor has the best record in this regard, for he celebrated only two Masses at which either he or some other priest did not use the pulpit. In explanation it may be said that there are excuses for this failure: the extremely hot weather at the late Masses in the summer months and the occasional curtailment of the time for the Mass because of delay from the previous Mass. When these qualifications are made, the priests of St. Mary's have a good record of conscientious service in this regard.

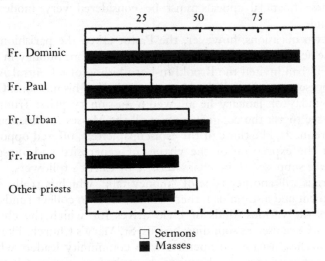

Fig. 53.—Distribution of the 318 Masses celebrated and the 168 sermons delivered on the Sundays of the year.

Figure 54 shows the different categories into which the use of the pulpit at St. Mary's Church may be divided.

The general objective of preaching in the Catholic parish may be said to be twofold: (*a*) to increase the knowledge and belief and (*b*) to improve the moral behavior of the parishioners. These two aspects are sometimes indistinguishable except in the abstract. They are both necessary and may be said to be mutually co-ordinated. The person who "believes" Catholicism but does not practice it is as much a moral contradiction as the person who practices the externals of Catholicism but disclaims belief. The sermons and instructions delivered from the pulpit of St. Mary's tend to weave both aspects of Catholicism together, and in the following subdivisions of "pulpit topics" this fact must be kept in mind.

From the point of view of the listener and recorder it was frequently difficult to discern the "leading idea" in the sermons. So far as we know, only on few occasions did the Sunday preacher have a prepared manuscript of his sermon. But even in these cases we did not ask for a copy of it. We were interested in what the congregation

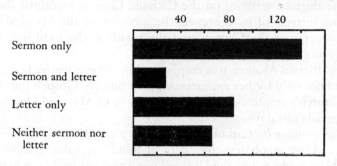

Fig. 54.—The number of times in which the pulpit was used variously at the 318 Sunday Masses.

TABLE 17

	Number of Sermons	Percentage of Total
A. Doctrinal (mainly informative)		
a) God	31	18.45
b) The Church	13	7.74
c) The Blessed Mother	16	9.52
B. Hortatory (mainly persuasive)		
a) Catholic beliefs	30	17.86
b) Behavior	35	20.83
c) Appeals	43	25.60
Total	168	100.00

heard rather than what the preacher intended to say. Perhaps the lack of careful preparation on the part of the priests made it difficult for our observers to summarize or outline the sermons. Most of the sermons showed a lack of unity and cohesion, touching on three or four main concepts and mixing together both doctrine and admonition.

Table 17 presents an outline based upon the main emphases in the year's sermons, but it is not meant to suggest that the sermons were exclusively on the topics mentioned.

God and His relations to human beings is the general subject of every Catholic sermon, even of those which specifically treat other topics. The majority of the sermons at St. Mary's in this category were on the Divinity of Christ, especially of His miraculous power as portrayed in the Sunday Gospels. The mystery of the Blessed Trinity, the Holy Spirit, and the fact of God's presence on earth were spoken of in the remaining discourses.

The thirteen sermons on the Catholic Church explained the continuous miracle of its existence, the meaning of the Mystical Body, the precepts of the Church, and the parish as the local unit of the parent-organization.

The Blessed Mother was emphasized in sixteen instructions, occasioned not only by her appearance in the Sunday Gospels but also by the Church's emphasis on her in the months of May and October and on special feast days.

The sermons on Catholic beliefs form a category of miscellaneous topics. They emphasize the "state of mind" or value system which Catholics ought to have and insisted upon supernatural faith in prayer, revelation, religion, and spiritual attitudes toward the whole economy of salvation as exhibited in the practices of the Church of Christ.

The various facets of Christian behavior were the main topics of thirty-five pulpit instructions and ranged from the virtues of sacrifice, chastity, humility, and love to the practical advantages of Catholic literature, Catholic education, and good example in the avoidance of sin and temptation.

Finally, there were forty-three sermons devoted mainly to appeals for the generous co-operation of parishioners in the physical and corporal works of charity. They asked for assistance in building a decent dwelling for the Sisters, in extending a generous hand to European war sufferers, and in helping to expand the foreign and domestic missionary activity of the Church.

In summary, it appears that the 168 sermons delivered in St. Mary's Church provide a tremendous amount of relatively unorganized information and advice for the people of the parish. The lay person who has no other source of instruction would learn a great deal about the teachings of the Catholic Church if he listened attentively to all sermons delivered during the course of a year. Actually, however, no lay person ever hears all these sermons. Since he attends one Mass on each Sunday, he would be fortunate if he heard 30 per cent of them.

Let us see what this means in terms of "listening time." Parishioners sometimes complained about the length of sermons preached by the

Pastor at Sunday Mass and preferred to hear Father Dominic, because he was "short and snappy." Table 18 gives the average length of time, in minutes and seconds, of the Mass and sermon by the various priests.

Since the average duration of the Sunday Mass is forty-six minutes and forty-two seconds, the lay person who attended only Sunday Mass spent about forty-one hours in church during the year. On the assumption that he heard a sermon every time he went to Sunday Mass, which is not likely, he received approximately twelve hours and thirty minutes of instruction in the Catholic faith during the course of the year. We have estimated that an average of 3,465 persons seven years and older attend Sunday Mass alone without going to other services. Unless these individuals have other sources of instruction, as Catholic books and periodicals, outside lectures and schooling

TABLE 18

Priest	Number of Sermons	Average Length of Mass	Average Length of Sermon
Fr. Urban	45	51:48	18:32
Fr. Dominic	23	42:45	12:28
Fr. Paul	28	46:42	11:49
Fr. Bruno	24	47:36	13:20
Guest priests	48	44:35	12:09
Total	168	46:42	13:48

in religion, they are certainly failing to receive the Word of God to the extent to which they need it.

This does not mean that the Pastor or the Church is failing them. The exigencies of time on a Sunday morning in an urban parish make it imperative that the Mass be completed within an hour. The distribution of Holy Communion, even when there is an assistant priest, is time-consuming. The exodus of hundreds of people from one Mass and the entrance of the new congregation for the next Mass must also be taken into consideration. This is noted on numerous Sundays when the nine o'clock Mass is delayed because of the "lengthy" sermons of the Pastor at the previous Mass; yet he averages less than nineteen minutes in his sermons. Under the present arrangement of hourly Masses on Sunday mornings there simply is not sufficient time for longer instructions.

Since the parishioners do not have previous knowledge of which priest is to celebrate Mass, they have no definite way of knowing when their favorite preacher will speak. In this regard, however, there is a rough pattern, since the Pastor usually says the eight o'clock Mass, a visiting priest the children's Mass, while the two curates alternate in celebrating the two earliest and the two late Masses. On the other hand, if a lay person wishes to hear an instruction every Sunday (or avoid one), which Mass should he try to attend? Figure 55 is an attempt to answer this question.

From the actual statistics of Sunday Mass attendance during the year it is seen that the children's Mass and the last Mass are almost

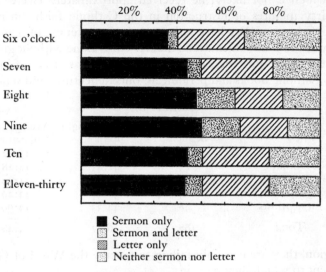

■ Sermon only
▤ Sermon and letter
▨ Letter only
▦ Neither sermon nor letter

FIG. 55.—Percentage distribution of the various uses of the pulpit at the six Sunday Masses.

invariably the most crowded. From the data in Figure 55 it is difficult to judge whether the attendance at these two Masses has any causal relation to preaching. Opinion among the parishioners indicates that they avoid the eight o'clock Mass because the Pastor is "so slow and talks so long" and the ten o'clock Mass because it is often a High Mass. Thus the relation between preaching and attendance is still not defined.

The quality of preaching in St. Mary's Church cannot be understood from a mere description or grouping of all the topics given during the year. Space does not allow a reproduction of even one full sermon, but a faithful transcription of some excerpts may be helpful. The following is an excerpt from Father Urban's sermon on the Feast of Christ the King, the last Sunday in October. It is spoken with a slight accent, with very little inflection, but with intense sincerity.

"In the name of the Father, and of the Son, and of the Holy Ghost, Amen. My dearly beloved in Christ: today is our opportunity to re-dedicate ourselves to the King of Kings, to Jesus Christ, Our Lord, King of the Universe. Why the Feast of the Kingship of Christ? It is not long ago since this feast was instituted, when people were driving their own king from his throne. Thinking at first that men could be looked up to and followed entirely, but finally realizing that after all they are only human and weak creatures. To realize that only One can lead us to final eternal happiness, One who can rule the world in justice, in holiness and in mercy, and guarantee that peace to the world which the world cannot give of itself and for which mankind yearns—and that is the King of Kings, Our Lord Jesus Christ.

"The kingdom of the world belongs to Him. He was born of the family of King David, and, being the Son of God, the Second Person of the Blessed Trinity, He is the King of the Universe. He made this world and everything in it, and He has a special right to the title 'King.' He redeemed every human being by paying the most sublime, the most expensive, price—His Precious Blood. Unless we adopt, un-less we adhere to this King, to Christ, the King of Kings, the world cannot hope for any permanent peace.

"Without Christ there is no justice, and the world can only end in war. If the world could only learn that once and for all! In the na-tional assemblies, in the United Nations, if they would open up to God. But, no, they have no room for that. If they would only say: 'You be the One to guide us, and teach us justice, charity, truthful-ness, and respect,' then, my friends, they will accomplish something for humanity. But they have nothing like that—only law, and insin-cere, unjust politicians, waiting for when they can grab.

"What you and I have between us in our individual life to be hap-py, so the whole nation must have. The world must recognize the divine truth. When we talk about men in public office who are not doing their duty, we are to blame, for we put them there. Like the election day coming up. People will say, 'Oh, I'll vote for So-and-so; he got my husband a job.' You know we never get anywhere acting against our conscience. Let us always choose those who help the majesty of the Lord to rule us. Choose the best and the just men, and then you yourself will be just."

Father Dominic is the clearest and most facile speaker of the three parish priests at St. Mary's. He preaches more rapidly than the Pastor and with more self-assurance than Father Paul. A sample of his preaching is taken from the sermon he gave on Mother's Day, the Sunday within the octave of the Ascension.

"As you all know, today is Mother's Day. It is an American out-growth of our feeling toward our mothers. The custom of celebrating this day isn't even forty years old, and so the church hasn't set aside the second Sunday of May for Mother's Day, and it's not a religious feast. During the month of May we Catholics do honor our mother in heaven, Mary, the Mother of God. We've been doing that for cen-turies.

"Now, how do we show our love? We don't scream and holler our love for our mothers or for Mary. We show it in the little things we do all year. And there's an awful lot we ought to do for her because she did so much for us.

"Your mother bore you, trained you, taught you, sent you to school. She encouraged your good marks and felt sorry because of bad marks. When you stepped out of the brood, she felt it deeply. All these things your mother did for you the Mother of God did too for Christ. But here the similitude ends, because the Mother of God knew what was going to happen to her Son.

"We turn to the Mother of God in times of trouble just as we turned to our own mothers when we were small. There is a false psy-chology in the United States today which claims that our mothers protect us too much. I say it is false, because most of the good that is in us was put there by our mothers, the good Catholic women who have devoted their lives to their children."

Father Paul usually tells a story of some moral significance in his sermons. His words and ideas are very simple and are delivered in the tense manner of one who is performing a necessary but difficult task. The following is taken from his sermon on humility, delivered on the tenth Sunday after Pentecost, the last Sunday in July.

" 'Everyone who exalteth himself shall be humbled, and he who humbleth himself shall be exalted.' In the name of the Father, and of the Son, and of the Holy Ghost. Amen. During the Civil War, Gen-eral Sherman called General Howard and told him that a certain pro-motion would not be his, and due to politics it would be given to someone else. Now, this meant that General Howard would have to relinquish his place at the head of his company and would no longer be able to lead them into battle.

"General Sherman knew that General Howard was a good Christian man, and able to take such disappointments, and told him as much. Well, he was so impressed with the way that General Howard took the disappointment that he allowed him to ride with him at the head of the entire army. Now, this fits right in with today's Gospel, and because he humbled himself he was exalted.

"Christ wants us to be humble. He wants us to be truthful. Many people have a foggy idea of Christ and His truth. But humility is truth—truth of one's self. A practical example of humility would be if the family is going on a picnic. And one person wants to go to the

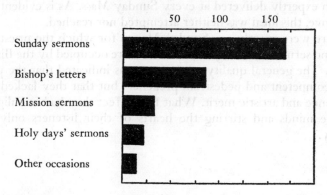

Fig. 56.—Distribution of the number and kind of instructions delivered from St. Mary's pulpit.

lake; another wants to go to the park; another somewhere else. The truly humble person will go wherever the rest want to go. He won't insist only on the place he wants to go to.

"The humble person always says 'Please' and 'Thank you,' for the truly courteous person also must be truly humble. The humble person is not afraid of work. Many people speak about the dignity of labor, but that's about as far as it gets. The humble person humbles himself by working hard and offering it all up to Christ. This doesn't mean that to be humble you have to make a doormat out of yourself. It just means that you should see yourself as you really are. If you're a good singer, humility doesn't say that you can't sing; but use your voice and recognize it for what it is, but no more."

All the above has been concerned with the use of the pulpit during Sunday Masses. St. Mary's Parish offers other times and occasions for hearing the Word of God. The weekly sermons during Lent, the

Forty Hours' Devotion, the parish mission, special feast days and ceremonies—all provide opportunities for conscientious parishioners to
obtain further knowledge and instruction in their religion. Figure 56
shows the number of instructions delivered in the parish during the
course of the year.

These instructions are discussed in other sections of this study and
need not be repeated here. At this point, however, the general question may be asked: Is the function of preaching pursued adequately
and successfully in St. Mary's Parish? From the point of view of the
preacher, it might be said that the ideal would require a well-prepared
sermon expertly delivered at every Sunday Mass. As is evident from
the above, this ideal was neither attempted nor reached.

There were exactly 150 Sunday Masses for which the priests prepared no sermons, although 84 of these were occupied by the Bishop's
letters. The general quality of the sermons indicated that the priests
were competent and pedestrian preachers but that they lacked great
eloquence and artistic merit. What final effect they had in enlighten-
ing the minds and stirring the hearts of their listeners only God
can say.

Chapter Seventeen

Catholic Revivalism

Every two years since he was appointed Pastor, Father Urban has invited missionary preachers to St. Mary's in order to "renew the spirit of the parish." The printed handbill which advertised the two-week services stated that "the object of the mission is to offer extraordinary opportunities for hearing the Word of God and for worthily receiving the sacraments." The Pastor, who had this handbill printed and distributed, said that "new priests with good sermons can bring the people closer to God and bring some of them back to the sacraments."

The Pastor's previous experience helped him to plan the mission at the proper time and to advertise it in the proper manner. Actually, he planned three missions, the first week for women, the second week for men, and a shorter mission for children to be given during the school hours on the first three days of the women's mission. He felt that he could get the "best results" during Lent, starting on the fourth Sunday and ending on Palm Sunday. The people would be more ready to sacrifice their time for religious purposes and would be in a more receptive spirit for the persuasive words of the preachers.

Although he had been talking to his friends and to the most active parishioners about the mission for almost two months, he made no formal announcement of public invitation until the second Sunday of Lent. On this day the handbills were first distributed, and at the first two Masses Father Dominic said that "the success of the mission does not depend on the eloquence of the priests giving the sermons but on the prayers of the people who are going to make the mission." He urged the people to "talk up the mission" and to contact those people whom the priests could not reach and to bring them to the mission. The Pastor said substantially the same at the eight o'clock Mass. Father Schmidt said the children's Mass and told the youngsters to "go home and tell your mother and dad about the mission and get them to go. Get your older brothers and sisters and anybody else you know and tell them that it's good for their souls. And don't forget to pray and ask God to bless the mission." Father Paul celebrated the two last Masses and briefly urged the congregation to pray for the mission.

On the third Sunday of Lent, because of the reading of the Bishop's letter on European war relief and the explanation of the parish census, there was time for only a short persuasive talk about the coming mission. At all the Masses this talk concentrated on the prospective spiritual advantages of the mission. "It is not only to bring sinners back to God. Even the daily communicants need this mission to help them lead a good life. You know that God is wonderful; all we need to do is call out to Him and He will help us. Every parishioner should come; the women and children the first week, and the men the second week."

The solemn opening of the women's mission took place at the eleven-thirty Mass on the fourth Sunday of Lent. The two missionaries, Fathers O'Hallohan and Carter, had arrived at St. Mary's the day before, and they occupied the pulpit at all the Masses. Although they alternated at the Masses, they gave basically the same sermon: an explanation of the mission, an invitation to come, and reasons why parishioners should accept the invitation. Next to the pulpit stood a cross ten feet high, painted black, with no corpus attached to it but having a long white cloth draped from the crosspiece. "The cross is black to remind us of the soul that is blackened with mortal sin. The white cloth symbolizes our baptismal innocence and the mercy of God. If your baptismal innocence has been lost to mortal sin, then you can regain it by making this mission."

"What is a mission? It is the way that God says: 'Peace be to you.' The grace of God brings peace, and you can receive that grace now. If you refuse now when it is offered to you, God may refuse later when you want it. . . . You had better make the mission now, for you may die, or move away into a parish where missions aren't given, and you may never have this opportunity again. . . . You receive ordinary grace through your priests and pastor, but you need extraordinary graces which come through the mission. It is a special call from God to you to bring you peace. . . . Three things will keep you from the mission: the world and its entertainments; the flesh, which tells you that it's too much trouble; and the devil, who tells you to make the mission the next time. . . .

"Don't just make half of the mission. Come for both the morning Mass and the evening service. All the sermons really form one discourse, and, if you happen to miss any part of it, you may be missing the part that God Almighty especially means for you. Therefore, it's necessary to come to both the morning and the evening sermons. . . . The mission will be for many a resurrection, while for others who refuse to come it will be a damnation. Which will it be for you? Tonight I want every woman in the parish to be present to co-operate with God's grace."[1]

The solemn opening of the mission consisted of the following ceremony which took place before the eleven o'clock Mass. A procession formed in the sanctuary made up of a cross-bearer and four acolytes with lighted candles, the two assistant pastors and the Pastor. They proceeded down the main aisle to the vestibule, where the two missionaries, dressed in cassock, surplice, and biretta, awaited them. The latter were greeted and welcomed by the Pastor, who sprinkled them with holy water. The procession then returned to the sanctuary, with a missionary on either side of the Pastor. At the altar the two preachers knelt before the Pastor, who placed the cord attached to a crucifix about each one's neck.

After praying briefly, the missioners turned and made the sign of the cross over the congregation, then went over to the sedilia while Father Urban ascended the pulpit. He welcomed the missionaries "who are about to begin a great work for the salvation of souls in the name of God. . . . The ceremony you have just witnessed signifies that I have given them full pastoral authority to come into the parish and use every means to bring God's grace to you. . . . Without your active co-operation, they cannot succeed. Come to the mission, but, above all, pray hard for its success and that God will bless our parish."

The program for the women's mission called for Rosary, sermon, and Benediction each night at seven-thirty, Mass and sermon each morning at seven forty-five. The two missionaries divided the work of preaching between them and had apparently planned the content and form of each sermon as well as of the whole mission. Only women were permitted in the church. The ushers were on duty each evening to direct the women to their places, but, as soon as the sermon started, they went into the vestibule and closed the doors. They sat there and

1. It was announced several times that the women's mission was for every "woman," including the high-school girls. This was a total of 2,428 Catholic females. The number of females present at all Masses on this Sunday was 1,804.

waited until time for Benediction and then returned to take up the collection.[2]

The following is a brief summary of the content of the mission sermons.

Sunday evening.—Father Carter explained the purpose of the mission, the need for prayer, and the method of saying the Rosary. After the Rosary was recited, and the hymn "Come, Holy Ghost" was sung, Father O'Hallohan preached on the most important thing in life—"to save your soul." Not pleasure, ease, comfort, making money, social prestige. Remove sin and come back to God. "The longer you stay away, the more unhappy you will be. . . . Go to confession now; give up mortal sin forever; do it now because you're not sure you'll have the chance again."

Monday morning.—Father O'Hallohan talked about the qualities of a good confession, the need for genuine sorrow and for the admission of all serious sins. "You must confess all your mortal sins. Omit one purposely and none is forgiven." He then defined the main species of mortal sins and the degrees of moral gravity contained in them.

Monday evening.—Father O'Hallohan encouraged the use of religious articles, medals, beads, crucifixes, pictures, statues, and holy water. He said that such articles could be purchased in the mission store set up in the school. Father Carter delivered the main sermon after the Rosary and hymn. His topic was the horror of mortal sin. "It is the greatest evil in the world because it offends God and sends you to hell. Poverty, loss of reputation, sickness—all of these are only temporary and minor evils in comparison with mortal sin. . . . It is deliberate disobedience against God, and by it we deserve to be thrown into eternal fire."

Tuesday morning.—Father O'Hallohan pursued the topic of confession further, dwelling particularly on the importance of good resolutions and the avoidance of the occasions of sin. "Do not dwell too long on what you have done in the past, but think about how you are going to live in the future."

Tuesday evening.—Father O'Hallohan talked to the married women in the church. It was a résumé of the Church's teaching on marriage as a life-vocation. He defined and explained the various sins that must be avoided by married women.[3] Meanwhile in the school auditorium

2. Two female observers attended all the services this week, while two male observers covered the men's mission the following week.

3. For further comments on this sermon see chap. 9, pp. 97–98.

Father Carter talked to the single women about their three main duties: to be practicing Catholics, to be obedient, and to be pure. "St. Alphonsus tells us that ninety-nine out of a hundred are in hell because of impurity, and the one hundredth is not there without impurity." Father then described the supernatural and natural means for preserving chastity, and the temptations and moral pitfalls of dating and courtship. He then warned them against marrying a non-Catholic because "forty-nine out of fifty mixed marriages turn out unhappily. . . . The Church teaches that those of nonmarriageable age are forbidden to keep steady company. For those of marriageable age, the policy is hands off. You can make a man an angel or a devil. Tell him, 'No sale, hands off.' Your bodies are temples of the Holy Ghost; therefore, do not let anyone expel God from your body."

Wednesday morning.—Father Carter gave a lecture on the manner of preparing for a general confession. It is absolutely necessary for those who have concealed a mortal sin in a past confession and is very helpful for those who are entering a new state of life. Those who are scrupulous should not make a general confession.

Wednesday evening.—Father O'Hallohan talked briefly on indulgences—what they are, how to gain them, what is the source of their merit. Confession and Communion made in conjunction with the mission brings a plenary indulgence. Father Carter gave the main sermon on the subject of death. "As I look over your faces, I see written on every forehead the words, 'Condemned to die.' Death is certain, but the time and the place are uncertain. . . . Perhaps tonight will be your last chance to go to confession. . . . The devil whispers that you won't die for a long time, but Christ says, 'At any hour which you know not.' "

Thursday seems to have been the turning point of the mission. The first three days concentrated on the negative aspects of the spiritual life, the sinfulness of human beings, the sanctions on sin, and the need for contrition and confession. For the remainder of the mission the priests emphasized the "Christian way of life," the virtues and rewards of Catholic behavior, the manner in which persons can remain in the friendship of God.

Thursday morning.—Father Carter talked about supernatural love of neighbor and demonstrated this with the words of the Lord's Prayer. "Christ was not only forgiving and kindly and friendly with everyone, He actually loved His enemies. . . . If you are willing to pray for your neighbor, you can be sure that there is no real hatred in your

heart for him." He talked of the need for making amends and of resti-
tution when evil has been done to others.

Thursday evening.—Father Carter gave the preliminary instruction
on the sacrament of extreme unction. He gave detailed information
about the manner in which the sickroom should be prepared. "Send
for the priest as soon as there is probable danger of death; do not
wait until a person is at death's door. . . . Then you will never have
cause to reproach yourself." Father O'Hallohan then gave the main
sermon on the Last Judgment. He described the kinds of women who
would be on Christ's right side: the woman who preferred parochial
activity to social climbing; the mother who was the queen of the
home and not a birth-controller; the young lady who knew how to
behave at a party and which men to date; the high-school girl who
followed her conscience rather than the crowd. "Get used to saying,
'Lord, I want to prepare now for the day when the books are open
for all to see.' "

Friday morning.—Father O'Hallohan talked about the "use of the
tongue" in both sinning and practicing virtue. He explained the Second, Sixth, and Eighth Commandments and how the faculty of speech
could be used in sins against God, in sins of impurity, and in sins
against one's neighbor.

Friday evening.—Father Urban took the pulpit to congratulate the
women in their faithful attendance and praised the missionaries for
"telling us divine truths even when we don't like them." He said that
envelopes would be distributed for offerings for the missionaries.
Father O'Hallohan then asked the ladies to do mission work of their
own by getting their menfolk out to next week's mission. He offered
to call on the home of any sick persons in the parish, "to bring the
mission to shut-ins." Father Carter delivered the main sermon, which
was on the precepts of the Church. He explained that we show our
gratitude and love of God by obeying the laws which His own
Church has set down. He discussed the obligations of Mass on Sundays and holy days, of fast and abstinence, of annual confession and
Communion, of the material support of the parish. The precept of
marriage was omitted here, since it had been explained in full detail
in a previous sermon.

Saturday morning.—Father O'Hallohan's sermon was on the Souls
in Purgatory. He taught the Church's doctrine on the need for expia-
tion of sins after death. "Let's not be too presumptuous about our
friends going straight to heaven. Let's give them the benefit of a doubt

and pray for them. You can't help their bodies but you can help their souls. . . . They want help—Masses, Communions, and prayers. This is something really monumental; not like the cold carved stones in the cemetery."

Saturday evening.—This was the last night of the mission, although the "formal closing" was to take place on Sunday afternoon. The usual shorter instruction was omitted. After the Rosary and hymn Father O'Hallohan preached on the Blessed Virgin under the title of Our Lady of Perpetual Help. "She has been with us all week and helped to make this a successful mission." He then spoke of the great power of Mary in heaven as our intercessor with her Son, Jesus Christ. "She is our main means of salvation. . . . No true servant of Mary has ever gone to hell." After the sermon six girls and six boys from the first grade, who were all dressed in white, stood up in the front pew which had been reserved for them. They dedicated themselves to Mary, repeating each phrase after Father O'Hallohan. The whole congregation of women then knelt down and repeated in unison the act of consecration to Mary.

A printed leaflet, *A Souvenir of the Mission,* was distributed to all the women. It was faced with a picture of Our Lady of Perpetual Help and contained advice on "how to spend the day in a Christian manner." It also listed the five means of perseverance and the five facts that every Christian must know.

On the next day, Passion Sunday, the missionaries alternated in speaking at all the Masses concerning the contents of this leaflet. Both priests also spoke in an effort to interest the men of the parish in the following week's mission. "Women have always been considered the weaker sex, but I'm not so sure about that. I was born in Missouri, and I'll have to be shown. I defy you men to show up the women by attending the mission in greater numbers than they did. They made a marvelous mission; and for some of them it was pretty hard to get here; but they did it. Now, let's see what the stronger sex can do this week. . . . Girls, kick the men out of the house at night and send them to the mission. Even if you have to hit him with the frying pan; don't worry about that; we'll give you absolution. Make them come to the mission.

"We are here to preach the word of God. He who is of God hears the word of God. If you don't make the mission, you are not of God. This is not my statement, or the Church's, but the words of Christ. . . . Tonight at seven-thirty when you hear the church bell ring, ask yourself the words, 'Am I of God?' And during the Benediction, when you hear the sinners' bell toll, ask yourself the question, 'Am I one of those sinners who refuses to make the mission?'"

The priests made a special plea to the former servicemen of the parish. "Have you thanked Almighty God sufficiently for your safe return from the war? We can have no peace in the world unless we have it in our own minds and hearts. With God's help we must avert another war. But, above all things, we must have a clear conscience so that we may have personal peace."[4]

The solemn closing of the women's mission took place at three-thirty on the afternoon of Passion Sunday. This "extra service" seemed almost an anticlimax, since the purpose of the mission had by that time been achieved in the large number of confessions and Communions and in the special services on the previous night. Father O'Hallohan preached a sermon of encouragement to all the women who had been at the mission, telling them that "the real mission begins for you today, for it is your mission in life to carry out all the good resolutions you have made in the past few days. The great obstacles to virtue—the world, the flesh, and the devil—still remain unchanged as they were last Sunday; but you have changed." After further repetition of good advice, Father thanked them all for their co-operation.

The congregation then knelt down for the papal blessing. This is a special privilege which missioners enjoy from the Pope and carries with it a plenary indulgence. It had been mentioned several times during the week. Finally, the Pastor, assisted by Fathers Dominic and Paul, conducted Solemn Benediction of the Blessed Sacrament. Thus ended the women's mission.

There was no solemn opening of the men's mission on Sunday as there had been on the previous Sunday for the women's mission. Apparently that ceremony sufficed for both missions, since it consisted essentially of the Pastor's formal invitation to the preachers to work in his parish. During the week of the men's mission the same sermons were given by the same preachers; they were delivered in the same order as in the foregoing week. The only noticeable difference was on Tuesday night, when the single men heard their sermon in the school auditorium and the married men in the church. The preachers had told the girls that they must protect their chastity

4. There had been 764 parishioners in the armed services during the war. Of these, 22 were killed, 38 were wounded, and 2 are still missing. No information could be obtained on 201 veterans.

from men; and they warned the boys that they must not lead girls into sin. The virtues of husband and father were logically emphasized for the married men.[5]

Since the majority of the male parishioners were employed, the brief morning sermons were arranged for the five-thirty Mass and repeated after the seven o'clock Mass. Except for the fact that the ushers remained inside the church for the sermons during this week and the female organist retired from the choir loft, the two missions were essentially alike.

It is generally assumed that the purpose of the bisexual division of the mission is that the preacher has things to say to the men that should not be heard by the women, and vice versa. A more practical reason seems to be the fact that parish churches usually are not large enough to accommodate the congregation if both men and women came at the same time. Furthermore, giving women chronological precedence over men has a psychological effect. The women can be relied upon to come in large numbers; but it is more difficult to attract large numbers of men to evening church services. The influence of the women was undoubtedly significant in urging the men to make the mission.

Figure 57 is a comparison by sexes of attendance at the evening services of the two-week mission, while Figure 58 is a comparison by sexes of attendance at the morning Masses and sermons during the two weeks of the mission; the figure for the men represents their attendance at both Masses each morning.

At this point we may ask whether the attendance at the mission is indicative of a high degree of spirituality in St. Mary's Parish. We note that an average of 189.6 women and 101.1 men were present for the morning services every day and that an average of 898.4 women and 453.5 men were present for the evening services. The missionaries had remarked that "those who do not come in the morning make only half of the mission," and, if we use this rigid criterion, we must admit that very few parishioners made the mission in the full sense of the term.

It is probably fair to say, however, that the missioners' words in this regard are a pious exaggeration, since the widespread definition of "making a mission" refers to the full course of evening sermons. The preachers also announced that those who stayed away from the mission were "not of God" and that the bell which tolled every night during Benediction of the Blessed Sacrament was meant for those

5. Two male observers were present at each service during the men's mission.

parishioners who did not attend the mission. They called it the "sinners' bell." Hence the absentees from the evening services were the sinners of the parish.

There are in St. Mary's Parish 2,428 Catholic females and 2,363 Catholic males fourteen years of age and over. All of these had been invited to attend the mission and, unless they had a reasonable excuse of absence, were to be included among the sinners of the parish.

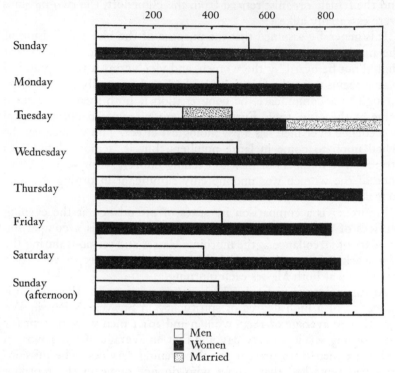

Fig. 57.—Attendance at the evening services of the parish mission according to sex (married and single separated only on Tuesday evenings).

If we subtract the average number in attendance at the evening sermons from the total number in these age categories, we find that 1,530 women (or 63.01 per cent) and 1,910 men (or 80.82 per cent) are sinners. This is, of course, an arbitrary definition of the term "sinner." Only God knows how many persons at any given time are in the state of mortal sin, and no human being can make a remotely reliable judgment in this regard. If the 3,440 persons who did not make the mission are to be called "sinners," this number probably includes the 1,117 persons who did not make their Easter duties. For them the mission bell tolled.

If the purpose of the mission for both men and women was to increase some kind of external measurable activity within the parish, we may judge its success by the membership of the Sodality of the Blessed Mother and the Holy Name Society. On Friday night of the women's mission the ushers distributed printed handbills inviting the young ladies to join the Sodality. Space was provided for name, address, and telephone number. We estimate that there were present

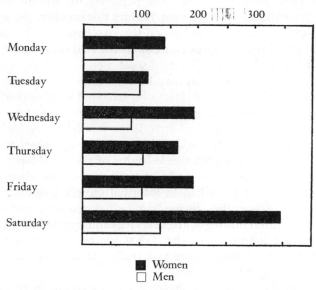

Fig. 58.—Attendance at the daily morning Mass and sermon of the parish mission according to sex.

about 275 girls and young ladies eligible for membership. The records of the Sodality meetings following the mission do not show one new application.

A similar printed invitation was distributed on the Saturday night of the men's mission, when 376 men were present. The same negative results were obtained. In his preliminary announcements on that night Father O'Hallohan praised the Holy Name men of the parish and asked them to make the following day another "Holy Name Sunday." Usually it was the second Sunday of the month when the organization received Communion as a group. "I invite all of you men to go to Communion with the Society, even if you aren't members. No doubt, you feel extra good and peaceful from this mission. Why don't you come together to the seven o'clock Mass tomorrow morning for the sake of Our Lord and our Blessed Mother.... Men going to Communion in a body make a tremendous impression on the rest of the parish." As a result of this plea, only fifty-three men received Communion at the seven o'clock Mass on Palm Sunday.

The number of confessions heard during these two weeks may be used as a partial criterion of the success of the mission. The missionaries frequently stressed the importance of the confessional, and during these two weeks they had 1,001 penitents, of whom 379 were women, 385 children, and 237 men. Besides this number, the assistant pastors also heard 257 confessions on the two Saturdays of the mission. This grand total of 1,258 confessions for two consecutive weeks is larger than that of any other two-week period in the year. From this point of view the mission may be considered highly successful. While it is true that not all of those who attended went to confession, and some may have gone to confession twice, the proportion of penitents in comparison to the total attendance was relatively high.

Quite aside from the reception of the sacraments, what effect did the mission have on the Christian behavior of the parishioners? This question can be answered only by the opinions of members of the congregation who were asked in informal sample interviews what they "thought about the mission." A half-dozen men gathered in front of the church one night after services and concluded that "missions don't get long-term results. What we need is more men on week-end retreats. That's where you really get time to think things over and make good resolutions."

In the "mission store," a converted meeting-room in the school, where several members of the Parish Council of Catholic Women sold religious articles during the mission, opinions were divided. One group of women thought that "this mission isn't as good as the one we had two years ago." Another woman, who said she made a mission every year, believed that "this is the best one I ever made." Another said that the two preachers "are too hard-boiled. I'd just have to leave my husband if I believed everything those priests say. I can't get absolution from them."

There was also some difference of opinion about the preaching abilities of the two missioners. Father Carter, the younger priest who had been preaching for about two years, was praised by both men and women as "a good, sincere man." The men thought that Father O'Hallohan was a much better preacher. "He tells you right straight out what he's thinking. He puts his points across much better. He don't pull any punches." The women said that Father O'Hallohan always had an undertone of sarcasm in his voice. "He couldn't stand anybody coughing, and he said once we ought to pass the cough drops around. . . . He was coarse in his language, especially when he talked to the married women on Tuesday night. . . . He doesn't understand women; he's too hard on us."

The immediate effectiveness of a preacher may be judged by his power to attract and hold an audience. By this criterion it may be said that the preachers were more effective in their sermons to women than to men. On the opening night there were 934 women present, but this number was surpassed on Tuesday, Wednesday, and Thursday nights. The men, on the other hand, started the mission on Sunday night with 528 present. On all the other nights the attendance was considerably smaller. These figures show that, even though the women expressed more dissatisfaction with the missionaries' preaching, they displayed a better regularity of attendance than the men.

Besides the comparison of the sexes it was also possible to make a comparison on the basis of marital status from the attendance figures for Tuesday nights. On that night 664 married women attended, which represents 34.49 per cent of the married women of the parish. The 360 single women represent 71.57 per cent of the single women fourteen years of age and over. The men show a much lower percentage in both categories. The 295 married men present are 15.32 per cent of the married men of the parish; while the 178 single men are 40.63 per cent of the single men fourteen years of age and older.

In summary of the conclusions concerning the two missions for adults, the following may be said: 28.22 per cent of the Catholics of fourteen years and older made the mission, the women showing a better percentage than the men. The numbers attending daily Mass were much smaller, but the numbers of those receiving the sacraments of penance and the Eucharist were relatively high. The result of the mission was not shown in the proposed extension into active parochial organizations, the Sodality and the Holy Name Society. The attitudes of parishioners toward the mission, as expressed by them, showed approximately even division of those who liked it and those who disliked it. The men generally thought that Father O'Hallohan was a better preacher, while the women preferred Father Carter.

For purposes of study the mission presented several difficulties.

Since the main purpose of the Catholic parish is to institute and forti-fy the religious relationship between God and man, we felt that the mission was an extremely important means toward this end. We could study and analyze the techniques of the preachers, the topics they discussed, the immediate numerical response of the parishioners during the mission. But the problem of measuring in some tangible way the effect of all this on the religious life of the parish was both important and difficult. The Pastor said that in his experience "a mission has a good effect for a couple of months, and then it wears off. People go to the sacraments more, some fallen-away Catholics come back, and some get their marriages fixed up."

Since it is impossible with the present tools of the social scientist to measure the internal spiritual effects of a religious action program, we had to rely on observation of external behavior. The inviolable seal of the confessional and the psychological reticence of Catholics about their spiritual experiences block even the most inquisitive inter-viewer from gaining statistical information. It would seem that we could measure the attendance at Mass and the number of Com-munions and confessions in the month following the mission and then compare these with other months in the year. If the mission had been held at any time except during Lent, this attempt could have been productive of relatively reliable information. But the mission ended on Palm Sunday, followed by Holy Week and Easter, and this is the very period of the year when the external observance of religious duties reaches a measurable climax. There was no way of distinguish-ing the causal influence of the mission from that of the Holy Week and Easter season.

A more subtle question of broader social import might be asked at this point. Quite apart from the religious behavior of the people within the walls of St. Mary's Church, was there any noticeable im-provement in their general social behavior? Did they come closer to the precepts of the Sermon on the Mount? Were their actions mark-edly more Christian than previously in their family affairs, business dealings, neighborhood, social, recreational, and political relations? These are questions which we cannot answer in a detailed, scientific way. There is some general evidence offered by individuals who said that the mission was a "wonderful spiritual tonic," that they had made strong resolutions "to lead a better life," and that from now on they were "going to be better Catholics."

Besides the missions for men and women, a short three-day mission was conducted for the school children of the parish. This took place

on Monday, Tuesday, and Wednesday of the same week on which
the women made their mission. An announcement was read at all the
Masses on Sunday, March 7, in which the children were told that
their mission services would be at nine o'clock in the morning and
at three-fifteen in the afternoon. "Parents of public-school children
are expected to see to it that their children attend this mission. The
Pastor has asked the superintendent of the public-school system for
general permission for the Catholic children attending public school
to be excused for the short morning meeting each day. For the first
time in twenty-seven years this permission has been refused. Parents
must write a note to the teacher or principal asking that they be excused. So, be sure to write these notes, so that your children may
attend."

The above announcement constituted a change from the instructions that had been given to the parochial school children on the
previous Friday afternoon. All children from the second to the
eighth grade had been told to come to Mass at seven forty-five on
the three days of their mission. The Sisters apparently did not realize
that the women's mission services would be conducted at that time
and that the priests could not talk to the children until eight forty-
five at the earliest. The switch in plans caused some confusion on
both Monday and Tuesday mornings. Many of the children came to
the seven forty-five Mass on those days and were taken from the
church at the last Gospel of the Mass by the Sisters in charge. They
waited in the school classrooms until eight-fifty, when the bell rang
for assembly in the church.

Meanwhile the Catholic children from the public schools came
into the church and occupied the pews at the sides and the rear of
the church. The Catholic school children took their accustomed
places off the middle aisles, as they do at the nine o'clock Mass on
Sundays.

On Monday morning Father O'Hallohan opened the mission with
a prayer, asking God's grace and assistance for all. He came down
from the altar to the middle aisle and talked from there as he walked
up and down so that the children could hear him better. He conducted the mission by asking questions, which the children were at
first very hesitant in answering. He asked why they were on earth,
what a mission was, what they could get out of a mission. He then
told them that certain numbers and letters were very important for
Catholics.

"The numbers are an automobile license so that you can go places as a Catholic. Remember 1, 3, 7, 10, and 6; and the letters *K, L, S,* and the letters *C* and *G*." He explained that the numbers stand for one God, three persons in one God, seven sacraments, ten commandments, six precepts; the letters stand for know, love, and serve God; and the other letters signify the cross and grace. These remarks seemed to catch the interest and attention of the children. They watched the priest closely as he walked up and down the aisle and became very animated as the half-hour went on, waving their hands vehemently to answer and talking among themselves about the questions.

On Monday afternoon Father Carter followed the same procedure of the catechetical form. The content of his discussion was "the greatest evil in the world," the same topic which was delivered at one of the night services in each adult mission. He told the children that some people think poverty, sickness, and loss of reputation are the greatest evils, and then asked a boy what he thought. The latter had no answer, but a girl spoke up and mentioned mortal sin. A whole series of questions on sin were then asked, and the children answered them quite readily and boldly. The same kind of excitement and talking which had existed at the morning lecture occurred again at this time.

This noisy exhibition was more than the Principal could allow. As soon as Father had said the Lord's Prayer to close the service, about fifty children rushed from the church. The Sister-Principal immediately came to the front of the pews and scolded the children for their "talking and giggling in church." She made them sit silently for five minutes before dismissing them. She told them, "This is no way to act in the House of God. If you don't act better tomorrow, I'll give you much more time to think about it."

Later in the afternoon the Principal asked the missionary preachers to speak from the microphone in the pulpit "because going up and down the aisle makes the children unruly." Father O'Hallohan said that they would comply with her wishes, but he asked whether it was not true that this kind of wild behavior was typical of southern school children. Sister restrained herself at this point but later told our observer that the children are all right. "These priests are just trying to put on an act for them so they'll go home and tell their parents how nice the missioners are and maybe get them to come at night time. . . . They ought to give them sermons—something to reflect on. . . . This generation of children are different. They shouldn't be talked to, or played with, like babies."

At any rate, Father Carter spoke from the pulpit on Tuesday morning. He still asked questions but in a more serious way and without attempting to make the children laugh. The topic was the sacrament of confession, particularly the preparation needed for it and the manner of going to confession. He told them several little stories about children who went to confession in the wrong way and then asked them to explain where the errors were. Some of the children then asked questions of the priest concerning the sin of stealing, one boy in particular asking how much they were "allowed to steal without committing a mortal sin." Father explained carefully that we are never allowed to sin in any way, and then he went on to a discussion of genuine sorrow for sins.

The Tuesday afternoon service was conducted from the pulpit by Father O'Hallohan, who asked questions about the precepts of the Church, paying special attention to those of Friday abstinence, and obligatory confession, Communion, and Mass attendance. The children showed a quite adequate knowledge of these points and were able to explain satisfactorily the meaning and purpose of the Holy Mass. Many of the children had gone to confession that day to the missionaries in preparation for the Communion Mass and closing of their mission on the following morning. Father explained to them that the rest would go to confession right after the service; but, if they had gone the previous week for First Friday and had not committed any serious sin, they would not need to go to confession again.

On Wednesday morning the children's Mass was held at seven o'clock so that it would not conflict with the women's mission Mass and service three-quarters of an hour later. At this Mass 321 children received Communion, and afterward most of them went to the school cafeteria for breakfast. Those who lived near by went home for breakfast, since they did not have to be back until nine o'clock for the closing of the mission.

Father O'Hallohan conducted the final service for the children. He distributed the leaflet *A Souvenir of the Mission* and spent most of the time explaining its contents (just as was done at the closing of both adult missions). This consisted of practical advice on how to live a good Catholic life, saying daily prayers, obeying parents and teachers, avoiding bad companions and occasions of sin, calling on God and the Blessed Mother for their help. He finally gave the papal blessing and asked them to hold up the various religions articles which they wanted blessed. After Father left the church, the Sister-

Principal led the children in prayers—Our Fathers and Hail Marys—for the "intention of the missionaries."

Was the children's mission successful in its avowed purpose of "reviving the Catholic spirit" of the parish? Table 19 shows the numbers of school children who were reached by the preachers on these three days. The poor attendance on Tuesday is accounted for by the fact of inclement, rainy weather.

TABLE 19

DAY	CATHOLIC SCHOOL		PUBLIC SCHOOL	
	Boys	Girls	Boys	Girls
Monday:				
Morning	183	234	16	24
Afternoon	192	231	9	21
Tuesday:				
Morning	124	197	2	6
Afternoon	176	212	7	18
Wednesday:				
Mass	117	198	16	21
Sermon	175	220	16	21
Average	141	215	11	18

TABLE 20

	In School	Average Attendance	Percentage Attending
St. Mary's	532*	356	67.01
Other Catholic schools	138	0	0.00
Public school	131	29	22.51
Total	801	386	48.18

* There are 549 children seven to thirteen years of age in St. Mary's Parochial School, of whom 17 come from other parishes.

This attendance record is, of course, meaningless unless a comparison is made with the numbers of children who were expected to attend. There are 801 children in the parish seven to thirteen years of age. These are the age groupings which represent the school children from the second to the eighth grade who had been invited to the mission in the Sunday announcements. The largest attendance at the mission services was on Monday, when 457 came in the morning and 453 in the afternoon. Thus, the highest attendance represents only 57.05 per cent of all the Catholic children of these ages in the parish. Table 20 shows what schools the children of St. Mary's

Parish, seven to thirteen years of age, attend and the percentage of each group attending the mission.

As far as the children who attend St. Mary's school are concerned, the mission preachers had a great deal of assistance from the teachers, who influenced their attendance. The teachers also helped the mission by reminding the children of the content of the sermons, giving further examples, and generally impressing upon the children the importance of the whole procedure. Attending a mission is a routine matter for parochial school children, but, even with this consideration, the average attendance was only 356, or 67.01 per cent of the children. No mention had been made concerning the St. Mary's children who attend other parochial schools, and, as far as we know, none of them made the mission. The public-school children, however, had been specifically invited, and the fact that they were required to bring a note from their parents to excuse them from class may account for the small percentage of 22.51 who came to the services.

There was a noticeable amount of "hooky-playing," especially among the boys who came late for the morning service and mingled with the other children going from the church to the school. The teachers' records show only a normal rate of absentees from the regular school classes. A comparison with the attendance at the pre-Communion and pre-confirmation retreats seems to indicate the difference in emphasis and incentive between missions and retreats. The latter contain much smaller and more easily controllable groups of children who have a clear objective toward which they are directed. This is also a sanction, for, if the children do not attend the retreat, they are warned that they cannot receive the sacrament.

A further difference lies in the whole atmosphere surrounding a retreat. The children spend much more time in church, and they are expected to keep silence, to meditate, and to pray during the retreat. From the above analysis of the preachers' talks it is difficult to judge that a mission offers the children anything that is more helpful spiritually than they would receive from the Sisters in their regular school-day program. As far as the external behavioral results may be judged, the Sisters indicated that the conduct of the children was somewhat more unruly during the mission than on ordinary school days.

Chapter Eighteen

Occasional Religious Activities

A COMPLETE picture of the purely religious functions of a Catholic parish cannot be obtained unless there is painted in also a great variety of occasional activities engaged in by priests and people. The main outlines have already been sketched in the previous chapters, but there are other activities which do not fall easily into the large categories. They are not so important as the essential sacramental and ritual proceedings of the parish, but they are absorbing of both time and energy. They tend to show in little ways the religious temper of the priests and parishioners of St. Mary's.

RECTORY VISITS

The incidental personal interactions of a religious nature that occur in the rectory may serve as an example. At any time of day, but particularly on Sunday mornings and on weekday nights, there are comings and goings of parishioners. Their most frequent request is to have medals, beads, prayer-books, crucifixes, and statuettes blessed. All three priests have these blessings memorized, and they get innumerable requests of this kind in and around the rectory and church. Several little schoolgirls who wore medals on chains around their necks competed with one another to see how many different priests they could get to bless their medals. The priests always comply with these requests and add a cheery, "God bless you too!"

Other parishioners come to the rectory to "pay" for holy water, even though there is a large container at the rear of the church from which they may freely help themselves. Some ask for blessed candles and for small vigil lights and cups which they use at home. Others bring Mass stipends and make arrangements for thanksgiving and Requiem Masses to be celebrated either at St. Mary's or elsewhere. Still others ask for copies of their baptismal records, which may be needed for employment, old age assistance, or prospective marriage in other parishes.

Spiritual advice and consolation are sought by parishioners, sometimes to "settle an argument" about some religious doctrine or Church ruling, more frequently to get help when they are in trouble. A delinquent son or daughter, a drunken husband or negligent wife, may be the focus of this trouble. The priest's pastoral counsel may be required for the person at fault. While the priests report that cases of profligacy and drunkenness have not decreased, there are fewer requests for the "pledge" to abstain from liquor. Only five were administered during the year.

St. Mary's contains a few religious "cranks" who complain about almost everything imaginable—from the way the flowers are arranged on the altar to the problem of Sunday-morning traffic in front of the church. These persons are a strain on any priest's charity. As Father Urban remarks: "If I decided to paint a statue, there would be some who would object." In spite of the irritating quality of these picayune complaints, the priests are remarkably patient and charitable. Father Paul had an experience with a "crank" of another kind, a woman who had been in a mental institution for several years. She claimed to have had a vision from heaven which appointed Father Paul her personal adviser, a job requiring several hours of spiritual consultation every day. After trying unsuccessfully to dissuade her from this notion, Father Paul attempted for several weeks to avoid her. He would not open the door without looking through the window to see who the caller was, and he finally induced her parents to return her to the asylum.

Besides the innumerable rectory meetings and discussions on economic, recreational, organizational, political, and other matters,[1] there are also many "friendship visits" to the priests. Former parishioners come in for a chat or to show their children to the Pastor. The inner circle of friends among the parishioners is present at odd times and for various personal and parochial reasons. Several families —the Meinhams, Patolis, and Lemardes—are very close to Father Urban, and are sometimes invited to dinner at the rectory. (Critics say that these are the people who "are really running the parish.") Fathers Dominic and Paul tend to visit in the homes of their particular friends rather than invite them to the rectory.

Finally, there are the "panhandlers," strange men and women who

1. These subjects are omitted here because they will be treated in a volume on the organizational life of the parish.

drift through Riverside and stop at the rectory for assistance. Although Catholic priests and rectories are notoriously "soft touches" for these beggars, the numbers who come to St. Mary's are remarkably small in comparison to those at other rectories. This may be because Riverside is far removed from the city's "Skid Row" and because the police have marked it "out of bounds" for vagrants. Or it may be because the attitude of Father Urban is one of discouragement. He never invites them to the kitchen for a sandwich or cup of coffee, and he only grudgingly gives them a coin, because he wants to "help the poor in our own parish first."

The following excerpt from our files is typical of this kind of eleemosynary visit to the rectory. "A little after nine-thirty at night, Father Urban answered the front-door bell. An unkempt man of about forty said he had just bummed a ride into town and needed some money to put up for the night. The Pastor asked him why he didn't work for a living. The man extended both hands and said, 'I've been working; look at them hands. I'm looking for a job now.' After giving some advice about diligence and respectability, Father put twenty cents in the man's hands. He looked at the money and said, 'Ya sure ya don't need this more than me?' The priest said, 'All right, my good man, if you don't want it, give it back to me,' which he did and departed. Father came back inside and said, 'That's the way these fellows are. They don't want to work, and they get insulted. All they want is money for a drink anyway.'"

Various other methods are used in treating beggars. Charlie, the houseboy and cook, usually tells them, "None of the priests are home." Bertha Meinham, the Pastor's secretary, asks them whether they live in the parish. Since they are all nonparishioners, she refers them to the public welfare agency or to a downtown parish. Fathers Dominic and Paul usually listen to their story and then give them a quarter or half-dollar of their own money. There is no change box or food-ticket arrangement in the rectory to provide for these itinerant beggars.[2]

CHURCH VISITS

A rough analogy can be drawn between the religious activities in the rectory and those in the church. The priests are busiest with personal relations in the evenings and on Sunday mornings, only relatively busy on weekday mornings after the Masses until lunchtime,

2. The St. Anthony Guild is charged with the material welfare of the parish poor. This activity will be discussed in another place.

and are least occupied with such calls in the afternoons of weekdays. Fathers Dominic and Paul alternate the days when they are "on duty" in the sense that they are responsible for taking care of rectory callers.

In the parish church itself, however, there is always someone "on duty." The church is opened by the sexton, Mr. Arnold, at five-thirty in the morning and closed at nine in the evening. What occurs there during those periods when public services are not being conducted? The Real Presence of Christ in the Blessed Sacrament is ideally a powerful attraction for parishioners. The ideal situation would be one in which large numbers of the faithful take the opportunity to "visit" and pray with Christ during the day. To observe this particular form of religious behavior, we made spot visits at different hours on weekdays throughout the year. We found that there were almost always a few parishioners present except in the early afternoon, from one to three, and at night from eight to nine.

What kind of people come to the church for private devotions and what do they do? Age and sex distinctions show some general patterns in this regard. During the morning young mothers who have been shopping on Main street come in occasionally with their pre-school children. During the lunch hour a few boys and girls from the parochial school may be seen in church. After three o'clock there may be a person of high-school or college age and several elderly men and women. Several young women who work in downtown offices regularly stop at the church before going home for dinner. Occasionally during the day a Negro nursemaid may come to the church briefly with her small white charges. Several elderly Negro women, who after almost thirty years still claim that St. Mary's is their parish church, make regular daily visits to the Blessed Sacrament.

The majority of the visitors to the church during the day appear to follow some private devotion. They are generally found kneeling in the forward pews or at the Communion rail before one of the statues or pictures there. There are four "side altars" in St. Mary's Church. On the Epistle side there is one in honor of the Sacred Heart and another in honor of Our Lady of Lourdes complete with a small statue of Bernadette. On the Gospel side are the altars in honor of St. Joseph and in honor of Our Lady of Perpetual Help. Lined up in front of these altars are a series of votive-light stands, each of which holds fifty lights and a sign suggesting: "Burn a Vigil Light in Honor of the Blessed Mother [or some other saint]. Offering 10¢." A metal box attached to the stand has a slot through which donations are made to pay for the candles. There are four stands in honor of the Blessed Mother, two for the Sacred Heart, one each for the Souls in Purgatory, St. Joseph, St. Rita, and "for your intention."

While the greatest number of offerings are made and candles lit at these stands when the large crowds are in church for the public services, it is characteristic of the daily visitors to burn vigil lights.[3] The people usually kneel to pray before one of the four altars which have statues or before the image of the saint for whom they have a special veneration. These statues stand on pedestals about four feet high, and they represent the Infant of Prague, St. Lucy, St. Cabrini, St. Rita, and St. Theresa, the Little Flower. Each statue has its donor's name attached, and at the base of three of them there are several small stone slabs with the word "Thanks" chiseled into them.

There are also two images at the back of the church which occasionally attract the daily visitor. One is a life-size crucifix attached to the wall near the baptistry, where people stand while praying and sometimes place their hand on the feet of Christ. A metal box for offerings is underneath. On the other side, near the choir stairs, stands a statue of St. Anthony, holding the Infant in his arms and consoling a poor beggar. Parishioners make special petitions to him for the recovery of lost articles, and the wide base on which the statue rests always displays an assortment of articles which have been left in the church. Father Dominic remarks that "the really valuable things, like sterling-silver rosaries or purses containing money, are brought by their finders to the rectory and claimed there. The junk is intrusted to St. Anthony."[4] In the pedestal of this statue there is

3. A little schoolboy came in one afternoon and lit eleven candles before the sexton chased him. The boy protested: "I put my nickel in the box." There are also several stands for large candles which burn seventy-two hours. The offering for these is one dollar, and they can be obtained only by going to the rectory.

4. Father Paul said that these things are allowed to accumulate until there is no more room; then they are given away or burned. Our observers made periodic listings of the objects left at the statue. One typical listing is as follows: a child's white purse, a pair of black gloves, three handkerchiefs, a white glove, an eighth-grader's songbook, a Lone Ranger comic book, a St. Christopher medal in leather case, four well-used Sunday missals, a child's prayer manual, three rosaries, four miscellaneous medals, a pamphlet, "Novena to the Sacred Heart," another called "Daily Pilgrimage to Purgatory," a gift card from a department store, a picture of the Blessed Mother, another of St. Patrick, a memorial prayer card, two coats belonging to very small children, four pieces of broken junk jewelry, a small black cloth purse, a Catholic Serviceman's Prayer-Book, and a Key to Heaven Prayer-Book.

also an offering box with the sign: "St. Anthony's Box for the Poor of the Parish." A pamphlet rack next to this statue carries the notice: "The regular supporters of the poor through St. Anthony's poor box, please take a Catholic paper to your home with Saint Anthony's blessing. Others are requested to make an offering."

The external symbols by which the daily visitors show their religious devotion are flowers and candles. Roughly from the beginning of March until the end of November there are always flowers at one or another of the statues in the church. They are not florists' bouquets but a handful of home-grown blossoms which sometimes remained three or four days before they were replaced or removed. On the feast days of Christ, Mary, and the various saints whose statues adorn the church there were more than two hundred vigil lights burning at one time. But on most weekdays of the year there were less than thirty. During Lent and in November the largest number of lights were on the stand commemorating the Poor Souls in Purgatory.

The above descriptions are an attempt to indicate what occurs in St. Mary's Church when no Masses or other public devotions are being celebrated. It must not give the impression that there is a constant stream of parishioners in and out of the church. A typical report of one of our observers, selected at random, may give a better understanding of St. Mary's Church in the daytime. "Wednesday, March 3, 10:48–11:05 A.M. The sexton was sweeping the left side aisle. An elderly man knelt at the altar rail before the Sacred Heart altar. One elderly woman was making the Way of the Cross. Two mothers with shopping bags and three children came in, walked to the front pew before the Blessed Virgin's altar, prayed for a few minutes, and left. There were fresh flowers before St. Rita's statue. Thirty-two vigil lights were burning and eleven large, three-day candles."

Another report tells us: "Friday, October 22, 5:45–6:03 P.M. As I walked up the steps, I saw Mr. Arnold in the shadow of the door. He was just standing there looking out into the street (apparently waiting to ring the 'Angelus'). A young man in a naval officer's uniform was kneeling in the front pew. He left while I was there. An elderly man came in at ten minutes to six, knelt in the last pew, and was still there when I left. He stood to say the 'Angelus' at six o'clock. A young lady (stenographer in a downtown office) entered a few minutes before six. She carried a large purse and two small bundles under her arm. She went to the altar rail, center, knelt for a moment in prayer, then to the altar of Our Lady of Perpetual Help, where she lit a vigil candle and remained a few minutes. Then she crossed to the other side, genuflecting at the center, and lit two candles before the statue of the Sacred Heart. After the 'Angelus' rang, she went to the back of the church, to the statue of St. Anthony, and was still standing there with her rosary in her hand when I left. There were forty-two votive lights burning and six three-day vigil lights. At the foot of St. Lucy's statue lay a bunch of red roses (not in a vase) which seemed to be two or three days old."

LITURGICAL ADHERENCE

The parishioners' devotion to Christ, the Blessed Mother, and the various saints would seem to suggest a year-round liturgical interest in the seasons and feasts of the Church calendar. This, however, is not the case. The "liturgical movement" in the sense of corporate public worship, in which the parishioners participate, pray, and act together, is hardly discernible in St. Mary's Parish. Of course, the parish has its official minimum liturgical functions according to seasons and feasts, but this seems to be the pursuit of the priests only in their official capacity at the altar. Except for the increasing use of missals by the younger people, there is little evidence of the so-called "liturgical spirit" at St. Mary's.[5]

The larger aspects of the sacramental and liturgical life of the parish have already been discussed in previous chapters. At this point, however, we may briefly glance at the ecclesiastical calendar as it is employed in St. Mary's Parish. The series of ember days which ought to serve as "penitential consecrations of each new season" are announced from the pulpit and are pointed out as periods of obligatory abstinence. The original significance of seasonal changes is generally lost upon an urban community, and it is doubtful whether more than one out of a hundred parishioners knows anything more than the fact that certain food prohibitions are placed upon them by the Church on these twelve days. Catholics who attend Mass on Sundays seem to be for the most part scrupulous about observing these regulations.

The annual cycle of dominical feasts is fairly well known to the parishioners and has already been mentioned in previous chapters. The feasts of Easter, Ascension, Pentecost, the Holy Trinity, Corpus

5. As we shall see in the volume on parochial organizations, the lay apostolate of Catholic Action, which is almost always the concomitant of the liturgical movement, is also at a low ebb.

Christi, the Sacred Heart, Christ the King, Christmas, and the Circumcision are carefully brought to the attention of the people. Others, like that of the Precious Blood, the Transfiguration, and the Holy Family, seem to pass unnoticed unless they occur on a Sunday. The Feast of the Holy Name, a Sunday, was simply the day after New Year's. The Epiphany, a Thursday, did not attract more than the normal attendance to Mass in the church, but it is a day still widely commemorated with "King Parties" among the families of French descent. The feature of these is a gaudily decorated ring cake into which an unshelled pecan has been baked. The person getting the piece containing the nut is supposed to have any reasonable request granted by the rest of the family. Any religious connotation of the feast day seems to have been forgotten.

Since the parish church is dedicated to Mary, the Mother of God, it would appear that all the Virgin's feast days should receive worthy prominence. During the first quarter-century of its existence, the church was called the "Nativity of the Blessed Mother," but this patronal feast (September 8) was inconspicuous except for the blue votive lights which Sister Berthold always places before Our Lady's altar on her feast days. The same may be said of other feasts which did not fall on a Sunday or were not holy days of obligation. The celebration of the Assumption and of the Immaculate Conception has already been discussed.[6]

The feasts of Our Lady of Perpetual Help, the Immaculate Heart of Mary, the Holy Name of Mary, and the Presentation all occurred on Sundays and were announced from the pulpit. The celebration of Our Lady of Lourdes conflicted with Ash Wednesday and the Annunciation with Holy Thursday and had to be postponed for the private devotion of the faithful. Other festival days, like the Purification, the Visitation, Our Lady of Mount Carmel, the Seven Sorrows, Our Lady of Mercy, and Maternity, passed almost unnoticed. The Feast of the Holy Rosary on Thursday, October 7, was not specifically mentioned, although the "month of the Rosary" was given worthy propaganda.

What can be said of the observable impact which the Blessed Mother might be expected to have on a parish dedicated to her honor? The public formulas are intact, Masses are celebrated in her honor, and the weekly Novena is recited;[7] the Children of Mary, the Sodality of the Blessed Virgin, and the Blessed Virgin's League are

6. See chap. 13, pp. 156–59.
7. See chap. 15, pp. 188–93.

named for her. In spite of all this, however, the devotion to Mary appears to be mainly a private affair, exhibited by the individual recitation of the Rosary during Mass and at odd times during the week.

For the most part, the same might be said of the saints whose statues adorn the church. Individuals who have these devotions request that Masses be celebrated on the feasts of St. Lucy, St. Cabrini, St. Rita, St. Anthony, and St. Theresa. Several other saints enter into the parish life in a public way, either because they receive public recognition from the Church or because they have been preserved in the folklore of the community.

The first of these is St. Blaise, on whose day, Tuesday, February 3, the blessing of throats occurred. On the previous Sunday it was announced that this blessing would be given by the priests at all the Masses, at four in the afternoon, and at seven-thirty at night. Two priests gave the blessing, a Latin formula which is recited for each person while the lower ends of the crossed candles are held against his throat. The people came up to the altar rail for this individual blessing after the three morning Masses. Just before school started, the Sisters brought the children over in orderly ranks, the kindergarten receiving the blessing first and the eighth-grade last. In the afternoon seventy-two adults, sixteen infants, thirty-four other preschool children, and twenty-six youths of high-school age came to the church for the blessing. For the evening blessing there were eighty-eight women, forty-one men, and seventeen children. Our observers noted that the great majority of those who honored St. Blaise on his feast day and asked his intervention were the faithful parishioners active in all functions of the church. The C.Y.L. Girls played in the school gymnasium that night at seven-thirty and did not go to the church at that time.

Another feast day of February, popular with the younger people, is St. Valentine's Day. It was the first Saturday of Lent, but neither the martyred saint nor the Lenten season seemed in any way connected with the celebration. This has become "Sweethearts' Day" and is marked in the parish by the exchange of amorous and humorous Valentine cards. Of the dozens we collected and observed in the homes and shops of the parish, as well as those made by the children in school, there was not one with a religious significance. Nor was there any that alluded to the saint himself. A few, because of the drawing or message on them, were in bad taste. It is safe to say that in this parish St. Valentine's Day has no longer a Catholic or religious meaning.

Two feast days in March, St. Patrick's and St. Joseph's, are also to some extent secularized in their celebration. They have national overtones which are not yet lost on the people of the parish. The "wearing of the green" characterizes St. Patrick's Day. Everyone of Irish ancestry, even though he may not have been at Mass for years, displays a bit of green on his person "to honor the saint." The day was a Wednesday in the midst of the men's mission during Lent. Some of the men who had "given up" liquor for Lent made an exception to their resolution on that day. The Irish were editorialized in the daily papers of the city, their feats were extolled, and numerous parties were held in homes of Riverside Catholics, but no specific religious function honoring the saint was held in St. Mary's.

ST. JOSEPH'S ALTARS

The Feast of St. Joseph, two days later, was widely celebrated by parishioners of Italian descent. The feature of this day is the erection of a "St. Joseph's Altar" in the home, a custom which is frowned upon by Father Urban because it is frequently a compound of superstition and money-making rather than a devotion to the saint. The Pastor was very articulate on this point, and he refused to bless all but three of the altars, the latter belonging to faithful parishioners he had known for many years.

The original purpose of the St. Joseph's Altar was the distribution of food in his name to poor and hungry people. Since the Italians, especially Sicilians, came to the city forty years ago, competition has gradually made the altars more elaborate and the purpose more remote. From March 15 to 18 notices appear in the "Personals" column of the daily press inviting the public to visit the St. Joseph's Altar in a particular home. One altar outside the parish, operated by a former Catholic, "opened for business" at four-thirty on March 18 and closed at two in the morning of the twentieth. Visitors helped themselves to the food delicacies, were given "lucky beans" and served wine, and were expected to leave an offering in one of the boxes placed in convenient spots around the altar.

For a week before the Feast of St. Joseph requests came to the rectory for one of the priests to bless these altars. All were refused except three. Two of our observers accompanied Father Urban on Friday morning when he went to the parishioners' homes to give this blessing. The altar prepared by Mrs. Farreyre and her daughter, who run a grocery store on the West Side, was typical of the two others. Upon arrival some time was spent in admiring the beauty of the altar, which consisted of four adjoining tables set against the wall. A small statue of St. Joseph holding the Child Jesus was elevated in a niche. Above it hung a crucifix, and next to it stood a miniature of the Infant Jesus of Prague. Three large candles, eight small candles, and six large votive lights, all decorated with pictures of Joseph and the Child, were lighted as soon as the Pastor arrived.

There were over fifty varieties of food displayed on the altar and four flagons of red wine. The various cooked, baked, and fried foods were made from vegetables, fish, fruit, and nuts, but not meat. Stuffed artichokes, olives, dates, figs, and stuffed peppers were piled high around mounds of breads, cakes, and pastries of varied size and shape. After Father Urban started to read the prayers, Mrs. Farreyre was seen putting a large bag (about fifteen pounds) of "lucky beans" on the edge of the table. About twenty persons, members and friends of the family, devoutly made the sign of the cross and stood at attention while the prayers were being read.

Nothing could be touched until the blessing was finished. Then the mother and daughter urged everyone to eat but were momentarily taken aback when Father Urban and his companions said that they could not eat between meals during Lent. This problem was solved when a paper bag was filled for each one "to eat for lunch." The visitors, after much urging, accepted a small glass of red wine before they departed. The same procedure was repeated at two other homes. In the afternoon one of the observers returned to take pictures and noted that Negroes were welcomed with the same cordiality as white persons and partook of the refreshments. At none of these three altars was a box for "offerings" at hand, although some of the neighborhood women had previously baked breads and cakes and offered other delicacies for the celebration.

Within the parish church itself there was no special devotion for the Feast of St. Joseph. Some of the school children, at the inspiration of the Sisters, had attended Mass and received Communion. They presented a spiritual bouquet to the Pastor for his birthday. That evening there were large numbers of men present for the mission sermon, but no external notice was taken of Joseph except for the relatively large number of votive lights burning before his statue. Since this feast occurred during Lent and since the Foster-Father of Christ is an important personage in the Catholic family of saints, the solemnity of his feast was celebrated on Wednesday, April 13. On this day a High Mass was celebrated by the Pastor, with the children's choir singing the Mass.

Since the feasts of St. Patrick and St. Joseph were accompanied by a remembrance of national origins, it was thought that parishioners of French ancestry might have special devotion to saints like the Curé of Ars or Joan of Arc, and those of German descent to saints like Boniface and Nicholas. Diligent inquiry among the families of the parish and observation of the church on their festivals uncovered no interest of this kind. It may be remarked in passing, however, that some of the more "liberal" members of the parish are developing a devotion to the South American Negro, Blessed Martin de Porres.

PARISH CENTENNIAL

One of the most elaborate religious celebrations of the year was planned to commemorate the centennial of St. Mary's Parish on September 18, 19, and 20. In early June, Father Urban had asked the Sisters in the school to prepare a pageant for presentation on these three nights[8] and had announced privately that there would be three Masses, one for children on Saturday, another for the parish on Sunday, and a Requiem Mass on Monday. Eventually, it was decided to omit the first day and to celebrate only on Sunday and Monday.

The Centennial Mass on Sunday, September 19, was begun with a procession from the rectory down the street to Riverside Drive and into the front of the church. Except for the confirmation ceremonies in April, this was the only occasion on which the Bishop made a public appearance in the parish. The procession was very impressive. The church bells started to ring at ten o'clock. Almost three hundred people stood at the curb watching the first group, composed of thirty-two nuns of various orders, who entered the church. Three seminarians in cassock and surplice then came down Union Street, one carrying the crucifix and two with lighted candles. Behind them walked two other seminarians ringing small hand chimes. Then came, in order, nine small altar boys in red cassocks, six in white cassocks, and fourteen in black cassocks. These were followed by eighteen parish ushers, nine priests from other city parishes, and seven monsignors.

An honor guard of twelve uniformed Catholic Forresters, with swords over their right shoulders, preceded the Pastor, who was flanked by the deacon and the subdeacon. Finally, the Bishop, accompanied by two priests and wearing his episcopal robes, blessed the people as he walked by. Most of them genuflected for the blessing. Four altar boys followed the Bishop and carried holy water, lighted

8. The pageant by the school children and the reception for the parishioners will be reported in another place.

candle, thurible, and incense boat. Inside the church the Forresters lined up along the center aisle and extended their swords over the head of the Bishop as the latter slowly walked up the aisle giving the "Asperges" to both sides of the congregation.

Father Urban had planned to make this celebration as parochial as possible. He had succeeded in bringing back for the occasion a number of the nuns and all the seminarians who came from the parish. Most of the priests, too, who had come from the parish or had at one time served there were invited. These and other priests could not all arrive on time because of their own pastoral and religious duties on this Sunday morning. The section of the front pews at the Gospel side reserved for priests gradually filled up during the Mass to a total of forty-two priests. The deacon was Father Scheidler, the subdeacon Father Naretti, and the preacher Father Schmidt, all former parishioners and products of St. Mary's Parochial School. Father Paul was master of ceremonies and Father Dominic the archpriest.

Father Schmidt preached for twenty-three minutes. He took his text from St. Paul: "Forgetting the things that are behind, and stretching forth myself to those that are before, I press toward the mark, to the prize of the supernal vocation of God in Christ Jesus" (Phil. 3:13-14).

"One hundred years have passed since the small foundation of a parish was laid in Riverside. All the joys and tears, hopes and fears, together with the sacrifices of thousands of souls have shared in the making of St. Mary's Parish. Just as the development of any living organism is the cumulation of a thousand complexities into a final unity, so also the growth of St. Mary's Parish is but the weaving of numberless threads into the beautiful fabric we appreciate today. In reaching this major milestone in the history of St. Mary's Parish, there is signaled the passage of the pioneer days.

"Little wonder then that we drop the anxieties, the sweat and the tears, of daily life, and pause today in joyful reminiscence of the past and hopeful contemplation of the future. There is a need that all men feel to raise the heart from the vain pursuits of earth to the praise of God and the desire of heaven. Today we satisfy that need in the solemn splendor of a centennial celebration."

Father Schmidt then gave a brief history of the parish, as seen "from the vantage ground of St. Mary's Guardian Angel, who has watched and shared in no small measure in the building of the parish." Since the time was limited, this Angel necessarily had to be selective in the facts observed and mentioned. The impact of the War between the States; the aftermath of the Franco-Prussian War, which split the parish into separate French and German churches; the composition of differences at the beginning of the century; the building of the present church edifice forty years ago; the early struggle of the nuns to start a parochial school; the administration of the various sacraments; the growth of the parish under its present Pastor—all of this was seen by the Guardian Angel.[9]

"We congratulate, now, the priests, the Sisters, and the people of St. Mary's Parish on the occasion of this celebration. We rejoice with them in the record of achievement that is theirs to uphold. We remember, too, the devotion and the sacrifices of countless men and women who have made this day possible. We pray with the congregation that the future will reveal an increase in the number of saints made in St. Mary's Parish." After a repetition of the sermon's text, Father Schmidt closed with the sign of the cross.

The Bishop, seated on the episcopal throne on the Gospel side of the sanctuary, listened attentively to this sermon. At the consecration of the Mass he knelt before the altar. Six altar boys knelt behind him holding hurricane candles; the Forresters in the pews presented arms. Immediately afterward, people began to leave the church, while others began to come in for the eleven-thirty Mass. When the Mass had ended and the people saw a microphone being placed before the Bishop, they began to leave in larger numbers.

Although it was already five minutes past the time for the next Mass to start, the Bishop spoke for twenty minutes. His theme was unity. "We are united before the throne of God this morning to thank him for the blessings He has given to us. St. Mary's Parish has become the symbol of religious activity and of Catholic unity. You Catholics of Riverside can be proud of the progress you have made here, building up the Catholic Church in this section of the city.... You have genuine leadership in your Pastor, Father Urban, who has worked so zealously on your behalf and has prayed so tirelessly to realize the Kingdom of Christ in this parish."

His Excellency then praised the united effort which the people had made to erect and maintain the parochial buildings and asked them to demonstrate the same spirit of sacrifice in the drive for the Sisters' Convent which would soon begin. After describing the "flowering of St. Mary's original parish into thirteen separate parishes," he spoke

9. The Guardian Angel overlooked the presence and the problem of Negro parishioners during the first sixty years of St. Mary's history. Unlike the differences between French and Germans, which ended in integration, the differences between white and colored ended in segregation.

briefly of the historical oneness of the Roman Catholic Church. "To-day, the world outside the Church lacks unity." As an indication of this disunity, he mentioned the recent conferences in Holland of representatives from more than a hundred and fifty different Christian sects, "whose varying beliefs are a proof of their disunity."

At the close of this sermon, the Bishop gave his triple blessing to the restless congregation. The procession formed again, went down the middle aisle, past the crowd still waiting for the next Mass, and along the sidewalk to the rectory. An elaborate dinner had been prepared for the visiting clergy and was served to them by a caterer in the school hall. The last Mass was over while this dinner was still in progress.

On the following morning a Solemn Requiem High Mass was sung by the Pastor, with Fathers Dominic and Paul as deacon and sub-deacon. It was celebrated at nine o'clock for the repose of the souls of St. Mary's parishioners "who are still suffering in Purgatory." About three-quarters of the school children were present (there was no school that day), and the children's choir performed under the direction of Sister Michael, Sister Angela, and Miss Koehl. There were 108 adults in the congregation, of whom almost a hundred were women.

It may be said in conclusion that the religious enthusiasm that might be expected on the occasion of a centennial celebration was ex-hibited only by those lay persons who are at the center of all paro-chial activities. The attendance at the ten o'clock Mass on Sunday was larger than that at the same Mass on other Sundays, and the increase is accounted for mainly by these active parishioners and a host of visitors. Monday was an ordinary business day, and it was not to be expected that employed persons could attend the Requiem Mass. Those who were present, however, were again the most faithful parishioners.

SECULAR HOLIDAYS

This chapter on the occasional activities of St. Mary's Parish would not be complete without a word about the relation between com-munity holidays and parochial religious activity. The general pattern is that the attendance at Mass on these days is much lower in children and slightly higher in adults. Parishioners seem to use these days for fishing trips, outings, "working around the house," and other secular activities. Shrove Tuesday was a city holiday, and attendance at Mass was slightly above average. Of the national holidays in February,

Lincoln's Birthday was ignored and Washington's fell on a Sunday. Memorial Day and Independence Day were also on Sundays.

Labor Day[10] was merely part of the last summer week end during which many parishioners were out of town, while Columbus Day meant little more than a school holiday for the children. On the Sunday before Thanksgiving an announcement was made at all the Masses urging the people to show their gratitude to God by coming to Mass and receiving Communion on Thursday. The Pastor had scheduled a Nuptial Mass for ten o'clock that morning, which he celebrated, with the result that the six o'clock Mass was omitted. A larger than average number, however, received Holy Communion at the two other Masses.

With the season of Advent the ecclesiastical year opens, while the secular year draws toward its end. The importance of "shopping" and of evergreen decorations on Main Street, and of Santa Claus within the family circle, seems to overshadow the spiritual significance of the Christ Child. This does not mean that the importance of Christmas is ignored or completely lost among the people of St. Mary's Parish,[11] but it indicates that the secular celebration of the Christmas season—up to and including New Year's Day—is given undue prominence.

We return to the place where we began this chapter, the rectory of St. Mary's. The busiest period of the year there is the Christmas season. The social as well as the religious demands made on the priests' time are excessive. It is also then that the priests and people of the parish seem to be in closest unity. Personal calls and expressions of thanks and appreciation are made in great numbers; gifts of all kinds pour into the rectory. The spirit of peace prevails, and in the midst of excitement there is a notable manifestation of parochial solidarity.

10. The Bishop's letter concerning social justice for the workingman was read at all the Masses on the previous day.

11. See chap. 13, pp. 155–56, 159–62.

Chapter Nineteen

Spiritual Exercises

THE layman's "retreat from the world" for the purpose of taking spiritual exercise is not a parochial activity in the strict sense of the term. The retreats do not take place at St. Mary's Church;[1] the parish priests do not conduct them and play only a secondary encouraging role in them; the retreatants do not attend the program together as parishioners. But the modern retreat movement is a serious attempt on the part of lay persons to achieve the ultimate individual and social ends of religion; and, since some of St. Mary's parishioners participate in them, they deserve our consideration in a study of this kind.

A spiritual retreat is called an "exercise of the soul." It is an active mental and volitional process in which the exercitant examines his relationship to God and creatures, seeks motives for sanctifying that relationship, and makes resolutions for a better life. For three days the retreat "master," or priest-director, gives inspirational talks to the group and between times makes himself available for private consultation.

In every retreat there are usually two personal highlights for the individuals who attend. The first is the general confession, either annual or lifetime, which all are encouraged to make. The second is the "election" or resolution concerning the person's future behavior. The latter is usually a specific decision to avoid a particular vice, practice some virtue more carefully, or even change one's state of life. The moral and psychological uplift is indicated in the propaganda of the movement. "You have an opportunity to be refreshed mentally and spiritually; to be all square with God and more duly appreciative of His daily love and protection."[2] "Take advantage of a

1. Except those made by the grammar-school children in preparation for Solemn Communion and confirmation.

2. From the publicity brochure of the Diocesan Retreat House, which serves the men of St. Mary's Parish.

beautiful opportunity you will never regret or forget. You will find physical rest, yet spiritual exercise. . . . No matter how great a sacrifice you have to make to attend one of these retreats, you will find it more than worth your while, we assure you."[3]

The original plan of St. Ignatius Loyola, whose *Spiritual Exercises* form the basis of modern retreats, called for an individual and personal retreat directed by a priest over a period of several weeks. The plan, however, has long since changed into a group activity, wherein from twenty to a hundred persons, usually of the same sex,[4] spend a week end together in prayer and silence. Some religious congregations order a retreat of thirty days for their members, but most of them make the retreat annually for a space of eight days. Most of them also have tridua, three-day retreats once or twice a year.

The modern retreat movement for lay persons has curtailed the process to three days, in which only the absolute essentials of the exercises can be presented. The "closed" retreats at the Diocesan Retreat House for men, and those at the various places which sponsor women's retreats, are always on week ends, from Thursday nights to Sunday nights. The "open" retreats, conducted annually at Catholic high schools and colleges, may be held on any three days of the week. The difference between the two is that the closed retreats are voluntary, the groups are smaller, the individuals keep silence from beginning to end; they eat, sleep, and pray in a secluded place. The open retreats are obligatory, the group may number hundreds, and the retreatants go home after the evening conference and cannot maintain the necessary silence and recollection.

One more preliminary remark must be made. Retreat "captains" are key factors in the success or failure of the whole movement for closed retreats. This is an individual layman (or laywoman) who phones, writes, or otherwise interviews Catholics in an attempt to persuade them to make a retreat with "his" group. This is a zealous, energetic, and thoroughly Catholic individual with leadership qualities. He gathers the retreatants, assures them transportation, collects the fees, and makes all arrangements with the authorities at the place of retreat and sometimes also with the priest-director of the retreat.

3. From a letter sent by Mrs. Rhatigan, head of a recently organized laywomen's retreat group, to one of the women of the parish.

4. Some dioceses have inaugurated the week-end retreat for married couples, but these have not yet been arranged for the diocese in which St. Mary's is located.

St. Mary's Parish has never had a woman retreat captain, but it has had three men in this capacity: the late Frank Boucher, Sr.; Henry Muhler, who took his place; and Warren Becker, who captains a group from Hendersonville.

MEN'S RETREATS

The men of St. Mary's Parish attend the Diocesan Retreat House located about sixty miles from Riverside. The building had once been a small Catholic boarding-school for boys and is situated in a relatively rural area. The grounds are spacious and quiet, ideally suited for contemplation. The building is in good repair but does not provide the numerous conveniences available at the usual week-end resort (and at some of the modern retreat houses in the United States). The retreatants seem to be satisfied with the present arrangements. As Tim Calahan remarked, "After all, we go for a retreat, not a vacation. We don't want a hotel and servants and fancy stuff. A bed, chair, and washbasin are good enough."

The retreat house is owned and operated by a religious order of priests, who provide both the spiritual and the physical accommodations. Since they conduct a retreat almost every week end of the year, there is a permanent staff in residence. The actual retreat master is changed from week to week according to the request of the captains or to the availability of priests of the order who give the retreats. They also maintain an office in a downtown business building, and this is the propaganda center for the whole layman's retreat movement in the diocese. The priest in charge of this office maintains a record of all the men who have made retreats, keeps in frequent communication with the captains, and personally helps the latter to complete their groups for each week end.

The retreatants arrive from the city on Thursday night for supper and for the first conference, which is an explanation of the purpose of a retreat. The group, which averages about thirty-five men, then maintains silence until Sunday night. The retreat master gives four or five talks in the chapel each day. He points out the pitfalls of temptation, the manner of avoiding sin, and the divine punishments for sin. He explains the proper use of created things, the motives for practicing virtue, the rewards God holds out for holiness, and gradually leads up to the final meditation on the love of God. The retreatants spend the time between talks reading a spiritual book, conferring with the director, reciting their beads, praying in the chapel, or simply walking around the grounds in silent meditation. They do not talk to one another even at meals.[5]

During the five-year period culminating in this study, seventy-nine men of St. Mary's Parish made 142 retreats. Three of them, M. D. Loisel, Charles Villere, and Henry Muhler, went to the retreat every year. Eight men, John Thames, Michael Pielier, Arthur Pielier, C. L. O'Brien, T. J. Schneider, James Marin, Karl Grusch, and Frank Boucher, went four times. Seven men made the retreat three times, thirteen went twice, and forty-eight went once.

Is it possible to say that these seventy-nine men are the "cream" of the parish, the most spiritual and the most Catholic of St. Mary's adult male parishioners? Experienced retreat masters generally agree that there are three rough categories of retreatants. About 25 per cent are the spiritual elite, conscientious, holy lay persons who frequent the sacraments and carefully fulfil all their religious obligations. About 50 per cent are mediocre Catholics who try to lead a fairly decent life and to "stay out of trouble" as much as possible. The remaining 25 per cent are individuals who "really need a retreat." They may be involved in an invalid marriage or have been away from the sacraments for a long time. Often they are induced by their friends to come up to the retreat and "get yourself straightened out."

As far as can be externally observed, without revealing strictly confidential information, the men retreatants from St. Mary's Parish do fall roughly into these three compartments. But there is still a further subdivision which must be made in each of the three groups. The pious, the mediocre, and the marginal Catholics can each be distinguished into "spiritual individualists" and parochial-minded Catholics. In other words, even among the upper fourth there are persons who do not participate actively in the social and organizational life of St. Mary's; while even among the lower fourth there are persons who take an active and interested part in parochial affairs.[6]

A similar conclusion may be made if we analyze the adult male retreatants from another point of view: that of active parochial leadership. Of this whole group of seventy-nine men, only thirteen can be said to have been prominently active in St. Mary's Parish in the five-year period under consideration. Most of the others are regular

5. Roughly speaking, this descriptive paragraph applies also to closed retreats made by boys, women, and girls and will not be repeated when these are discussed.

6. These observations seem to be roughly applicable also to the other groups in the parish who make closed retreats. The younger people who make open retreats at their schools cannot be so easily classified.

churchgoers and may have a nominal membership in one or more of the parochial organizations. The names of some few are not even known to the Pastor and his assistants.

Of the thirteen laymen who demonstrated active leadership in this five-year period, one, Dr. Boucher, died just before our study began; Dr. Lennon, C. O'Brien, and Thomas Flint have withdrawn more and more from strictly parochial functions. The remaining nine are Hasele, Greve, Calahan, Feuerling, Pielier, Schneider, Meinham, Becker, and Muhler. These names occur again and again in our reports. They are part of the small nucleus of laymen who support the Pastor's plans, co-operate with the priests in all activities, and play a prominent part in the Holy Name Society, the St. Anthony Guild, the Ushers' Society, and other groups. By any sociological standard they must be called solidaristic and parochial-minded.

Until he died in the year before the study began, Dr. Boucher was not only the most highly respected and active layman in St. Mary's Parish but also one of the most energetic and successful retreat captains in the diocese. He induced men from many other parishes to make retreats, and it was largely through his own personal effort that the number of men retreatants from St. Mary's increased successively during the four years before his death as follows: nineteen, twenty-eight, thirty-three, and thirty-three. It is true, of course, that in the first two of these four years many of the men were absent from the parish and in the armed services. But it is also true that in the year after his death, when Henry Muhler took his place as captain, the number dropped back to twenty-nine.

Lest a misunderstanding arise concerning the composition of these retreat groups, one curious fact must be mentioned here. Even though the Doctor was a successful retreat captain, and Muhler after him, the men from St. Mary's Parish do not form a united group making the retreat on the same week end. This is true also of the relatively few women from the parish who make closed retreats. The twenty-nine men who made the retreat during the year of the survey were spread out on seven different week ends. Thus it is clear that the retreat movement cuts across parochial lines and that the lay persons attend closed retreats not as parishioners but as members of other groups. We shall return to this concept at the end of the chapter.

BOYS' RETREATS

A study of the retreat movement among the young men of the parish shows that several aspects must be considered separately. A distinction must be made between high-school boys and college men and between those who go to the retreat house of the diocese and those who make the retreat at the school which they attend.

The three Catholic high schools which attract boys from St. Mary's Parish have gradually developed the custom of sending their graduating seniors annually to the same retreat house which the men of the parish patronize. This closed retreat, however, is not obligatory, and those boys who do not attend it must make the annual retreat at the school itself with the other students. Thus, over a period of five years, seventy-four boys from St. Mary's Parish went to the retreat house at the behest of their school authorities. Among them there was no need for a retreat captain, since all arrangements were made by their schools.

The fact that these closed retreats are voluntary and that they are made much more "seriously" than the retreats conducted in the school might indicate that these boys are the "better Catholics" among the youth of the parish. For the most part, this is true. The proportion of marginal Cahtolics among them is much smaller than among the men who go to the retreat house. Among them we find the names of well-known and active families of the parish: Greve, Tureaux, Marrait, Green, Lennon, Santos, Neil, Harmon, Smithson, Mann, Redon, and others.

For some unaccountable reason, the records at the retreat house show that the numbers of boys from St. Mary's Parish are declining. In the five successive years the totals have been: seventeen, eighteen, eighteen, eleven, and ten. The numbers of male parishioners who graduated from Catholic high schools during these years do not show a similar decline. Some of the boys said that they did not "have the money" to go (they are expected to pay from five to ten dollars for the three-day retreat), and others said they could make "just as good a retreat" at school. It may be that some of the school authorities are not stressing the need of a retreat as they have in past years. A partial explanation lies in the fact that the increasing number of men's retreats makes it difficult to schedule week ends for boys at the retreat house.

The age category which these 74 boy retreatants represent contains 234 male parishioners. The young men in this five-year group have 141 graduates from Catholic high schools and 47 from public high schools. This means that 52.55 per cent of the Catholic high-school graduates, 39.36 per cent of all high-school graduates, and 31.62 per cent of the whole five-year age category have made at least one closed retreat during this period.[7] If all these could have been induced to continue the custom of an annual retreat, the spiritual effect upon themselves, their families, and the parish might be quite noticeable.

During the year of the study 109 boys of the parish were attending Catholic high schools, and 36 were going to public high schools. We have already seen that 10 of these 109 left town for a closed week-end retreat. All the rest (99) were obliged to make the retreat which is an annual feature of their school. This spiritual experience is quite different from the more or less intense program at the retreat house. All classes are suspended for three days. The boys are expected to attend Mass in the morning at the school chapel, and they listen to four talks by the priest-director during the day. Otherwise their time is supervised by teachers in the study halls, cafeteria, and playground. They are told to keep silence both in the school building and at home during this three-day period. The distractions are so great, however, that it is doubtful whether this suggestion can be well observed after school hours.

The spiritual benefits achieved from this kind of "open" retreat are not likely to be so great as those experienced by the boys who go to the retreat house for a week end. Yet even this type of curtailed spiritual exercise is better than no retreat at all. There are seventy boys of high-school age in the parish who have contact with neither kind of retreat. In other words, 39.1 per cent of all boys of this age category are not attending Catholic school. It is no mere coincidence that the fifty-five boys who did not make their Easter duties and the twenty-seven boys who regularly miss Mass are all from among this number.

The question of youths of college age in the parish who make retreats becomes somewhat involved when we realize that these "youths" range in age from eighteen to thirty-five. The many veterans who are attending college have temporarily made this category meaningless as an age group. It St. Mary's Parish there are 137 men who list themselves as college students; and, of this number, 59 are attending Catholic colleges. Since an annual retreat is obligatory for all Catholic college students, we know that at least this number of men went through this spiritual experience during the year of the survey.[8] These

7. Some of these who are now attending Catholic colleges have since made annual retreats, a few at the retreat house, the rest at the school.

8. The records of the retreat house show that three of these men made a closed retreat there during the year.

retreats are similar to the ones given in high school in that four spiritual talks are presented during each of three days, but the opportunities for silence and meditation are negligible.

WOMEN'S RETREATS

The women's retreat movement of the city is younger than that of the men, has no central diocesan organization, and, in general, fewer women make retreats than men. There is no religious order of women[9] in the diocese to maintain a year-round retreat house similar to that which is available to Catholic men. The Sisters who teach in Catholic colleges for women and boarding schools for girls will upon request open their facilities for occasional week-end retreats in the summertime. They may sponsor such retreats for their alumnae, but otherwise they do not concern themselves with preliminary arrangements. The lack of a central office makes it almost impossible to coordinate effort, and, as a result, laywomen generally are neither encouraged nor able to enjoy the spiritual experience of a retreat.

There are three groups of women in the city who are interested in changing this situation so that the retreat opportunities for Catholic women will improve. The St. Anne Society has been sponsoring laywomen's week-end retreats at their rest home in the country. They have averaged two retreats each year for eleven years. The Sisters of St. Angela's Academy in the city have had six retreats in the last five years, mainly for their own alumnae. An independent group of women, headed by Mrs. Rhatigan, has sponsored seven retreats in four years at St. Gertrude's Convent, about forty miles from Riverside. Mrs. Rhatigan has been inspired by the success of her husband, who captains a group of more than twenty men each year. This group seems to be the nucleus of a growing diocesan retreat movement for Catholic laywomen.

During the year of the survey eleven women from St. Mary's Parish made these closed retreats, distributed at the three different places. The technique and the daily program are essentially the same as those for men's retreats, except that at St. Gertrude's the program starts on Thursdays and lasts for four days. Another incidental difference is in the numbers attending. The men's retreat house limits each retreat to thirty-five, while the women's retreats in some instances accommodate close to one hundred.

St. Mary's Parish does not send its proportionate share of women

9. Like the Sisters of the Cenacle, who are active in this work in some dioceses.

to these retreats. In the five-year period twenty-seven women made 34 retreats at the three retreat houses. In the same period seventy-nine men made 142 retreats. Not only did more men of the parish make retreats, but they made them more frequently. It is interesting to note that only four of these women are wives of men who go to retreats. There seems to be no explanation for this except the typical sex pattern of spirituality in the parish, which is especially accentuated in the parochial organizations.[10]

Of all the observable religious behavior in St. Mary's Parish, the retreat movement is the only one in which men are more active than women. In all other spiritual activities the women outnumber the men approximately seven to three. Besides the other reasons already mentioned (lack of a year-round retreat house, a religious order in charge, and a central diocesan organization), it may be that the woman's position in the home is a partial factor of this disproportion. In an urban society the husband's responsibilities are mainly occupational and extra-domestic. The daily routine of the home depends entirely on his wife, who cannot easily abandon it for a space of three or four days. Of course, this explanation cannot be used for unattached females.

The twenty-seven female parishioners who made retreats during the last five years are not all noticeable for their parochial activity. Several of the names are familiar in other parochial affairs and belong to leaders: O'Brien, Zeurling, Neil, Gannon, and McGuffey. Most of the others are women who take at best a halfhearted interest in the parish itself, and some are not even known to the priests as members of St. Mary's. Thus it would seem that the spiritual exercises of the retreat draw not only the spiritual elite of the parish but many other ostensibly less religious women as well.

At this point there must be mentioned another program of religious exercises akin to retreats and engaged in mainly by women parishioners. The reference is to "Days of Recollection" which are held on occasional Sundays throughout the diocese. These are conducted at schools or academies where a chapel, dining-hall, and lecture-room are available and consist of Mass, breakfast, two conferences by a priest, luncheon, and two afternoon conferences ending with Benediction of the Blessed Sacrament.

The purpose of the Day of Recollection is self-examination and renewal of spirit. In these it is similar to a week-end retreat. Silence is observed. There is, however, much less opportunity for private con-

10. The only society to which the husband and wife jointly belong is the Parents' Club.

sultation with the priest-director and hardly ever time for confession. As may be expected, the women of St. Mary's Parish make these Days of Recollection more frequently than they make retreats. Our records show that a great variety of groups sponsored these one-day programs during the last five years, among them the St. Anne Society, the Daughters of Isabella, sodalities, and professional groups like nurses, teachers, librarians, and others.

Since the initiating arrangements are sporadic and often very informal, it was impossible to obtain a complete listing of all the parishioners who attended these spiritual programs. The information at hand, however, allows for a conservative estimate that about forty-five women made almost a hundred Days of Recollection during the five-year period. No group of women from St. Mary's went to either a retreat or a Day of Recollection as a parochial group. No St. Mary's woman was either a leader or an originator of such a program, but all seem to have become interested through their friendship, school, or other relationship with Catholic women outside the parish.

GIRLS' RETREATS

Most of the difficulties that impede the laywomen's retreat movement also impede those for girls, with the exception that all of the girls in the parish who attend high school and college are obliged to make an annual retreat at their respective schools. During the year of the survey 124 girls from St. Mary's made the retreat in high school, and 45 in college. These retreats last for three days and are similar to those already described for the boys. The priest-director expounds the same principles but attempts to apply them to the specific needs and situations of young Catholic women.

There are 206 girls of high-school age in the parish, of whom 39.8 per cent do not attend Catholic schools and therefore do not have the benefit of an annual retreat. This is approximately the same percentage as that of the boys in the parish who are not going to Catholic schools. There are 63 college girls in the parish, of whom 45 attend Catholic colleges, where the annual retreat is obligatory.

Aside from these school retreats, an independent retreat movement has sprung up among the girls of St. Mary's Parish under the inspiration of Sister Berthold. This nun says that she is primarily interested in helping the young girls of the parish to discover their true vocation in life. As the moderator of the Children of Mary, she arranges a closed retreat for them at St. Gertrude's Convent. For the last three

years she has chosen the first week end in August and has had successively eight, eleven, and fourteen girls. Some of these were "repeat-
ers," so that actually only twenty-eight girls have made the retreats.
On the last retreat eight of the girls had just graduated from St.
Mary's Parochial School in June, while the five others were older.[11]

Other Sisters from the same religious order who teach in various
parochial schools are co-operating with Sister Berthold in this attempt
to help young girls and women. The fourteen who went from St.
Mary's were only part of the fifty-eight who came from five different
parishes. The program started on Thursday night with the first conference by the priest-director and continued until the last conference
at eleven-thirty on Sunday morning. Sister Berthold was with the
girls the whole time and helped to supervise their spiritual reading
and to encourage them in both the general confession and the "election" which are features of every retreat. She returned with them on
the late afternoon of Sunday.

The only other age group in the parish are the school children.
While there is no annual program of spiritual exercises for them, they
do make a quasi-retreat in preparation for their first Solemn Communion and for the reception of the sacrament of confirmation. These
have already been discussed in previous chapters.[12]

SUMMATION

The description and analysis of the various retreat groups of St.
Mary's Parish lead us to several conclusions. In the first place, it is
commonly believed to be a "sign of a good Catholic" when a man or
woman retires from the busy world to pray and contemplate in silence
for several days. This is supposed to indicate a constant, active interest in the deeper aspects of religion as they relate to the individual's
own spiritual advancement. In other words, the popular theory seems
to be that only pious people, the members of the inner parochial circle,
make retreats.

The observable facts lead to a different conclusion. On the high-
school and college level where all Catholic students are obliged to
make the annual retreat there are also all grades of Catholics, from
the most pious to the most negligent. To some extent, the same can be
said of those who make closed retreats at a retreat house. Those who
go annually, or every other year, are generally numbered among

11. See chap. 10, pp. 117–18.

12. See chap. 6, pp. 58–60, and chap. 8, pp. 87–90.

the spiritual elite of a parish, while the others are more likely to be mediocre or even negligent Catholics. This does not mean that all the holy lay persons in the parish make retreats. There are some highly spiritual parishioners of both sexes who have never made a closed retreat. Thus attendance at retreats cannot be used as an autonomous index of constant and deep-seated religiosity.

Second, the role of retreat captain in the whole structure of the lay retreat movement requires further analysis. Of course, where the retreats are open and obligatory, as in the schools, there is no question of a captain. In the closed retreats for both men and women these captains are of central importance. They are the most enthusiastic and active retreatants, individuals with friendly personalities, a wide circle of acquaintances, and a tendency toward persuasive leadership. Without them the whole movement would not be nearly so successful.

The third conclusion is that the composition of any retreat group depends largely upon the retreat captain. Theoretically, there are numerous bases upon which a retreat group may be formed. Four of them are of interest to us here: the academic, the professional, the friendship, and the parochial. The first two are sometimes the actual bases used in the composition of a retreat group. The third and fourth, however, seem to be more logically fitted to the social structure of both the community and the Church, as understood by Catholic sociologists.

It is quite evident that the basis of the retreat groups in Catholic high schools and colleges, whether open or closed, is the individual's membership in, or attendance at, the particular school. Of course, this academic bond may incidentally be linked with some of the others. Some of the persons making the retreat may be close friends; they may be fellow-parishioners, and they may even have the same professional interests. But the fundamental bond which brings them together in a retreat, especially where it is obligatory, is none of these three.

It is also quite clear that in the closed retreats for both laymen and laywomen, friendship relations are the gravitational center around which the retreat group clusters. The retreat captain makes up his own group from among his friends and associates. Individuals go to closed retreats with their friends, whether or not they are neighbors and fellow-parishioners. The priest in charge of the central office for laymen's retreats and the extant records of the laywomen's retreats both indicate that Catholics who make frequent closed retreats like to come back each year with the same group. Thus, while there is time for conversation only at the beginning and the end of a retreat, these individuals tend to form and maintain friendships that cross parochial lines.

Even in those rare instances when the composition of a retreat group is based on occupational or professional status, the whole group tends to follow lines that are supra-parochial. Closed retreats for various professional groups are common in other dioceses, but the Diocesan Retreat House which serves St. Mary's has only one annual retreat of this kind, that of lawyers, and only one of St. Mary's men attends it. The laywomen's Days of Recollection tend to follow this pattern of professional composition with greater frequency. Wherever this occurs, the lay person attends the retreat as a member of an interest group which may have no direct relation to his role as a parishioner.

It may be argued that any basis for membership in a retreat group ultimately has a beneficial effect on parochial solidarity. The interior spiritual experience of a retreat is supposed to make a lay person more fully aware of his obligation as a Catholic and inspire in him an active improvement in social behavior with fellow-parishioners. Since, in theory, virtue is characteristically diffusive, it may be said that spiritual progress in one's academic or friendship or occupational relations should directly effect improvement in one's familial, parochial, and other relations. But in practice the clearly defined segmental structure of modern urban life does not give satisfactory evidence of this diffusion.

The statement has sometimes been made that, "when a person becomes a better Catholic (for example, by means of a retreat), he becomes a better parishioner." Two observations may be made to show that this statement is in need of revision. (*a*) A large number of parishioners who had the advantage of making one or more retreats during the five-year period do not give evidence of greater parochial activity and solidarity. Among the outstanding parishioners who did make a retreat, it is doubtful in which direction the causal influence was greater, that is, whether they are better parishioners for having made a retreat, or made a retreat because they were good parishioners. (*b*) A significant number of active lay parishioners did not make a retreat in the last five years. Hence, in their case, it cannot be said that the retreat movement had any direct influence on their external, active Catholicism.

Chapter Twenty

The Catholic Mind of the Parish

THROUGHOUT this book we have observed and analyzed the overt religious behavior of the people of St. Mary's Parish. We have limited our judgments objectively to that external behavior as a measurable expression of their religious beliefs and values. From a scientific point of view this empirical approach is probably the most valid and reliable in any attempt to discover the concordance between the official ideals of the Catholic Church and the actual practices of its members.

Besides this objective observational and statistical method, there is also the personal technique of interviews and questionnaires. Instead of accurately observing and analyzing the conduct of parishioners, it asks them directly or indirectly to express their minds. This is admittedly open to subjective and rationalized answers by the interviewee. Mere speech reactions, that is, expected answers, may be given to such questions. Statements made by people concerning their own thoughts and beliefs are frequently colored by what they think "ought to be" rather than by "what is."

In spite of the inherent shortcomings of the technique of opinion surveys, we decided to conduct one among a selected group of parishioners who had demonstrated the "most Catholic" behavior. We felt that, if we could reach their attitudes, opinions, and values, we could understand better the highest practical ideology of the parish and that the rest of the parishioners could be judged as deviants from this ideal. In other words, the results of these interviews represent the subjective ideal type as actually existing in the minds of the inner circle of parishioners. They do not represent either the average attitudes of all the parishioners or the full teaching of the Catholic Church.

The conceptual scheme on which these conclusions are evaluated suggests three levels of scientific abstraction which must be recognized and compared. (*a*) The *complete Christian ideology* is the pure super-

259

natural culture as taught and promoted by the Catholic Church. It is the unattainable positive ideal of spiritual perfection toward which all parishioners "should" be striving. It is the true spirit of Catholicism, accepted without mental reservation only by saintly persons and overtly approximated only by them. (*b*) The *practical ideology* of the parishioners is the value system which guides them in everyday life. This is difficult to assay because it is variable in the individual Catholic and differs from person to person. It seems to be a mental working compromise between the spirituality of the Church and the materialistic philosophy of the world. (*c*) The *actual behavior* of parishioners is usually assumed to be in accord with the second ideology, although it is "expected" to follow the first. This is learned by patient, accurate, detailed, and objective observation.

In the previous chapters of this book we have attempted to recount the actual behavior of the parishioners as it centered around the primary functions of the Church. By comparing this with the complete Christian ideology, we were able to make rough conclusions concerning the various grades of practical ideology. The parishioners thus exhibited in their conduct their proximity to or remoteness from the ideals taught by the Church. In order to supplement these conclusions by the actual statements of parishioners, we interviewed forty men and twenty-eight women from among the inner circle of the people of St. Mary's. All interviews were conducted by priests, who simply asked a series of sixteen questions without advancing any explanation of their meaning or giving any indication of the "correct" answers.[1]

The material which these questions treated may be divided into two kinds: (*a*) *authoritative* matters which had been clearly decided upon by the Church authority and should be known by well-informed parishioners as the official teaching of their Church, and (*b*) *interpretable* matters, in which there are permissible differences of opinion according to circumstances. In these latter questions, however, although the answers may vary, they may also be measured against the ideal of the complete Christian ideology.

We assumed that the highest Christian ideology, unattainable for all but the most saintly person, would contain the following statements. We assumed also that the thoroughly trained and fully believing Catholic would agree with them even though his behavior may not be in conformity with them: (1) Murder is never permis-

1. The questionnaire was the last part of the interviews made with parish leaders and exemplary Catholics which will be analyzed and reported in a subsequent volume.

sible. (2) The Church laws on divorce are right and just. (3) God is just if He condemns mortal sinners to hell. (4) The devil is a real person. (5) Catholic children should not attend public schools. (6) Children are more valuable than material standards of living. (7) The practice of rhythm is allowed only for grave reasons. (8) Catholics should not marry persons of a different religion. (9) Catholics have a moral obligation to vote. (10) Expenditures for social welfare are to be approved. (11) Municipal low-rent housing projects are desirable where needed. (12) Catholic workers should join labor unions. (13) The atomic bomb should not be dropped on civilians. (14) Parochial schools should not be racially segregated. (15) Catholic parishes should be racially integrated. (16) Modern practices of fast and abstinence are lax.

These assumptions were the bases for the questions asked, although the wording of the questions was done in such wise that the expected answer was not indicated. In the analysis of answers there is no intention to state that a parishioner could not be a practicing Catholic if he disagreed with the assumptions. His disagreement may indicate a certain amount of ignorance, a relative degree of compromise, or simply a conscious reluctance to "go all the way" in the spirit of Christianity.

QUESTIONS WITH AUTHORITATIVE ANSWERS[2]

1. "In the case of prolonged and painful cancer do you think that it would be all right for a doctor to give the patient an overdose of sleeping pills?" The great majority of persons immediately recognized this action as outright murder. The teaching of the Church and the mores of American society more or less coincide on this question. Most people instinctively recoil from the responsibility of taking another's life regardless of the circumstances. Sixty-two thought it would be wrong, three (all women) thought it would be all right, and two men and one woman had no answer.   *91.17*

2. "Do you think that the laws of the Church regarding divorce ought to be relaxed for people who are unhappily married?" The Catholic Church's "unpopular" doctrine on the question of divorce is probably at the present time its most publicized moral teaching. Even persons outside the Church know well that Catholics may not divorce with the intention of remarrying. We would expect that among Catholic parishioners there would be unanimous agreement

---

2. The italicized score at the end of each question represents the percentage of persons who answered correctly according to our assumptions.

on this question. Fifty-nine persons answered that the Church law should remain unchanged; four women said that it should be relaxed; three men and two women did not give an opinion.   86.76

3. "Do you think that God is just if He condemns a person to hell for committing only one mortal sin?" An appreciation of the serious-ness of an offense against God is needed to answer this question cor-rectly according to the mind of the Catholic Church. No imaginable penalty is too great to pay for the commission of a mortal sin. Fifty-two parishioners agreed that God is perfectly justified in condemning the mortal sinner to hell. Nine (eight of them men) thought that God would be unjust if He did this; seven declined to answer.   76.47

4. "Do you believe that the devil is a real person?" The popular disbelief of the devil as a really existing person seems to have influ-enced the thinking of Catholics. It is very common to explain the con-cept of devil as an imaginary being, or as one's own lower impulses, or as a combination of baneful circumstances. Twenty-two of these Catholic laymen denied that the devil is a personal being and thus showed that they either forgot the doctrine of the Church in this regard or never knew it. Twenty of the women acknowledge the devil as a real person. Of the whole group of sixty-eight interviewees, thirty-seven held the Catholic doctrine, thirty denied it, and one man did not know.   54.41

5. "If you wanted to send your child to a public school, would you bother to ask the permission of the Bishop?" The canon law of the Church expressly forbids Catholic children's attendance at public schools when Catholic facilities are available. The assumption is that there is at least remote danger to faith and morals in a secular school system. It seems that the Bishop has neither publicized this ruling of the Church nor insisted that it be followed to the letter of the law. At any rate, St. Mary's parochial leaders show a decided ignorance of it. This is the first question to which more than half of the inter-viewees gave the wrong answer. Thirty-three said they would not ask permission; thirty said they would; five did not know what to say.   44.11

QUESTIONS ABOUT INTERPRETABLE MATTERS

The three following questions concern marriage and family and are framed in such wise that a great latitude of interpretation may be found among Catholics. Where secular and material values are ac-cepted, people tend to move away from the ideals of the Church. These questions are charged with emotional overtones, and the answers indicate that the full spirit of Catholicism, or of the Christian virtues, is lacking in many of the persons interviewed.

6. "Do you think that it is better to raise two children in comfortable circumstances than five children in decent poverty?" This is a test question that clearly shows the influence of materialism over the spiritual teaching of Catholicism. No one had any hesitancy or doubt about it; twenty-two answered affirmatively, and forty-six answered negatively. The problem offers a choice between popular secular values and Catholic values, between a higher material standard of living with fewer children, on the one side, and a lower standard of living with more children, on the other. Anyone who understands and accepts the supernatural criteria of Christianity would not place comfortable advantages above children and would realize that decent poverty is a virtue which Christ deliberately chose. A little more than two-thirds of these parishioners accept the complete ideal.   *67.64*

7. "Do you think that it is a good idea for persons of limited income to practice rhythm for the first few years of marriage?" There appears to be a wide misunderstanding in the American Catholic mind that "it is perfectly all right" for married people to practice rhythm. The Church, of course, does not approve it, but teaches that it is morally permissible only when there is a grave reason involved. Thirty-five persons understood this and disapproved the practice even for couples with limited income. Twenty-six approved it, while seven did not know what to answer. Here, again, it was clearly a matter of approaching, or withdrawing from, an ideal of Christian behavior.   *51.47*

8. "When two young people are very much in love, do you think that they should marry even if they are not of the same religion?" The Church's constant warning against mixed marriage is well known even to non-Catholics. Canon law forbids the practice, priests preach against it, and social scientists demonstrate its disrupting consequences. Despite all this, the popular romantic theme of plays and stories and songs that "love conquers all" seems to be deeply imbedded in the minds of these urban Catholics. Only twenty-four of them disapproved mixed marriage; thirty-eight were in favor of it when people are very much in love; and six offered no opinion. *35.29*

OTHER QUESTIONS

The remaining questions treat a wide range of religious, social, political, and economic problems, on which well-instructed and spiritually formed Catholics may be expected to have ideal answers. They are arranged in a descending order from those matters on which the parishioners had the "most Catholic" attitude to those on which they had the "least Catholic" attitude.

9. "Do you think that all Catholics of voting age, both men and women, have a moral obligation to vote?" No one hesitated to answer this question, and it is the one which received the greatest number of "correct" answers. Sixty-four agreed that it is a Catholic's duty to vote, while four said that it is not. Strictly interpreted, this is not a loaded question. Implied in it, however, is the fact that the person who believes that voting is a moral obligation commits a sin when he fails to vote.[3] The Church encourages good citizenship and wishes its members to participate in civic and political activities. In certain public issues which affect the moral and social life of the community, the Catholic may be under serious obligation not only to vote but to vote conscientiously.   *94.11*

10. "Do you think that more tax money should be expended for social welfare, such as maternity hospitals for the poor, clinics for disabled persons, etc.?" These parishioners showed here an attitude of generosity toward the underprivileged which might be called typically Christian. Sixty-two were in favor of such expenditures even though it would mean higher tax payments from their own income. Five were against it, and one had no opinion. These answers seem to indicate a consciousness of the need for such facilities in the parish and city where they live. Implied in this question is the fact that most of the beneficiaries of an extended program of social welfare in Riverside would be Negroes. In view of the answers to Questions 14 and 15 below, it would be interesting to guess what the score would be if the word "Negro" had been expressly stated in the question. *91.17*

11. "Would you approve the city's putting up a low-rent housing project in the poorer sections of St. Mary's Parish? Fifty-six answered in favor of the proposition, ten were against it, and two declined to answer. Here, again, a fairly large proportion gave the answer to be expected from religious-minded and socially conscious Catholics. The poorer sections of the parish are the areas of high Negro concentration, but this fact was only implied in the question. A suspicion may be reasonably entertained that the score would drop if this racial aspect were deliberately mentioned in the question.   *82.35*

12. "Do you think that every Catholic workingman ought to belong to a good labor union?" The principle of labor organization has

3. See chap. 3, p. 29, for the ratio between potential and actual voters in Riverside.

been so frequently approved by official Church spokesmen that one would expect a unanimously affirmative answer by knowledgeable and faithful Catholics. Actually only thirty-six gave this expected Catholic answer; twenty-five answered negatively; while seven gave no opinion. Here again one may note the influence of conservative social thinking so prevalent in the community of Riverside.   *52.94*

13. "If Russia declared war against the United States, would you be in favor of dropping the atom bomb on Moscow?" This question shows the greatest disparity of opinion between the sexes; 57 per cent of the women disapproved the bomb, while 70 per cent of the men approved its use on Moscow. It may be reasonably assumed that a thoroughly religious person is immediately repelled by the relatively barbaric horror of exploding the atomic bomb on a group of his fellow human beings. The contemporary antagonism between Americans and Russians and the Catholic fight against communism evidently supplied undertones influencing thirty-six persons to give the wrong answer. Twenty-six were against the use of the bomb, while six gave no opinion.   *38.23*

14. "If the kindergartens of the parochial schools were opened to Catholic Negro children, would you allow your own children to attend them?" The doctrine of the Mystical Body, with its insistence upon the moral integration of all Catholics into a recognizable and co-operative unity, has been widely publicized in modern times. Racial segregation among Catholics is directly counter to this doctrine, and community patterns of thought and behavior, accepted by Catholics, have quite successfully prevented the application of the principle of integration and unity. Forty-seven persons said they would not send their children to a racially mixed Catholic kindergarten. Presumably they would prefer public-school education for their children. Only eighteen gave the correct answer in conformity with the ideal of the Church; while three expressed no opinion. *26.47*

15. "Are you in favor of the present arrangement whereby the Negro Catholics of the city have their own parishes?" The parishioners questioned were even more opposed to racially integrated Catholic parishes than they were to integrated kindergartens. Around the first decade of this century it had been found expedient to allow segregated parishes for Negroes, although in principle there are no racial barriers within the Catholic Church.[4] This question involves

4. In a city-wide survey it was found that about 14 per cent of the Catholic Negro churchgoers attend Mass in "white parishes." At St. Mary's Parish there have never been more than a dozen Negroes attending Mass at any one time.

the breaking-down of these barriers as they now exist, at least to the extent that whites and Negroes would attend the same religious services. Sixty of the interviewees wanted to keep the Catholic parishes segregated as they are now. Only eight wanted integration.   *11.76*

16. "Do you think that the laws of fast and abstinence as promulgated in this diocese ought to be made more strict?" This question was asked in order to discover whether the spirit of penance and self-sacrifice is seriously accepted by the interviewees. It is common knowledge that the Lenten penance requirements have gradually become more relaxed in modern times. The regulations issued by the Bishop of this diocese are substantially the same as those in most other dioceses. An affirmative answer would indicate an understanding of the meaning of penance and a willingness to do more than the simple obligations now imposed by the Church. A negative answer might indicate a preference for a more comfortable and convenient practice of fast and abstinence. Sixty persons (including all of the women) thought that the regulations should not be made stricter. Five men wanted sterner regulations; three men had no opinion.   *7.35*

In recapitulation of the above information we may attempt to interpret the scores nearest to both ends of the scale. It is interesting to note that those questions which have scores below 40 all touch the personal convenience of these parishioners or the prejudices prevalent in the community. Three of these involve anti-Russian and anti-Negro attitudes. Two concern fasting and the matter of mixed marriages. If we combine the scores for all these answers, we find that the average score is 23.82. This is certainly a long distance from the full ideal of Catholicism.

At the other end of the scale, the scores show that matters which do not particularly touch the parishioner personally, that is, the duty of voting, the need for hospital facilities and housing, and those doctrinal questions which have been emphasized by the Church—mercy killing and divorce—were correctly answered in most instances. The average score for these five questions was 89.11. The remaining six questions have an average score of 57.84, with the question on permission to attend public schools the lowest at 44.11, and that on the reality of the devil at 54.11.

It may be tentatively suggested (with the special caution that statistics cannot adequately measure opinions and attitudes and beliefs) that these leaders of St. Mary's Parish are a little more than half-Catholic in their thinking. In other words, the average score on all these questions was 56.98.

The above analysis is an attempt to compute the degree of acceptance or rejection which the various Catholic values and beliefs have among these selected parishioners. We may look at this whole problem of the mind of the parish from a different point of view. Instead of scoring the questions, as above, we may score the interviewees. In other words, each of the sixty-eight persons interviewed is given a score indicating the number of correct answers. No individual made a perfect score. No man gave more than fourteen correct answers, and no woman gave more than twelve. The worst score among the men was five correct answers and the worst among the women was six. Nine persons scored above 70; forty scored between 50 and 70; nineteen scored below 50 points (Fig. 59).

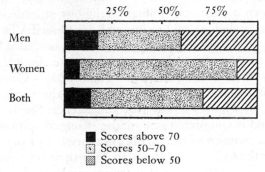

Fig. 59.—Percentage comparison by sex of the scores for the complete Christian ideology as exhibited in an adult sample of parishioners.

It may be repeated here that, while this analysis is subject to the deficiencies inherent in opinion surveys, it may be used to indicate in general the practical ideology of these parishioners as admitted by themselves. If it is true that individuals tend to favor themselves in giving answers of this kind, then the scores must be lowered and the people interviewed may be even further removed from the complete Christian ideology than the scores suggest. On the other hand, it may be more scientific to surmise that some of the persons interviewed did not understand the full implications of the questions asked and that, if given an explanation of each question, they would tend to show higher scores.

For purposes of clarifying this difficult subjective point, let us consider the personal qualities and actions of a few individuals at either end of the scoring. Warren Becker, who had the highest score of all, appears to live according to his high convictions. He is the father of five young children and a frequent communicant and faithful worker in parochial organizations. He is a graduate of a secular college and seems to have obtained most of his knowledge from his parental home and by reading Catholic books. He does not believe in a personal devil. Emile Roudge is one of the most active men in the parish, having at one time or other been an officer in each of the men's organizations. He is also prominent in civic, political, and business groups. He had a Catholic education but finished only one year of college. He says that he believes in offering economic opportunities to Negroes but does not want to attend the same church with them or send his children to school with them.

Catherine McGuffey is a women in her late forties. After finishing Catholic high school she went to work in an office where she has always shown a relatively militant religious attitude. Her central interests are a religious study club and the Blessed Virgin's League. She did not know that the Bishop's permission is needed before sending a child to the public school and is not sure about the obligation to join labor unions. She attends Mass and receives Communion several times a week. Mrs. George Schmidt is the mother of twelve children, all of whom are now past adolescence. She is a daily communicant and is considered one of the strongest spiritual influences among the laywomen of the parish. As a member of the "older" generation, she thinks Negroes ought to have their own parishes and is doubtful about rhythm, mixed marriage, and the mixed attendance of Negro and white children in the parochial kindergarten.

At the other end of the score are several persons who seem to be furthest removed from the true Catholic philosophy of life. Paul Harleau is a successful businessman, a former well-known singer, and one of the most popular men in the parish. He is active in the parish when there is need of fund-raising or encouragement to youthful athletic clubs. He had a repertory of jokes and stories which he enjoys telling. He is in his forties and the father of three children. He was very definite in his answers with the exception of the one concerning the Church's laws against divorce. He appears to be anti-Negro and anti-labor and to be in favor of "modern" views on marriage and family, is willing to drop the bomb on Moscow, and believes that God is unjust for condemning a person to hell for one mortal sin.

An equally poor score was made by Harold Dobson, who is better known on the diocesan level than in his own parish. He is an extremely successful professional man and tends to demonstrate all the attitudes of an urban American with high social mobility and ambition. He, too, is called on as a fund-raiser although not otherwise active in any parish organization. He is a self-made man with two children of college age who attend secular universities. His attitudes are almost identical with Mr. Harleau's in so far as they can be judged from this questionnaire and are certainly far removed from the ideals of Catholicism.

The woman with the lowest score was Mrs. Carp, the wife of a lawyer and a member of a family of long residence in Riverside. She herself never finished college but sent her two daughters through a Catholic high school and a secular college. She is very active in community organizations, is one of the hardest workers in the Parents' Club, and still does voluntary work in the school cafeteria. She bemoans the fact that she was never able to attend a Catholic school, and this may account for her inability to answer three of the questions. She thought it would be all right to administer a mercy-killing drug and did not believe that a personal devil exists.

In the final analysis, what can be said of the Catholic mind of St. Mary's Parish as it is derived from this selected sample of forty men and twenty-eight women? If this study is representative of the attitudes and beliefs of the "best Catholics," what can be said of the parish at large? On the scale we have devised above, very few of them approach 100 per cent Catholicism, while some of them are less than one-third Catholic. The average score for the women interviewed is 59.82 per cent; for the men the average is 55.00 per cent; while for both combined it is 56.98 per cent.

At this point an interesting comparison may be made between the actual religious behavior of the parishioners, as recorded in other chapters of this book, and the opinions and beliefs expressed by a select group of parishioners in this chapter. It must be remembered, however, that we are comparing not only behavior with belief but also the large number of parishioners in their behavior with a small group of parochial leaders in their beliefs.

The first rough similarity between the two is that in both behavior and belief the women parishioners have a better record and a higher average. They attend the various devotions, Mass, Novena, Mission, etc., more frequently and also receive the sacraments of confession and Communion in greater numbers than the men. In answering the questions about their beliefs and values, they show a better score than the men (59.82 to 55.00 per cent). The sex difference in the actual religious observance is much more in favor of the women than the difference shown in the interviews.

Disregarding the sex difference, we note that the whole group of parishioners interviewed made an average score of 56.98 per cent on their knowledge and opinions. In other words, they are somewhat better than "half-Catholic" in their thinking. Let us compare this percentage with various evaluations of external religious activities. (*a*) As far as can be determined, about 45 per cent of parishioners, seven years of age and older, go to confession semiannually or oftener. (*b*) Approximately 57 per cent of the same parochial category receive Holy Communion semiannually or oftener. (*c*) About 57 per cent of the same group attend Mass regularly every Sunday.[5]

By this admittedly rough technique of measuring attitudes and opinions and beliefs, we may estimate that the Catholic mind of these outstanding parishioners is about two-thirds Catholic and one-third pagan. If these persons may be used as a criterion, a sample of the other parishioners would probably show a much lower rating.

These three indexes of confession, Communion, and Sunday Mass attendance can be employed as simple criteria of the Catholic's external adherence to his faith. Of course, the criteria could be placed on a higher level; for example, monthly instead of semiannual confession and Communion, and the numbers who attend Mass on both Sundays and holy days of obligation. If these stricter interpretations of Catholic observance were selected, the percentage evaluation of the whole parish would necessarily be lowered.

We may conclude, therefore, that the religious observance of parishioners corresponds roughly with their religious thinking. In the conceptual scheme with which this chapter began, this means that the practical ideology of the parishioners is in approximate balance with their actual behavior patterns, while both of them are at considerable distance from the complete Christian ideology of the Catholic Church.

Can the facts and generalizations of this book be summarized in Father Schmidt's statement that we would find a "hollow shell of Catholicism" in St. Mary's Parish? Perhaps it would be more accurate to say that this parish has not been awakened to its full religious possibilities. When the standard of parochial accomplishment is set as high as it has been in this book, it is certain that no parish anywhere reaches the ideal.

As long as the personal and institutional blocks to spiritual values remain in our urban and secular culture, it will be extremely difficult

5. See chap. 5, p. 55; chap. 6, p. 68; and chap. 12, p. 152.

to achieve parochial progress of a high nature. We are only beginning to appreciate, by careful study and research, what those blocks are. We need more facts concerning the actual practice of religion on the parochial level. We need more and scientific understanding of the social patterns and institutions in the midst of which the parish operates.

Always there remains the mystery of God's grace and His co-operation with human beings. In the inscrutable providence of God, He may, without assistance of social research, change the face of the parish overnight. But persons who are concerned with the maintenance and progress of parochial religious functions cannot presume on such an occurrence. Admitting always the tremendous importance of divine grace in the workings of the Church, we may suggest that a parish is what people are.

Index

and altar boys, 100 f.
external display, 102 f.
at home, 103 f.
and Nuptial Mass, 110
Wednesday night Lenten services,
170 f.
Western culture, elements of, 2 f.
"Women's Mass," 141

Women's mission
program of, 213 f.
single ladies' talk, 215
solemn closing, 218
solemn opening, 212 f.
summary of contents, 214–17
Women's retreats, 253 f.
Workingmen, and unions, 264 f.

PRINTED
IN U·S·A·

[298]